Graham Latimer

Graham Latimer

a biography

Noel Harrison

First published in 2002 by Huia Publishers,
This edition published in 2016.
39 Pipitea Street, PO Box 12-280,
Wellington, Aotearoa New Zealand.
www.huia.co.nz

ISBN 1-877283-68-1

Copyright © Noel Harrison 2002

Cover image: Sir Graham Latimer, 1991. *Northern Advocate,* January 30 1991.

All rights reserved. No part of this publication may be reproduced, stored in a retrieval system, or transmitted in any form or by any means, electronic, mechanical, including photocopying, recording or otherwise, without prior permission of the copyright owner.

National Library of New Zealand Cataloguing-in-Publication Data
Harrison, Noel, 1929-
Graham Latimer : a biography / by Noel Harrison.
Includes bibliographical references.
ISBN 1-877283-68-1
1. Latimer, Graham Stanley, Sir, 1926- 2. Maori (New Zealand people)—Biography. 3. Maori (New Zealand people)—Politics and government—20th century. I. Title.
305.8994420092—dc 21

Contents

Preface
    Sir Henare Ngata   VII
    Heather Ayrton   X

Introduction   1

1   Beginnings: 1926–1946   7

2   Trooper in Japan: 1946–1947   15

3   Maori Identity: 1947–1956   41

4   Becoming a National Leader: 1956–1987   73

5   The Treaty Legacy: 1840–1987   103

6   The Treaty Goes to Court: 1987   119

7   Tupuna Maori – Item 181: 1988   129

8   First Fruits and Backlash: 1987–2001   141

9   Race Relations – a Minor Miracle: 1926–2001   159

10   Reputations: 1987–2001   183

Epilogue: 2002   205

Glossary of Maori Terms   215

References   217

Bibliography   223

Chronology   227

Preface

NOEL HARRISON HAS PAID A HANDSOME TRIBUTE TO ONE OF MAORIDOM'S outstanding leaders in his biography of Sir Graham Latimer.

I came to know Sir Graham when he joined the New Zealand Maori Council in 1964. I retired in 1985, so we had a long association together on the Council. He rose through the ranks of the Council becoming its vice-president in the late sixties and president in 1973, a position he continues to hold in 2002. In 1980, in recognition of his leadership of the Council and the contribution to Maori affairs by both the Council and himself, he was knighted.

Like his predecessors as president, Sir Graham was a National Party supporter. All three in fact – Sir Turi Carroll, Dr Pei Jones and Sir Graham – had been parliamentary candidates for the National Party. Unlike Sir Turi, who endeavoured to maintain the independence of the Council by putting some distance between himself and the Party, Sir Graham retained his party affiliation, and so rejected the advice of friends in the New Zealand Maori Council.

In the event, I don't believe any harm was done. Looking back over the years, I observe that Maori had never been given serious consideration in the National Party's designs anyway. On the other hand, Maori political aspirations never regarded the National Party as a friendly contender.

It was after the Labour Party returned to power in 1984 that Sir Graham gained wider prominence as a Maori leader.

Noel Harrison sets out in some detail the challenge Sir Graham led against the Government's plan in 1987 to transfer Crown assets to newly established state-owned enterprises, a move that he regarded as a crucial threat to Treaty of Waitangi settlements.

The Court of Appeal verdict in favour of the New Zealand Maori Council was, according to Noel Harrison, the crowning achievement in Sir Graham's career. All the elements of high drama were certainly present: eminent counsel, prestigious judges, and a successful challenge against the power and the authority of the Crown mounted by an individual who possessed little more than his strong belief that what he was doing was right, and his faith and courage to see it through.

However, while one agrees that the Court of Appeal decision established a new benchmark in relations between the Crown and Maori, one cannot readily erase from one's mind the long history of dubious practices by the Crown that Maori have had to bear. More often than not in the past the course that politicians have set has been determined more by expediency than by principle.

There has, however, been a curious contradiction in the course of recent Treaty settlements. While Labour governments have set the stage in enacting epoch-making legislation, as it were, it has in fact been National governments which have led the way in effecting actual settlements: with Tainui, with Ngai Tahu, and in the acquisition of substantial fisheries assets.

Currently, there has been speculation that changes in the constitution of the Waitangi Tribunal are under consideration, and that these may be more favourable to the Crown than to its Maori Treaty partner.

But, for me, the most revealing insight into the character and quality of Sir Graham was his involvement in the 'mokomokai' issue. With little if anything to gain, and at some considerable financial cost, he stopped the sale in England of the tattooed head of a Maori warrior. He said he was offended that human body parts should be regarded as saleable commodities. The tattooed head was 'tapu' and should be returned home and given a decent burial. With no help either from the Government or the National Museum, that was precisely what Sir Graham did.

Before I conclude, I must say something about the New Zealand Maori Council – the platform and motivating force in Sir Graham's life for nearly forty years.

Set up in 1962, with high hopes and lofty aspirations, the Council was for years regarded as a National Party puppet. In fact, its membership has been drawn from a wide range of political creeds. Political bias has never been a dominant concern of the Council.

Sir Graham has been an adviser on Maori issues to both Muldoon and Bolger during their respective terms as prime minister. Lange and Palmer have also sought his advice, as has Prime Minister Helen Clark, according to the media. This bears testimony to the independence of the Council, and to the integrity and independence of Sir Graham.

A monthly news publication recently quoted one of the members of Labour's Maori caucus as saying, in reference to Sir Graham's efforts to persuade the Prime Minister to return to Waitangi for the 2002 Waitangi Day ceremonies, that he thought 'it was really outrageous that a bloke who goes into print against Dover Samuels, has taken the Government to court more than anyone else, all of a sudden is now a champion'. However unintended, this statement must surely be a remarkable affirmation of Sir Graham's and the Maori Council's independence.

In recent years, however, the Council seems to have lost its 'fizz'. There are reports of internal bickering. Yet, more than ever, the Council is needed.

Since Sir Hepi Te Heuheu passed away a few years ago, the Maori Congress (established in 1990) has almost disappeared from sight.

Runanga profess to act for Maori, but as they are organisations set up by government under the Rununga Iwi Act 1990 to carry out government policy, and which receive government funds to do so, it is highly questionable as to how runanga can keep faith with both Crown and Maori.

I end these comments with a tribute to Lady Emily Latimer: a gentle person, but always strong in her support of her husband and of the Maori Council.

Noel Harrison's book makes good reading.

Kia ora Ta Kereama korua ko to hoa rangatira. Ma te Kaihanga korua e manaaki.

Sir Henare Ngata, 2002

THE COMPLEXITIES OF MAORI THINKING ARE OFTEN DIFFICULT FOR Pakeha to comprehend.

When the late Dame Whina Cooper imperiously summoned Sir Graham Latimer to her bedside at Middlemore Hospital shortly before her return home to Panguru to die, she purportedly transferred the mantle of her responsibilities for Maoridom to him. She was also emphasising her own mana as well as her achievements and hopes for her people together with the betterment of all New Zealanders.

Dame Whina's fearlessly untiring work for Maoridom was self-imposed. Law unto herself, she trod where neither angels nor other women dared.

Sir Graham, on the other hand, was directed, charged and challenged by his elders into the most daunting of tasks. Essentially humble, painfully aware of his shortcomings and inadequacies, he found himself thrust into the turmoil of significant and crucial times of change and the associated needs of Maoridom.

Dame Whina was a Maori woman and proud of it. Of mixed blood, Sir Graham grew up more as Pakeha but was strongly influenced by his Maori heritage. His elders saw him as a strong bridge between the two cultures, someone who would be able to walk with dignity in both worlds.

He always endeavoured never to let his elders or his tupuna down.

His way has not been without immense difficulties. At times his burden has been heartbreaking to the point of bitter despair but he has barely faltered. Often his sense of humour aided him.

Sir Graham has a reputation for kindliness, for compassionate understanding but also for shrewdness. His infinite patience, his preparedness to compromise where necessary, are coupled with a determination comparable with that of the indomitable Dame Whina.

While he may be secretly pleased with his successes, he is more concerned that there is still room for improvements with much yet to be done.

He frets at the restrictions and effects of advancing years but has confidence that there are people to follow his aspirations.

There can be no doubt of the influence of Sir Graham in many spheres, in Maoridom, politics, the Anglican Church and his kindly assistance in many lives.

In writing of the life of Sir Graham, Noel Harrison has provided an insight into the moulding of what New Zealand history will regard as the man chosen for the times and how that man to the best of his ability dealt with the challenges imposed upon him.

Heather Ayrton, 2002

Introduction

SIR GRAHAM LATIMER WAS CHOSEN IN THE LATE 1960S BY HIS ELDERS TO help them seek justice for Maori, to gain equal citizenship rights, and to resolve their ancient grievances. They wanted him to transform a neglected treaty, signed in 1840, into a cornerstone of the country's constitution, and use it to right the wrongs committed against Maori for more than 100 years.

The elders did not express their wishes in quite those words, and they were not sure Latimer could do it. They did know, however, that they needed a new approach, and a new type of leader: hardheaded, pragmatic, grounded in the modern world, not tied to iwi responsibilities but still committed to their cause. The elders and their predecessors had tried sweet reason, petitions to the Crown and appeals to honour. All had failed. They needed a younger leader, able to learn the devious ways of politicians and bureaucrats and to beat them at their own game – a new Maui, a warrior-leader in a suit.

What the elders got was a strong-minded, independent thinker – willing to act without always waiting for full consensus, a man determined to fulfil the New Zealand Maori Council's aims, but in his own way. To some he was a maverick, not one of the herd, an innovator ready to take risks. To others he was an autocrat, using the Maori Council for his own purposes. The New Zealand Maori Council was set up under the Maori Welfare Act 1962, 'to consider and, as far as possible, give effect to any measures that will conserve and promote harmonious and friendly relations between members of the Maori race and other members of the community'.

This is the story of Sir Graham's latter-day Pilgrim's Progress, slowly coming to understand the Treaty of Waitangi and its history, walking through a wasteland of injustice and missed opportunities and, finally, using the Pakeha judicial system to force the Pakeha majority to carry out the promises made so long ago in the name of Queen Victoria.

It's also the story of a personal and political partnership. Sir Graham and Lady Latimer (known as Lady Emily) have worked together as a team on all the main issues facing Maoridom and the New Zealand Maori Council. The pair stood on the shoulders of giants and built on the past achievements of many others, almost all unsung and unhonoured, invisible participants in the country's history.

Lady Emily has shared all the risks at each stage of Sir Graham's journey. She alone made it possible for him to be president of the Maori Council by accepting heavier responsibilities for their family and their farm. Lady Emily insisted that Sir Graham stay on as a national leader in spite of all the burdens that this placed on their family and the personal abuse he received for his policies.

Together they made the crucial decision in 1987, with the help of others, to stop the Labour government implementing its state-owned enterprises policy – mortgaging their farm to ensure that their case (*New Zealand Maori Council v Attorney-General*) reached the Court of Appeal. Lady Emily knew that if the decision went against them the Latimers would lose everything they had slowly and painfully accumulated in forty years of married life, and that Maori would lose many millions (probably billions) of dollars of assets. She thought it was well worth the risk. She was right.

In the words of the former minister of justice and Labour prime minister Sir Geoffrey Palmer, the Court's decision shifted the 'tectonic plates of New Zealand law'[1] and, in the Latimers' words, 'nothing was ever the same again'. The Treaty's significance was acknowledged, Maori rights were recognised, and governments agreed, however reluctantly, to enter into a new partnership with Maori.

The Latimer's story has never been told. Sir Graham has deliberately rejected celebrity status in the news media and has refused to debate complex and sensitive issues through newspaper headlines and soundbites. As a result he is less well-known than those Maori leaders and commentators who swim easily through their fifteen minutes of fame without putting at risk their personal assets or reputations. Lady Emily is widely respected and warmly loved in Maori communities but has always rejected media prominence.

Sir Graham asked me in 1992 if I was interested in writing the story of his life. We had worked closely together at Northland Polytechnic from 1978. He was council chairman of Northland Polytechnic from 1978 till 1987 and I was chief executive officer from 1978 till 1990. I'd worked with Maori organisations and communities over the previous thirty years. We'd cooperated on major projects on housing in Northland, local histories, employment and poverty, Maori language, and Maori Council activities. Sir Graham was aware of my long interest in New Zealand history, including the Treaty of Waitangi and the conflict between Maori and the new settlers and their descendants.

Sir Graham was very hesitant about having a biography written. He has always tried to preserve his privacy. And he did not want his family exposed to public view. However, he was concerned about the almost complete absence of books on Maori leaders and their impact on New Zealand's cultural, political and economic environment.

I talked with a number of Maori leaders, including some who had opposed his policies strongly in the past. They said, without hesitation, that Sir Graham's life should be recorded because of his central position in Maori affairs, and agreed that there were too few biographies of Maori. Also, they said, the story should be written as soon as possible. Too many kaumatua and kuia had died without leaving a written account of their lives.

When I agreed to write his story I reminded Sir Graham of my whiteness (I am a New Zealand-born Anglo-Saxon Celt). The distinguished Pakeha historian, Michael King, had been harshly criticised for writing biographies of Maori leaders. One very angry Tainui said it was better that Maori history be not recorded at all rather than have Pakeha do it.

Sir Graham replied that his mother, Lillian (née Kenworthy) Latimer, had Celtic ancestry. He made his belief very plain that a Maori is not the only person who can write about Maori.

I also reminded Sir Graham I was pro-Labour – while he was then Maori vice-president of the National Party. His response was that most of his family were Labour supporters. He thought I could be objective, that I had worked with Maori for a long time, had first-hand knowledge of current issues, and already knew him very well.

This book is the result. It is not a commissioned, authorised, official biography. The Latimers cannot insist on anything being put in or left out. They promised to answer all questions frankly, and have. They know I don't share some of their political, social and religious views, that I could not write from a Maori perspective, and that I would need to include comments from people hostile to Sir Graham or his policies.

During the intervening years I had many interviews with Sir Graham, with Lady Emily, family members, friends, other Maori leaders, government officials, politicians, church members, farmers and people who did not know Sir Graham personally – just through the news media. I read most of the minutes of the New Zealand Maori Council during its formative years, a host of publications relating to race relations, and the most important legal decisions relating to the Treaty.

I've touched only on the main features of Sir Graham's political life and have deliberately kept the book short to make it accessible to a wide audience. A much more detailed study is needed to record and evaluate Sir Graham's national role as a leader not dependent on iwi support, and his work with the wider community, particularly the Anglican Church. His involvement with the New Zealand Maori Council over thirty-eight years, most of it as president, requires a book of its own.

I've recounted very briefly his early life in the Far North; his time in Japan as an occupation soldier; his marriage to Emily Moore; his time with New Zealand Railways and how this led indirectly to his identification as Maori; and his rise to a leadership role with the Maori Council while he and Lady Emily were developing a dairy farm on Kaipara Harbour scrubland.

Most of the book's attention has been given to Sir Graham's Treaty of Waitangi strategy, using the judicial system against hostile politicians; his attempts to improve race relations; his retrieval, with Lady

Emily, of the head of a Maori warrior when it was about to be auctioned in London; and his reputation, personal and political.

The epilogue leaves the Latimers at home in the Far North, still fully involved, often controversially, with the Maori Council, the Crown Forest Rental Trust, with Muriwhenua hapu politics, and with the Treaty issues Sir Graham inherited from his grandfather and other leaders of the past.

Sir Graham continues to be a target for constant attacks from those who resent the importance now irreversibly placed on the Treaty of Waitangi and on the country's social and legal obligation to recognise the place of tangata whenua in New Zealand society.

Sir Graham's place in history can be assessed only from the perspective of time. He is currently seen by some as the most outstanding and effective Maori leader of the twentieth century. His court actions over the last fifteen years have begun a new era not only in constitutional law but also in the relationships between Maori and Pakeha. His negotiating skills have helped to gain billions of dollars of resources for Maori in land, forest and fisheries settlements.

And he's only yet seventy-six.

CHAPTER ONE

Beginnings
1926–1946

GRAHAM STANLEY LATIMER WAS BORN BESIDE A DIRT TRACK ON THE Aupouri Peninsula, 7 February 1926, in the early years of the Great Depression that lasted till the outbreak of the Second World War in 1939. His family had so little cash that it barely noticed the collapse of the world's economy. Anyone who owned a horse was considered well off in the Far North gumfields.

Graham Latimer was the third son of a young mother (Lillian, twenty-one – married at sixteen) of mixed Irish–Scottish descent and an almost equally young father (Graham, twenty-six – married at twenty-one) of mixed Anglo-Saxon and Maori descent. Their marriage was a public scandal because a Pakeha had married a Maori, and was an additional trauma for both families because the bride was Catholic and the groom Anglican (the couple married in the local police station). The young Latimer's first home was in a wasteland area: according to legend Sir Apirana Ngata, the country's most prominent Maori leader, refused to concede it was part of New Zealand. He is popularly said to have claimed without fear of too much argument that New Zealand ended just north of Kaitaia (the northernmost town in the country). The remaining land was a long narrow peninsula of sand dunes and scrub a few kilometres wide. Very few people lived on the tail of Te Ika-a-Maui (the fish of Maui, the North Island). Most of the land, formerly covered by kauri, was sterile and too acidic for conventional farming. Since the turn of the century it had been systematically ripped up by Croatian, English and Maori gumdiggers.

When Ngata travelled north of Kaitaia in 1931 as minister of native affairs the land was a jumbled mass of kauri stumps, pits filled with stagnant water, sand dunes, tussock and ti-tree. It had no roads, just tracks. It was, however, blessed with a soft, temperate climate which led a property developer with a sense of humour to coin the term Winterless North for the whole peninsula.

Those living on the peninsula were the poorest of the poor. In the 1920s, although the Maori infant death rate was declining, one Maori child in seven did not survive the first year; a rate three times that of non-Maori. In the Far North the death rate was much higher. At Te Kao, just north of the squatters' camp where the Latimers lived, as many as one in five children died without reaching the age of five. There were no health services, nor was there a hospital. Graham's two older brothers were born in a shack with an earth floor.

Graham was born while his mother was travelling in the mail buggy to Kaitaia where she hoped to have the luxury of giving birth in the small maternity annexe. His mother thought she had plenty of time, at least two weeks. Her pains began, however, at the tiny settlement of Waiharara, about thirty kilometres away from Kaitaia, and the baby was born on a rug on the side of the track. The Cochrane family living nearby helped Lillian and she went home a few days later with the same driver on his return trip north. This open-air birth was not unusual on the gumfields, not a great crisis. Lillian's family extended its sympathy to the driver for his duties as midwife. The new baby thrived in spite of the odds.

The Latimers lived near Houhora, well north of Ngata's frontier line. Pukenui was a little further south. About a kilometre away to the west of the Latimer's home lay the Tasman Sea and Te Oneroa-a-Tohe, the long beach of Tohe. Also known as Ninety Mile Beach, this is referred to as the pathway used by the spirits of the dead going to Te Rerenga Wairua, the departure point for Hawaiki.

The land all round the Latimers was rich in history. Moa hunters had left traces at Houhora. Early settlements had been established at river mouths, creeks, beaches and harbours. Fishing had later been developed to a fine art, with ocean-going canoes and nets of awe-inspiring size. Great kauri logs lay submerged beneath their feet, waiting to provide settlers with a new industry – gum for varnishing the world's high-grade furniture.

The Latimers lived on fish, eels, toheroa, vegetables from their gardens, fruit from their trees, and food bought from the sale of gum nuggets and their father's irregular labouring work (7s 6d a day). Older brother Joe remembers eating turnips often: 'Everything tastes good when you're hungry.' Nothing was wasted.

The family was, in Latimer's words, 'very, very poor'. They lived in an unofficial settlement of about thirty shacks on land leased by three Europeans with the initials RST, unofficially amplified to Rip, Shit and Tear. The family's clothes were mostly home-made, they had no shoes or socks and their blankets were sacks. Butter was for visitors; gravy and dripping was for family. Sir Graham's parents put great value on every penny they earned, and so did he. The children rarely received Christmas presents and made their own fun, like most people at that time.

The region was undeveloped, understandably neglected by central and provincial governments. The soil was poor – hard, cold clay in most places. Pockets of good land were rare. The first Pakeha settlers arriving in the second half of the nineteenth century had burned the bush to allow for quick growth of grass. Gumdiggers who arrived at the end of the century burned what was left to expose the clay to their long spades.

The land that the Latimers roamed in the late 1920s was described by some travellers as desolate, isolated, harsh, romantic, unromantic. It was made up of sombre patches of undulating country covered sparsely with bracken, fern and manuka, and littered with gaunt, half-burned dead trunks of kauri.

The young Graham was not then aware he was descended from a long line of rangatira who had lived in the Far North for hundreds of years, or that he had Irish, Scottish and English ancestors. From his birth he was surrounded by people of mixed origins from different parts of New Zealand, Europe and America; Scots, Irish, English, Germans, Portuguese, Poles, Jews and Dalmatians from Croatia. They called themselves a League of Nations. If blood is equated with race, as it was at that time, then his ancestry was just slightly more European than Maori. Ethnically, culturally and racially he was Northern Gumfields Squatter, circa 1920s.

Latimer grew up happily with people he identified as family: mother, father, brothers (three), sisters (two), grandfathers, grandmothers, uncles and aunts, cousins – seeing them as individuals, not as members of any racial group. Not till he went to the last of three primary schools can he remember being called Maori. He attended one small native school briefly when he was young but his parents were determined that he and his brothers and sisters be taught in public schools.

By that time, the 1930s, the family had moved south across Ngata's border, back into New Zealand. Gum prices had dropped on international markets over the previous ten years, and the fields had been almost worked out because of the intensive mining methods used by Dalmatian gangs.

The family lived on collectively-owned land at Pamapuria, about seven kilometres from Kaitaia, then a rough frontier town of fewer than 500 people. Later, his mother's Kenworthy clan also moved south, both families commuting to the gumfields from time to time.

The country was in the middle of a worldwide economic depression. Unemployed men rioted in Auckland's Queen Street. The number registered as out of work was about 100,000 in a population of 1.4 million. Women were not counted amongst the unemployed. Most Maori were unemployed, many living in extreme poverty in rural slums.

In Europe, years of economic collapse left that region vulnerable to leadership by Mussolini in Italy and Hitler in Germany. In Asia, the Japanese had already invaded Manchuria and were preparing to take over much of China. In the United States, President Roosevelt was applying his New Deal policies, promising to give all families at least one square meal a day. In New Zealand, the conservative coalition government, led by George W Forbes, responded to hard times by making them worse. It cut spending, sacked civil servants, stopped one year's intake into schools, and told citizens to be self-reliant.

The Latimer–Kenworthy families knew all about self-reliance. For years they had lived independently, mostly beyond the authority of the state. They welcomed the Labour Party's election victory in 1935 but believed it would make little immediate difference to them. They were still seriously poor but, according to Latimer and his brothers and sisters, healthy and happy – a close-knit, supportive group.

Life at Pamapuria was dramatically different from that on the gum fields. The family had access to shops, a hospital, an Anglican Church just across the road, a dairy factory, a billiard parlour, rugby fields with real posts, and a pub. The fact that Kaitaia had no public water supply system, no borough drainage, and no septic tanks (a night cart was used to dispose of waste) was no hardship. The Latimers had joined small-town mainstream New Zealand.

The children went to the local cinema and saw films then being angrily condemned by Sir Truby King, the founder of the Plunket Society. Sir Truby thought picture palaces showed all that was despicable, damning, vile and beastly in human nature. While he wanted to stop children seeing films, the Latimers, with the rest of the country, enjoyed gaining a view of a wider world.

Radio provided another new dimension. The isolation of the backblocks was relieved by the music, the news and the sounds of the whole country, all contributing to a sense of a common culture, no matter how common. Aunt Daisy, who became an enduring radio personality, and Uncle Scrim, a minister of religion with a political message, came into every home, along with politicians when Parliament was broadcast daily.

The Latimer's lives again changed dramatically with the outbreak of the Second World War when Graham was thirteen. His two older brothers joined the army (one served in the Maori Battalion) and his father, then thirty-nine, too old for active service, became a recruitment officer. Graham left Kaitaia District High School when he was fourteen, after spending about two weeks in the third form breaking-in his first pair of shoes. He was needed at home to hand-milk the family's small dairy herd of fourteen cows on forty-eight acres.

He had no regrets. He had already decided he wanted to be a farmer. He liked animals. He liked being outside, and envied what he then believed was the free and independent life farmers led – being their own bosses. Though he enjoyed school he had no special desire to stay for three years and gain School Certificate. Older brother

Frank who was a top student (and later a school principal) said Graham was an average student.

After working on the home farm for a year Graham hired out as a labourer when the herd was sold because of disputes among the whanau (extended family). He had the option of going back to school, at fifteen, or continuing to work on farms. He chose work: the family needed money. Even though his father was then earning a regular income his mother still had very little housekeeping money to care for the three children still at home, and the others she always seemed to be looking after.

One Pakeha farmer treated Graham very well. Another, married to a Maori, overworked him mercilessly. Latimer: 'He was quick-tempered. If anything went wrong or you weren't quick enough he'd just hit you.' His uncle, Frank Kenworthy, took Graham home when he saw the bruises and cuts on his face. These experiences confirmed what Graham already knew: some people are decent, friendly folk; others are not.

When he was seventeen, in 1943, Graham went first into the Territorial Army and then into the New Zealand Army. Stationed at the Papakura military camp near Auckland he learned how to cope with army life. By the end of the war, late 1945, he had become an experienced poker player (his father had taught him, playing for matches), and in one long, spectacular game which began in the early afternoon he had a 'golden run'. He gave much of his winnings to his mother, with whom he had an extremely strong bond. 'I realised from a very early age that she was my salvation.'

While still in the army, Graham met Emily Patricia Moore at a Trades Hall dance in Auckland. She was sixteen, three years younger, fresh from working in the vegetable gardens at Pukekohe as part of the war effort. Emily's mother was from the Whakatohea iwi at Opotiki in the Bay of Plenty, and her father, Romeo Romano Moananui, was Ngati Wai from Northland. The family name was changed to Moore, later, for simplicity. The Catholic Church was a big part of Emily's early life in much the same way that the Church of England was part of Graham's background. 'If you missed Holy Communion on Sunday you had to go to church through the week,' she says.

Emily grew up in Opotiki with nine brothers and sisters (she was seventh). Everyone was sports mad. She remembers being dragged into a rugby game when she was seven, as halfback, and being flattened. ('There were no beg-your-pardons.') She played hockey, tennis and basketball and anything else that was going. 'I enjoyed school but wasn't a scholar. We had a happy childhood, lots of friends, Pakeha and Maori.'

She left school when she was fifteen to work in Pukekohe. For the first time she met and worked with Maori from other areas — and realised that Maori are not all alike. The town was also racially divided. Local and other Maori were not given credit by Pakeha shop-keepers, but were looked on as outcasts. She got along well with her Pakeha workmates.

When the war ended she went to Auckland, the 'big smoke'. She had no trouble getting work, first in a home for servicemen from the First World War and then in hospital laundries. She lived with other young Maori women in a flat in Hobson Street, in the middle of the city, thoroughly enjoyed her social life and became a representative basketball player.

Latimer had by this time decided to go to Japan as part of the Allied occupation force so they had little time to get to know each other.

CHAPTER TWO

Trooper In Japan
1946–1947

It is the duty of New Zealand not only to take part in the victorious occupation of Japan but to play its part so well that the Japanese people will learn to respect the ways of free democracy, and, let us hope, to adopt them as a new and better way of life for themselves. Our J Force has done exceptionally well in tedious circumstances in a foreign land.

– Fred Jones, minister of defence, *Jayforce Times*,
14 December 1946

We couldn't escape the horror all round us. We tried to help but there was little we could do. We were observers. We saw the terrible results of war, and of atomic warfare. Some of us became serious, old, before our time.

– Sir Graham Latimer, Pamapuria, May 2000, talking of his time in Japan with the occupation forces in 1946–1947

Knowing ... that you have performed faithfully and well a difficult and onerous but essential task in the service of your country, you will, I hope, in years to come be able to look back with pleasure at the time you have spent in Japan.

– Fred Jones, minister of defence, *Jayforce Times*,
12 July 1948

GRAHAM LATIMER WENT TO JAPAN WITH J FORCE (JAYFORCE) WHEN HE WAS twenty, a country boy with a little experience of one small city, Auckland, and no knowledge of New Zealand south of Papakura military camp. He came back just over a year later feeling, he says, ten years older. 'Japan wasn't the place to grow old gracefully. Many of us felt we'd aged a lifetime between arrival and departure.'

Fifty-six years later he still has painful memories of a people and a country devastated by war, humiliated by defeat and the boots of a well-fed occupying army trampling on their deeply held customs. His experiences helped to shape his beliefs, and taught him that people are capable of almost casual cruelty and also of remarkable generosity and warmth.

More than anything else, he learnt a lot about the resilience of the human spirit. He realised that people can survive almost anything. He saw men, women and children suffering from malnutrition, brutalised by starvation, with hardly any resources – all desperately struggling to survive.

Latimer saw and smelt Hiroshima a year after a small atomic bomb equal to 20,000 tons of TNT almost obliterated the city. Three days later an even more powerful bomb was dropped on Nagasaki. 'We killed innocent people.'

He and his fellow-soldiers were misled by those in authority whose fundamental duty should have been to protect the soldiers from needless harm. He learned later that information about radiation sickness was deliberately withheld by American authorities, and that his own government had either gone along with the cover-up or had taken no independent steps to determine the facts. He believes now that he and others stationed near Hiroshima were exposed to potential dangers from atomic radiation.

Though the city was declared out of bounds no steps were taken to enforce the ban. Troop trains ran through Hiroshima regularly and stopped at the station, giving everyone the chance to walk about in the ruins.

Latimer also learned a lot about people who had too much power too early. He witnessed the arrogance of some soldiers who regarded Japanese as inferior and treated them with indifference or contempt. 'Some of our men just looked at them as though they were animals; not really human. They suffered from a power complex.'

He saw all the rules broken. Black markets flourished. Officers and men exchanged money illegally and some traded food, petrol, and cigarettes for money, jewellery, samurai swords and sex. Fraternisation bans were ignored from the moment the occupying force landed.

Girls and women were badly treated by their own men and by their own municipal authorities – and exploited by troops of all the occupying armies.

Latimer believes most New Zealanders behaved well. They worked easily with the Japanese they met in their official capacity, with those who delivered goods, drivers, cleaners, shop-owners, and thousands of labourers hired to maintain buildings, build roads and repair sewers. Some became so friendly that there were tears when the soldiers went back to New Zealand.

He had time to think about his own past, particularly the hard life his mother had led and was still leading at Pamapuria, and about how people of one ethnic or racial group found it so easy to despise those of another.

Possibly, more than anything else, however, he became, in his own words, a 'loner'. He could depend only on himself. 'I realised that I had to be responsible, that I couldn't just hope that things would work out well. If I wanted something then I would have to make sure it happened.'

There was an inevitability about going to Japan. Since 1943 Latimer had been waiting to be old enough to go to the front in Europe or the Pacific. Just before the war ended in Europe, New Zealand had agreed to join an invasion force with an army of 16,000 men as part of a combined Commonwealth operation, and another 8,000 men for fighter and bomber squadrons.

Latimer, nineteen in 1945, fully expected to be sent overseas and was, with his age group, looking forward to it. War was still an adventure, and the Allies were winning. Propaganda films showed German and Japanese cities in flaming ruins, though nothing was said about the use of phosphorous bombs which burnt hundreds of thousands to death – a war atrocity.

Volunteers were needed when Japan surrendered. Latimer looked at the advertisements that promised good rates of pay, jobs would be held open for those in employment, and opportunities would be given for recreation and study ('games, educational facilities, entertainment and sight-seeing will be amply provided for'). Enlist NOW. Age limits were set: twenty to forty. Preference was given to single men.

No reference was made to women, though some did serve, mostly as nurses and in the Women's Auxiliary Army Corps. One poster showed the Pacific Ocean with an over-sized New Zealand lying to the south, facing an equally over-sized Japan to the north. A banner girdled the Pacific with the legend: Our Ocean and Our Job. 'There is an important and interesting job ahead for every man who enlists in J Force.'[1]

Fred Jones, the minister of defence, urged young men to enlist, saying they would be helping to make the Pacific safe from future aggression. The Hiroshima area, where the British Commonwealth Occupation Force was to be stationed, was reported to be very healthy, he said.

Latimer talked with his parents about volunteering and gained their consent, necessary because he was still under twenty-one. He saw the occupation army as a great experience. He had missed the war but he could still see Japan. He was young enough to think he could do his bit disarming the hated soldiers, keeping the peace and generally having a great time.

He also remembered receiving a white feather two years earlier. It had appeared on the doorstep of the Latimer's small farmhouse – a feather from a domestic fowl, inside an ordinary envelope with his name on it. No other message was included or needed. The feather was sufficiently eloquent. He was a coward, a fit young man playing pool in his Kenworthy grandfather's billiard parlour while brave men died in foreign countries.

Lillian Latimer was stunned by the malice and the stupidity. She was so shocked she decided that Graham's father and brothers must not know: it was too shameful and unjust. Nobody was told.

Graham thought for a long time about who could have left it. 'I never grieved about it. I knew someone was telling me I had to go overseas. It lingered in my mind and I kept on wondering which one of the people who knew me sent it. I came to the conclusion that it was probably a neighbour, someone in the district. The envelope didn't come through the mail. It was placed on the doorstep. I don't think someone would have come a long distance to do that. My father always said to me that if you're looking for enemies you usually don't have to look far.'

He believed it probably came from a woman. Some mothers, wives and sisters complained bitterly about apparently able-bodied men not in uniform, accepting all the benefits of civilian life in wartime, including the enjoyment of the company of many single and some married women. At the same time their own men were suffering on the battlefields of northern Italy, dying in the bloodbath at Monte Cassino or maybe coming home injured for life.

White feathers appeared immediately after war was declared. Some were even sent to returned servicemen from the First World War. Sidney Holland, leader of the National Party, received one and showed it angrily in a parliamentary debate. He wanted this act of intimidation and insult made a heavily punishable offence. It wasn't.

The National Council of Women condemned feather-giving. Queen Elizabeth II made a rare public statement against the practice, a revival from the First World War. A White Feather Movement had then encouraged squads of young women to give these tokens of cowardice to all young men not in uniform. Baroness Orczy, author of *The Scarlet Pimpernel*, founded the Women of England's Active Service League with the sole purpose of forcing men to enlist immediately. White feathers were part of its armoury.

No such organisation was set up in New Zealand during the Second World War but individuals acted willingly on their own.

For Graham Latimer, seen as a Maori, the insult was compounded by the fact that he had no legal or historical obligation to fight for a government representing colonial authorities which had taken land unjustly, rejected valid grievances and refused to confer to Maori many civic rights guaranteed to all other citizens. Nor did he have to fight for a Crown that had ignored all petitions to redress the wrongs done to Maori.

This was, however, certainly not how he saw himself. He and his family had proved how anxious they were to fight if given the chance. So were most Maori. The least enthusiastic, Waikato and Taranaki, had strong and fresh memories of illegal land confiscations which still affected them daily. Before conscription was introduced nationally (though not for Maori) almost four out of every ten Maori men of military service age had already volunteered – a very high percentage.

A white feather signified another level of abuse for Latimer. This symbol for cowardice evolved from breeding game birds for recreational slaughter. When such feathers were found in the tail of game birds, bred to be shot, this indicated mixed (and therefore bad) breeding. These birds were inferior, low standard, second-rate. White feathers sent in wartime branded a man as a mongrel, not up to scratch, a coward not doing his bit – such as Graham Latimer, technically a half-caste.

While the feather was not a major influence, his decision to enlist was a clear response to the anonymous person who wanted to shame him.

He went to the Whangarei recruiting office, filled in his occupation as farmer, and was accepted after a medical examination. He said goodbye to Emily and promised to write. He then sailed off to become part of an army made up of 150,000 American troops and 40,000 from the Commonwealth (Britain, Australia, India and New Zealand).

Latimer was completely unprepared for what he found when he landed in southern Japan in June 1946. He knew very little about the country or the devastation caused by saturation bombing of its cities and ports, and virtually nothing about Hiroshima. During the two-week voyage from New Zealand he had relaxed, drilled regularly (because of the danger from floating mines), and enjoyed the sensation of sailing over a great ocean. Some of his fellow-soldiers changed the name of J Force to Joyforce, anticipating that a good time would be had by all. Wartime propaganda had painted the Japanese as monsters ruled by a fanatical emperor, Hirohito. Japanese armies were accused of atrocities: murder, rape, torture. Soldiers were stereotyped as slit-eyed yellow monkeys with big teeth. Racist slogans portrayed them as depraved and inferior. General Tojo and other senior officers and politicians were then on trial in Tokyo for war crimes.

Peter Fraser's Labour government put all the blame for the war on the Japanese in an effort to build up a climate of fear, and to maintain hostility to an enemy state. For some New Zealanders it was a natural extension of earlier colonial campaigns to save the country from the 'Yellow Peril', from unrestricted immigration from

Asia, and to preserve racial purity by implementing a White New Zealand policy.

After four or five years of censored news and Hollywood epics the cumulative effect was a distorted and ignorant view of what had been happening in Asia and in Japan. The New Zealand Army did little to fill the gaps. Latimer says that even as a youngster he was not impressed by the racist caricatures that had been screened. He did not believe that the Japanese were inferior racially, or as soldiers. They had conquered so much of Asia and the Pacific and held it for so long from such a small base, a country the size of New Zealand. What Latimer saw immediately he landed was a defeated people, many on the verge of starvation – scratching out a living in bombed cities and on poor farms lacking in fertilisers, equipment and seeds. Most were peasants or people from the lowest classes. They had never had any democratic rights. They had not voted for war. They were still living in a feudal economy, controlled by a ruling class.

He arrived ten months after the war ended and could see the results of bombing raids on the southern ports and cities. Wrecked ships stuck out of the water. Wharves and docks were shattered, as were most of the buildings nearby. More than 700,000 Japanese were estimated to have died in the fire-bombing of cities all over Japan in preparation for the invasion. (Japanese casualties during fourteen years of fighting, from 1931, were about 3.5 million.)

Even though no official figures were given of those who died at Hiroshima and Nagasaki, or the effect of radiation on the survivors, Latimer and his mates realised instantly that the occupying armies were in no danger from the Japanese. Defeat was total. Emperor Hirohito had publicly declared he was no longer divine and told his subjects to cooperate in every way with their new rulers. Endure the unendurable, he said. Suffer the insufferable. And they did.

Latimer says that the returning Japanese soldiers were sullen and always low in spirits, but were no trouble. About six million soldiers and civilians were finally repatriated. 'They'd known nothing of what had been happening outside their own area of action. Their government censored all news to keep them ignorant and obedient.' Many of the first Japanese he saw were still in shock. They had been numbed by years of deprivation during the war and their pride was gone. He saw people dying on the side of the road and was unable to do anything about it.

He sympathised. For years these peasants had been forced to produce as much as they could for the home front and for their armies in other countries. Students and young girls and boys had been conscripted to help the war effort, as a land army.

Japanese had seen newsreels and photos of brave young soldiers fighting their enemies all over Asia. Young girls waved cherry blossoms to airmen taking off on kamikaze suicide missions against American ships. Boys and girls were trained with rifles and sharpened bamboo spears to defend Japan against the barbarian invaders.

Civilians were told that the enemy was vicious and inhuman, that they would rape and kill without mercy. Women and girls were told to wear loose-fitting dresses or floppy trousers to avoid rape. Slogans and posters demanded that everyone fight to the finish, and never surrender.

By the time Latimer arrived morale had collapsed. 'People no longer believed in the Emperor or their leaders. They didn't want to believe that their sons, husbands and brothers had been part of armies that were accused of atrocities. Where was the honour? Many felt betrayed.' The last thing they needed, he said, was a huge occupation army.

Latimer slowly realised that the Commonwealth force was not really needed. The Americans had more than enough men and resources and did not need help from a small army made up of four different national units. General MacArthur, as supreme commander, made all decisions with very little interference from the United States government and with no significant input from his allies. The Commonwealth presence simply enabled the occupation to be described as a joint enterprise – not just an American show. It was in fact totally under American orders. It was there, as its first commander put in his final report, to 'assist the American forces'.[2]

The Americans had been in complete control since September 1945. Commonwealth troops were there solely for political reasons. Britain had emerged from the war with much of its international authority permanently weakened. It was still a 'great power' but only just. In Asia it wanted to reaffirm its status by taking part in the occupation of Japan.

The British government asked its Commonwealth allies for help. Australia responded enthusiastically, offering the greatest number of servicemen and women. The New Zealand prime minister, Peter Fraser, wanted to assert New Zealand's right to take part in making Asian and Pacific policy along with the United States and Britain but did not want to spend too much. The result was a token force of about 4,000, relieved each year till 1948. Its purpose was to be seen, to place New Zealand on the international stage as a player, even if only in a bit part.

When J Force arrived in two stages in March and June 1946 all the action was over. The Commonwealth force had been initially intended to occupy only one area, the prefecture of Hiroshima. Immediately after its arrival, however, MacArthur asked the Commonwealth force to take over all of southern Honshu. At that time MacArthur had few troops in the area. It was of no economic or political importance, with no industries of any significance, and the civilian population was calm in spite of the horrific bombing of Hiroshima. Latimer describes the Yamaguchi prefecture, where J Force was based, as sad and depressing. It was an area of about 5000 square kilometres with about 1.4 million people (the total New Zealand population when he was born in 1926). Health standards were dangerously low, sanitation was poor (human waste was used as farm fertiliser). The incidence of tuberculosis and venereal disease (VD) was high.

Latimer was part of D Squadron, a Maori Battalion unit of 135 men, stationed at Yanai on the coast fewer than forty kilometres from Hiroshima. With other Commonwealth troops, D Squadron was assigned to what he felt was the dirty work of sending home Korean prisoners of war and Korean workers, many of them slave labourers. Those who tried to re-enter Japan had to be stopped and sent back.

'We had to patrol the coast at night and watch for small boats,' he says. 'Life was so hard in Korea, which had been occupied for years by the Japanese, that some people thought that Japan under the American occupation would give them a better chance, not now but in the future. They were desperate and they were probably right. We arrested them and shipped them back whenever we could catch them.'

'This wasn't what I expected,' he says. 'We'd been told that the main reason we were there was to subdue the enemy population and to prevent uprisings or demonstrations. It was more a police job, rounding up starving refugees to send them back to a place that was even worse – in the interests of racial purity among other things. The Japanese treated Koreans as though they were inferior.'

The closest Latimer came to disarming the enemy was searching for hidden weapons and war supplies. These included samurai swords, coveted as souvenirs by the occupation troops rather than because of their destructive potential.

Direct personal contact with Japanese was difficult at first. General Northcott, the Australian commander of the Commonwealth force, issued a fraternisation directive designed to reduce contact to a minimum.

'Your relations with this defeated enemy,' he said in March 1946, 'must be guided by your own initiative, your own individual good judgement, and your own sense of discipline. You must at ALL times be formal and correct. You must not enter their homes and take part in their family lives. Your unofficial dealings with the Japanese must be kept to a minimum. You must obey strictly all instructions regarding establishments or areas which are placed out of bounds to all personnel forming part of the BCOF.'[3]

'The authorities discouraged contact,' says Latimer. 'It wasn't actually banned but we were told we couldn't have anything to do with them because they were a conquered enemy who had caused terrible suffering and loss in many thousands of homes in the British Empire. We were also told that language difficulties would make it hard for us to become friendly with them and that we had little in common anyway. We were told, particularly, to keep away from their women because they had venereal disease.'

Latimer says the official position was quite plain. The Japanese were still the enemy and 'we were to avoid them as much as possible. In other words, fraternisation was banned'.

This policy led to farcical scenes. On one occasion J Force men on leave were mingling with Japanese at a beach when New Zealand military police arrived. An observer wrote: 'We could see our boys with Japanese families, some with towels over their heads, and one was even being buried in sand by a group of Japanese youngsters. No one gave them away and none were identified. At that time to fraternise with the enemy was a serious offence.'

Latimer: 'What made it even sillier was that we all knew that Northcott's policy was directly opposed to MacArthur's. He publicly told his troops to fraternise, to get to know the Japanese, to not treat them as enemies but as future allies and friends.'

MacArthur was trying to destroy the power of the big industrial combines, which had supported the Japanese war effort, and to reduce the country's military potential. He wanted to break down the old feudal class structure and to introduce democratic government. Banning social contact with a defeated population was poor policy. Soldiers, he said, would be soldiers. MacArthur encouraged friendly relations, including sex. 'My father [also a general] told me never to give an order unless I was certain it would be carried out. I wouldn't issue a non-fraternization order for all the tea in China.'[4]

American soldiers had no difficulty communicating with Japanese women and fraternised enthusiastically. So did Commonwealth troops. Northcott's directive was comprehensively ignored, and his authority weakened. He finally accepted reality. He was so concerned about the high rate of VD that he made more resources available for sex education and hygiene. Any Commonwealth force officer with VD would be sent home in disgrace (ten at least were repatriated).

Latimer says that VD was just part of the way of life. One officer set up a supervised brothel for his men, to keep them healthy, but was forced to close it when a chaplain objected that it was immoral, and threatened to tell the authorities in New Zealand.

Latimer claimed the Army health service provided no prophylactics, no condoms. The official view seemed to be that intimate contact with Japanese women was unthinkable and so nothing practical was done to stop the spread of VD among J Force troops. According to the unit's official history the VD rate caused 'considerable concern'. It was highest among the Maori members of the New Zealand force, 'eight times greater than among European members'. The health of the occupation troops would have suffered more than it did but for what was described as 'constant vigilance on the part of authority'.[5]

Latimer says living conditions were so bad that women and children prostituted themselves so they could feed their families, keep warm, stay alive. Many soldiers inevitably took advantage of their desperate need. 'Women were available all the time.'

Hone Tuwhare, the poet, was in J Force at the same time and confirms the human traffic in flesh. In his biography, written by Janet Hunt, he recalls how he and some other Maori sang for American officers in Tokyo and were shown the good life. 'By the good life they meant prostitutes – and girls were thoroughly available, okay? That's the good life, which was up there as far as the Americans were concerned. And which we found, to our astonishment, was there, you know, at our gates.' Tuwhare acknowledged that some of the women were 'just forced into that kind of thing, not by choice'.[6]

He says VD was 'rife' but differs from Latimer in saying that 'heavy sorts of films were put on about how to avoid VD and so on, that was compulsory, anyone on leave, to get condoms and so on'.[7]

Local authorities were so afraid that occupation troops would, as they had been warned, loot and rape, that they quickly built and funded official brothels for the protection and reassurance of the city's 'respectable' female population who felt themselves threatened.

They called them Houses of Consolation, arranged a system for running them with brothel keepers and then set about filling them with 'comfort women'. Police were sent round the countryside and outlying islands to buy women and girls from parents or relations who had lost everything in the war. Hundreds of recruits were collected from Hiroshima, some former prostitutes, but most victims of poverty and their own families.

The authorities believed, with the record of history on their side, that all occupation troops everywhere rape women. They institutionalised rape by providing low-caste, abandoned or unwanted females for the victors to use in supervised surroundings.

They were not entirely successful. Latimer says flatly that rape was common. He saw more than one soldier just grab a woman off the street. He was ashamed and angry and would lose his temper. Once he saw a New Zealander trying to rape a child. 'I had my bayonet through the man's uniform and starting to go into his flesh when I stopped. He knew I would have stabbed him. He let the girl go.'

Other observers told similar stories of random rapes. A young Japanese bomb survivor: 'Recently a stenographer was raped by three soldiers [Australian], one after the other. I heard tell that one of the laundry girls had simply been kidnapped, taken off to one of the barrack huts, and was kept locked up in there.'[8] The same man mentioned acts of kindness by Australians at the same base, two even protecting him after he struck a soldier who abused him. He added that some Japanese women were pleased to be able to sell themselves to soldiers, and he called them traitors. Others called them family saviours.

Latimer kept his promise to write to Emily but said nothing about the horrors around him. 'We just didn't talk about it. It didn't seem possible to explain to people who weren't there.'

Very little was said by anyone at the time about rape or cruel treatment of local people. Japanese authorities refused to complain. The Allied occupation was benign when compared with the brutal treatment conquered people had received from the Japanese military.

The war crimes trials were then revealing to Japan and the world details of atrocities, including the repeated rape of hundreds of thousands of 'comfort women' in territory occupied by their armies during the previous eight years. They did not want to offend their all-powerful victors with criticisms that some women were being raped or prostituted when so many of their own people were publicly cooperating with the soldiers.

Almost fifty years later a Japanese professor at Melbourne University claimed, in 1993, that Commonwealth troops, including New Zealanders, raped and brutalised women during the occupation.[9] He called on the allies to apologise, compensate the victims and join research to learn why soldiers raped women in war. The New Zealand Returned Servicemen's Association denied the claim, questioned the professor's credibility and said it was strange that the allegation had not been made earlier.

Latimer finds nothing strange about the claim or the fact that it did not come sooner. He knows it is true, though he has no knowledge of how often it happened. Official records confirm that rapes, assaults and even murders were committed. One soldier was said to have declared, after a heavy drinking session, that he was going to get himself a 'gook'. He then took a truck and ran down and killed two Japanese. No charges were laid.

Latimer believes he knows why some soldiers rape. 'They're a long way from home. Women are defenceless. It's lust and power. Their own commanders often ignore the behaviour. They're not living under the ordinary rules of their own community in peacetime. They usually get away with it. All armies do it. It is terrible.' Northcott believed that the behaviour of the Commonwealth force was, on the whole, good but was concerned about a minority. In his final report in July 1946 he said that these soldiers had 'let their comrades down very badly by unruly, even criminal acts.' Whenever possible offenders were dealt with severely. Convicted criminals were removed from Japan. 'Prompt action has produced good results both by maintaining law and order and by increased confidence on the part of the civil population.'[10]

Latimer, and other soldiers, did not need to read Northcott's report. Evidence of good and bad behaviour was all around them. One Australian soldier shot at a Japanese man trying to beg cigarettes from men on a troopship. A New Zealander turned a high-pressure hose on a small boat containing three women, a baby and a man when they begged for cigarettes. The baby and one woman were nearly drowned. Some soldiers were angry at the treatment received by the women and baby but had no sympathy for the man. Latimer believes that the two soldiers would not have been reprimanded by their superiors. 'That sort of behaviour was common.'

Laurie Brocklebank, who wrote the only full account of J Force, reports that serious crimes committed by New Zealand troops 'included, in addition to rape, arson, assault on Japanese civilians, robbery and wilful damage'.[11] He also records one case of murder and a whole range of black-market offences.

Latimer says that the black market brought everyone closer together. Most soldiers took part to some extent. The rate of monetary exchange was so low that everyone used it. As a result, many New Zealanders came to know Japanese outside the official boundaries. Some set up in business, stealing supplies and establishing a network of buyers. One J Force member wrote years later that he had been introduced on his arrival in 1947 to a number of Japanese by soldiers about to return home. He did not realise for some months that they were intended to be his black-market contacts.

Relations between the New Zealanders and the Japanese eased as the occupation continued. Latimer became friends with a doctor and a dentist who lived close to one of his bases. Neither could legally practise their skills, but did so unofficially. He visited them in their homes, sitting on the floor round their low tables, getting to know their families. Both men had travelled and had knowledge of the English language. Latimer had picked up some words quite quickly and though he never considered that he was able to speak even elementary Japanese he made himself understood at a simple level.

He found them to be like most people: struggling to cope with the problems of the day, worried about the future, relieved that the occupation troops were not the monsters they had been taught to expect. They were willing to talk about the war. 'They were apologetic. It was the worst thing that could have happened to them. And all their efforts, their deaths, all the destruction, all for nothing. But they still didn't criticise the Emperor.'

They admired MacArthur and thought he was trying to give them a vision for the future. 'It was as though they saw him as another sort of emperor, or at least as someone who had the same sort of role – to give them hope. He gave back some of their pride. Plant one bunch of rice a day. Believe in yourselves.'

The Japanese had been amazed at the friendliness and tolerance of the Americans. They were mostly kind, using their vehicles to take ill Japanese to hospitals, returning lost children to their homes, and giving up their streetcar seats to older women.

Latimer said that most New Zealand soldiers also gave as much help as they could. Some soldiers arranged Christmas parties for children. One trooper noted that they consumed food as though they had not eaten for weeks: 'One little chap of about seven caused much interest in the steady methodical manner in which he put away an immense amount of food without the slightest sign of any emotion. His hands reached out, his jaws functioned. He was very much a person hard at work.'

Latimer admired the resilience and integrity of the peasant women. 'They worked terribly hard. They kept on planting rice in the paddy fields. They carried huge packs of wood on their backs. They were determined they and their families were going to survive no matter what they had to put up with.' *Time* magazine and some Western observers often described Japanese women as ants, a dehumanising comparison which Latimer did not accept. He saw the women as survivors.

The Japanese women had long been regarded as inferior to men, by male tradition, and had few civil rights and no political rights till MacArthur gave them the vote in the new constitution he imposed. Latimer respected them as workers and builders at a time when many of their men sat back, defeated and angry. They reminded him of his mother. They were small, like her, and they never gave up.

Hiroshima is still the strongest memory he has of Japan. Latimer knew that the Japanese called what happened the pikadon, the day of lightning (pika) and thunder (don).

The *Jayforce Times*, a news and information publication, printed just one article on Hiroshima in two years. It described the size of the atomic bomb and how it was made but said nothing about any possible dangers from radiation. American military authorities were determined to suppress details of the health hazards which followed. They discouraged (if not actually banned) the publication in Japan of John Hersey's internationally famous book on Hiroshima.[12]

President Truman had already been fiercely criticised for ordering the destruction of Hiroshima and Nagasaki (one demonstration bomb over an uninhabited area, would, it was argued, have been sufficient to force surrender). The United States government did not want to be accused of biological warfare, worse even than poison gas.

At the time, Latimer heard the rumours which circulated about terrible wounds, of sores called cheloids spreading all over the bodies of victims, of strange vegetation, and of genetic deformities in humans and animals. Poison gases were mentioned and claims made that the land itself could not be used for generations.

He learned the truth many years later. About 80,000 people, the great majority of them civilians in Hiroshima, died in the blast. Later about another 60,000 or 70,000 died as a result of radiation sickness. A city of about 250,000 to 300,000 people was reduced to ashes in the instant after many saw a great flash, a man-made sun, appear in the sky above them.

A few days after he arrived in Japan, Latimer went through the city by train. Hersey, sent by *The New Yorker* magazine, had arrived a month earlier (his account of what he saw was first published in August 1946). Like others, Latimer saw a wasteland, dotted with remnants of buildings, rough shacks, and the beginnings of fresh vegetation.

Hone Tuwhare, who passed through at the same time, says he wandered around quite innocently. 'There was only just shacks beginning to be put up and people who had escaped and people who were related were drifting back.' They were 'little, pitiful things'. There were no streets. People built where they thought they had lived. He saw beggars. 'I didn't hang round. It was too bleak a landscape.'[13]

A few months earlier the first J Force soldiers, from Italy, had made the same journey. One senior officer, Frank Rennie, said the complete devastation wrought by the bomb was still apparent. 'The silhouette, on the surface of a sealed road, of a horse, cart and driver told the whole horrific story; they had provided only fleeting resistance to the blinding, scorching flash.'[14] Rennie said that few were unaffected by what they saw and little was said during the rest of their journey.

Latimer recalls driving into Hiroshima with a friend in a truck. 'There was still absolute devastation a year after the bomb was dropped.' He recalls the stench of carbon and human flesh. Unaware, he had driven up to a family cremating a bomb victim in a homemade incinerator. He had heard chanting but did not know what was happening till he was quite close. Relatives had built a frame on which the body was placed and had lit a big fire underneath. 'I turned the truck and left quickly.' He says the city still had no cremation facilities. 'People had to burn their dead any way they could. It was utterly sad.'

Many J Force men and women visited the city, some on organised trips. Some fossicked in the rubble looking for souvenirs such as fused glass. A senior officer recalled that one of his group had, by chance, a geiger counter: 'it made clacking noises but no one was concerned about it all.'

Laurie Brocklebank, author of *Jayforce: New Zealand and the Military Occupation of Japan 1945–48*, says that one of his informants told him that official leave parties stopped late in 1946 because of concerns about safety.[15] Opportunities to go to Hiroshima continued however through 1947 and 1948, and it remained a popular centre for black-market activities.

Latimer believes that some members of J Force could have been affected by radiation. His own health has always been good but he has wondered why he and Emily had only four children, and then no more. Sterility, permanent or temporary, has been experienced by others affected by radiation, and he thinks this could have been the reason the Latimers had no more children.

He knows of other returned soldiers who, with their children, have had illnesses which could have resulted from war service. Two friends both had children fairly late in their lives. 'I knew that these children had defects but I didn't make the connection between their health and our time in Japan till I saw them together. One had bone weaknesses and couldn't stand upright. Another had something like Down's syndrome. That was when I began to think these children of veterans could have been affected by radiation.'

Hone Tuwhare also believes he could have been affected. He says in his biography that 'there must have been some damage to the New Zealanders' when they walked around the city. 'I get these damn things on my eyebrow, you know – it breaks out now and again, this damn thing just on here – never had it before, eh.'[16]

Latimer's friend, Rutene Irwin, says that for many years his eyes 'are always weeping', his head aches and he 'can't sleep at night dreaming of dead people'.[17] He is now on a 37 per cent disability pension.

Another soldier, Lloyd Griffiths, the regimental artist, spent hours of free time in the rubble because his colonel wanted paintings for the mess. His thyroid is no longer functioning but he cannot prove conclusively that this is related to his time in Hiroshima.[18]

Australian troops were stationed even nearer than the New Zealanders to the epicentre of the bomb blast, only eight kilometres away. They often went into the city and poked round the ruins. They drank beer made in Hiroshima, and played football there. Some claimed later that there had been a high incidence of cancer among veterans, though actual figures were not known. One spokesman said in 1992 that he believed the Australian authorities used them as guinea pigs to test their reaction to radiation. He rejected the official response that no radiation damage was possible because the troops had arrived there five months after the bomb exploded.

Latimer believes that the New Zealand government should approve an independent study into the health of surviving members of J Force. He is concerned not so much for the men themselves but for any genetic consequences of exposure to radiation. Servicemen in other countries have made similar requests. 'Our own commanders and government must have known something about what happened. Otherwise why would they have told us to keep out of the city. Why did the Americans pull out? We were exposed to a completely new biological hazard.'

He refers to Chernobyl, where a nuclear reactor exploded in Russia about fourteen years ago. 'The full effect is only now starting to be felt as more and more people who were exposed are getting sick.'

The Japanese he knew said little about the bomb. 'They didn't want to talk about it. It was too painful.' He saw nobody with cheloid scars. 'They tended to be kept out of sight. The Japanese themselves seemed to be ashamed of them.' Later he heard that some victims had not been well treated because the scars were seen as signs of defeat, of humiliation, of guilt. Some years passed before these sufferers were accorded respect, and Hiroshima came to be a symbol of peace in the world. No more bombs was the slogan.

Most of Latimer's time in Japan was spent on the usual duties of soldiers, maintaining their own units, their equipment, vehicles and buildings, and going on patrols. Inevitably much of it was boring. Recreation was arranged, mostly rugby, soccer and cricket. Few took advantage of the educational programmes promised in the recruiting publicity. American and British films were shown each week.

Some units were accused of slackness, indiscipline and unmilitary behaviour. Latimer says one reason was that soldiers simply did not have much to do that was seen as important. 'We were told before we came that we were being sent to finish the job – meaning that we were going to make sure that the Japanese were never going to be a threat again,' he says. 'But when we got to Japan our main tasks were looking after ourselves, repairing our old trucks, making sure we got all our supplies. We had a lot of time on our hands.'

This was true for officers as well as soldiers. Some found it hard to maintain discipline when they were not confronted by any real enemy, when there was no danger and when one of their biggest problems was ensuring the quality of their daily food.

Responsibility for what was described as low morale among the force belonged, however, to the New Zealand government, not those in Japan. Almost 40,000 Commonwealth troops stationed in one relatively small area of Japan were constantly stumbling over one another. The New Zealand government had begun having second thoughts about the value of J Force as a political pawn soon after it arrived in Japan. As early as the end of 1946 Fraser considered pulling out but was persuaded to hold on a little longer (almost two more years in fact). Britain was, instead, the first to start withdrawing its forces the following year.

Latimer says J Force, and the whole Commonwealth army, was under-employed and that soldiers could not be blamed for not taking their army duties seriously. Latimer: 'For the Japanese we were something like a new industry. We hired a lot of people and so we were a source of employment at a time when there were very few paid jobs. The country was bankrupt.'

A complete break in routine came when Latimer was chosen for ceremonial guard duty in Tokyo outside the imperial palace. This was a rotating function with the Americans. For the Commonwealth troops it was a chance to see Tokyo. The city had not recovered from the intensive raids carried out before the atomic bombs were dropped. Phosphorous bombs had caused fire storms.

Latimer saw destruction and poverty but also signs of regeneration. Parts of the city were still intact. New buildings were being erected, streets laid out, gardens planted. MacArthur wanted a new Japan created quickly and gave all the support he could.

Hirohito's palace had not been damaged but it was not what Latimer had expected. Instead of a grand structure the imperial buildings were small, clustered in gardens and ornamental lakes, and completely hidden behind walls surrounded by a moat. Palace? What palace?

No guard was necessary for security. The Emperor was safe from the occupying forces, and his own people still accorded him respect in spite of his revelation that he was just one of them. The most exciting incident during Latimer's guard duty was when a Maori soldier shot a swan in the moat. Latimer was the corporal on duty so had to take responsibility.

He remembers his twenty-first birthday, 7 February 1947. He felt as though he was freezing to death. Knowing that he was probably as smartly dressed as he had ever been – spic and span, everything polished which could be polished – did not make him feel any warmer.

The guards were on show all the time. MacArthur inspected them more than once and expressed his satisfaction. His command headquarters was immediately opposite the palace, in one of the few big buildings that survived the bombing. Formerly used by an insurance company, the building became known as Dai Ichi (Number One) by the Japanese and everyone else.

Latimer was impressed by MacArthur's bearing. The General saw himself as an exceptional man, singled out by destiny to be a great leader. He had all the arrogance and self-righteousness of an absolute dictator. Latimer said he had a tremendous presence. 'When we were on guard duty he would speak to us, quite casually – you know, like, been here long? He knew his power. He knew what he was trying to do.'

When it was time to leave in mid-1947 Latimer had no regrets. Some of his fellow-soldiers had volunteered, they said, for King and Country. He had gone mostly for the adventure, for a chance to see the world, or at least part of it.

The fact that he got more than he had bargained for did not make him feel he should have stayed home. He made good friends. Jim Pou, a Ngapuhi from Kaikohe, later became a senior welfare officer for the Department of Maori Affairs. Lieutenant-Colonel Duncan McIntyre, one of his officers, later became minister of Maori affairs. Captain Ross Wright, Te Uri-o-Hau from the Kaipara, worked with him for many years on hapu affairs and submissions to the Waitangi Tribunal.

He had also had a lot of time to think about his own future. He knew he would not go back to the Far North. There was no work there. He still hoped some day to become a farmer but he needed a job.

When asked what he brought back with him from Japan he smiles. His only memento is a gold wisdom tooth. He says he took little part in the black market but did swap milk for false teeth being sold by the roadside.

Soldiers who sold stolen supplies on the black market could not bring back large wads of currency or expensive goods because they could not explain how they got them. Some left money in Japan, hoping to be able to use it much later, as New Zealand soldiers had done in Italy late in the war.

Latimer says his time in the army and in Japan changed his life permanently. His experiences at Papakura military camp gave him a chance to grow up within a stable environment at just that time in his life, late teens, when he could have got into trouble living in a city for the first time. He understands young people who get offside with the police, who are involved in petty crime and who end up in jail for short terms – and become permanently alienated. 'It isn't hard. Just get drunk with your mates, convert a car, get busted by a cop, and you end up in jail with a lot of people who are much worse.'

Because of his time in the army, Latimer favours the introduction of some form of compulsory military training for three months or six months, for young Maori. He knows this is unfashionable but says that so little is being done to help young unemployed Maori that a short period of training could build up their health, their skills and their self-confidence.

Latimer had not gone to Japan as a complete innocent. His early years on the Aupouri Peninsula had, in many ways, been tough. He had seen gumdiggers spend money on drink at the Houhora pub, and then prove how manly they were by fighting each other. He still remembers seeing diggers challenge others to hit them as hard as they could on their tight-muscled bellies. He remembers the beatings he took from one of his first bosses when he was just fifteen. But Japan was different, not just because of the scale of the suffering but its type. He says it was nearly impossible for anyone to treat their service there as just a job, whether it was called peace-keeping or police duties. 'We couldn't escape the horror all round us. We were observers. We saw the terrible results of war, and of atomic warfare.'

This was not the view of all those who served with J Force. Some saw their time there as an interlude, almost like a holiday. They visited different parts of the country on their leave breaks. They picked up souvenirs. They gained little understanding of Japanese people.

Hone Tuwhare put the thoughts and feelings of some of them into one of his best-known poems, 'No Ordinary Sun'.[19] Others spoke and wrote later of what they saw, and of their realisation that a massive new force of destruction and toxic pollution had been released — and could be used again.

Latimer also learned that governments do not always mean what they say, and that promises can have a very short life-span. Your country needs you, the Labour government said. In a Christmas message in 1946 the minister of defence, Fred Jones, reassured J Force that they had done 'exceptionally well in tedious circumstances in a foreign land' but did not tell them that his government was even then thinking of pulling them out because they were not needed.

Nor did Jones tell them that when they returned home they would be denied recognition as war veterans — they were not part of the Second New Zealand Expeditionary Force (2NZEF) and they were not on active service. They were, therefore, refused pension rights and service medals.

They had to wait till 1994 to be accepted as veterans largely because of a campaign carried out by Lloyd Griffiths, a retired Carrington Polytechnic lecturer. He argued that J Force was legally part of 2NZEF and that it was on active duty, a view finally supported by the Crown Law Office.[20] Members are now entitled to war pensions and have received the New Zealand Service Medal, concessions given only reluctantly and without grace about fifty years late.

Successive governments also refused requests for a full inquiry into J Force exposure to radiation. Latimer: 'We were never in any danger from the Japanese. It was our own government which exposed us to possible dangers from radiation sickness whether they knew it or not. This is like being hit by "friendly fire", when your own side accidentally shells you.'

On his return Latimer decided he was finished with the military and with official functions and so did not go to the special welcome arranged for northern J Force members at Otiria. Instead, he went straight to Auckland to Emily Moore.

He has been back to Japan six or seven times since then, usually with Emily, and in rather more style. His first visit was in the early 1980s as part of a group negotiating a box-net fishing deal. The Latimers stayed in the Palace Hotel, about 100 metres from his guard post in front of the imperial palace where he celebrated his coming of age. He was astonished by the redevelopment of the city, raised literally from the ashes.

He still has some knowledge of the language. He respects the competence of Japanese in business and finds them easy to deal with, not unlike Maori in the way in which they want to go away and think about things in their own time.

The war was never a topic of conversation on visits to Japan. Nobody wanted to talk about it and he saw no reason to raise it after thirty-five or forty years. 'There were a lot of war crimes on both sides. The use of atom bombs on Hiroshima and Nagasaki are often described as two of the greatest atrocities. Now we're just meeting each other as ordinary people, not former enemies. All the resentment we saw in 1946 on the faces of the young men has long gone.'

He is pleased that the status of women has risen greatly. MacArthur shocked the country when he gave Japanese women the vote. But MacArthur believed that democracy could not work unless men and women were equal. Latimer: 'I'm sure there are all sorts of invisible restrictions on women but the progress has been tremendous.'

He has never returned to southern Japan and to Hiroshima, now bigger than when it was destroyed in 1945. Its population has grown from about 300,000 to almost a million. Other veterans have gone back and revisited their old barrack towns.

Japanese have never happily accepted mixed-race children. Some of those children born as a result of fraternisation would not have lived through the hardest times after the war. They would have had the lowest priority for food or care. Those who did survive would have had low status. Part-Japanese, part-foreign children today are likely to be insulted with terms such as 'round-eyes'.

Latimer still wants governments to recognise the dangers J Force men and women were exposed to in Japan. He welcomes the decision by Mark Burton, the Minister of Defence and Veterans' Affairs (on 29 April 2001) to award special treatment to Vietnam War veterans with health problems linked to Agent Orange and would like to see those who served in Japan treated in the same way.

CHAPTER THREE

Maori Identity
1947–1956

> As the person who has the responsibility to speak for the Maori people I quite often find myself arguing with the various bloods that run through my body. My Irish and Scottish and English blood puts my Maori blood under so much pressure that I am forced to champion the Maori side and I will continue to do that while I believe that the threat to my Maori ancestral side is there.
> – Sir Graham Latimer, speaking at a resource consent hearing related to the Karikari Peninsula, Northland, in the 1980s

GRAHAM LATIMER BECAME DISTINCTIVELY AND PUBLICLY MAORI IN THE early hours of the morning during a Ngati Whatua hui at Oruawharo in the Kaipara in 1956. He was thirty. He was asleep. When he woke he joined friends for breakfast in the marae dining hall and asked who had been elected as an iwi spokesman. You, they said.

Though he had kinship connections with Ngati Whatua, Latimer had lived in the area for only three years. His own hapu is Ngati Kahu from the Aupouri Peninsula. He says nobody had asked him if he wanted the position, which was to speak on practical issues as distinct from spiritual ones. He had not even considered it. He could not speak Maori, though he understood quite a bit. He had not been brought up on a marae and was not fully familiar with protocol. He was not highly educated (two weeks in secondary school) and he held a minor job as New Zealand Railways stationmaster at Kaiwaka. Some kaumatua and kuia had, however, already decided that he had the potential to be one of their leaders on policies and strategies. He was young, energetic, popular, a good husband and caring father, a rugby player, and a churchgoer. Emily was an asset to the community, respected as a mother, and admired as a representative tennis and basketball player. Elders had watched them both, talked with them, and judged them. They decided they needed them.

Latimer's evolution as a Maori spokesman occurred slowly and as a result of circumstances over which he felt he had little control. For many years he had no special consciousness of being Maori or anything else. He was a New Zealander of mixed ancestry, like lots of other people.

When he was born, in 1926, he was statistically something less than Maori in terms of the definitions then used. Anyone with half or more Maori blood was classified as Maori. Anyone with a lesser quantity could be defined as quarter-caste or European.

There are no longer any blood rules: Maoriness is a matter of personal choice. Someone can decide to be Maori for a particular purpose, such as registering on the Maori electoral roll. The same person could also choose to be on the general roll. Decisions about ethnicity depend on the context. The exception is when someone wishes to assert membership of a hapu or iwi; then it is necessary to provide their whakapapa, their genealogy, their bloodline.

Because Latimer had a Pakeha mother and a Maori father with some English ancestry he was less-than-half, as determined by the 1926 blood definition, and was not, consequently, a Maori for census purposes. However, nobody checked statements people made then, or now, so he could just as easily have been entered on the electoral role as either Maori or European.

During his years on the gumfields Latimer was much closer to members of his mother's family than to his father's, who lived near Kaitaia. By the time he was four he had as much or more contact with Croatians and Boer War veterans of various nationalities as with Maori. After 1930, when the family moved south to Pamapuria, he spent more time with his Maori relatives but did not feel as close to them as to his mother's parents because of those impressionable first years. He still remembers the warmth, affection and easy humour of the Kenworthy family.

'Nobody could have had better grandparents,' he says. 'They always took time to talk with us, to look after us when Mum was busy or not at home. They always made sure they had a boiled lolly.' His older brother Joe has an equally great love and affection for his Pakeha grandparents. He describes Joseph Kenworthy as a 'great old bugger'. Graham Latimer agrees: 'He was tough.'

Latimer's memories of his Maori grandparents are of the strong emphasis they gave to evening Bible readings, to compulsory Sunday school attendance, and other Anglican Church activities. His grandmother was the first Maori Sunday school teacher in the Far North and he remembers her presence and her elegance with awe. 'They were all very serious.' Joe recalls his Maori grandfather as someone who, to a child, was distant, aloof, unapproachable, unrelenting, strict and humourless – a total contrast to his Irish grandfather.

Latimer's strongest and most lasting impressions came from his mother. His father was often away – either on other parts of the gumfields or as a labourer or contractor on road works. This resulted in the first three children spending much of their early lives actually living in the Kenworthy home.

Latimer vividly recalls one incident when he was about four. Lillian saw the local policeman from Houhora coming toward their home, told her son to tell him she was out, and then hid inside their small hut. Graham did as he was told. The policeman said loudly that he knew Mrs Latimer was there and that unless she paid an outstanding debt to the storekeeper he'd be back.

The boy knew his mother was very upset, and he felt angry that she had been shamed by the policeman. Latimer: 'I realised a lot later that the policeman had been used to intimidate my mother. He was acting like a debt collector and so he made himself into an enemy of people like my parents. Even though I was very young I felt that I had to defend her. The debt was paid later when my father came back.'

His feelings for his mother were further strengthened when he realised later she had broken all the racial and social taboos of her time, at great personal cost, to leave her Catholic upbringing at sixteen to marry an Anglican Maori not much older than herself.

Early cartoons depicted Maori holding wild moa chariot races. Posed photographs showed children in the Far North drinking alcohol and smoking tobacco in pipes. Cartoons showed scowling 'chinks' sitting in trams while sturdy Anglo-Saxons (returned servicemen and workers) had to stand up. One showed a young white woman holding hands with a thin, knock-kneed Indian in a turban. They were standing in front of a large black heart topped by a ribbon saying True Love. The caption: 'Your Daughter?' The Indian could just as easily have been Maori.[1]

In 1927 a well-known journalist-writer, Pat Lawlor, published a classic book of Maori as buffoons, a bestseller that went through five editions in nine months. His *Maori Tales*, over 100 stories from 'Artists and Writers from every Centre in New Zealand' was described, falsely, as a collection of Maori wit and humour to add a little 'to the gaiety of a world sadly in need of it'.[2]

The stories were full of throw-away lines: 'The only part of Hori that had ever been known to work was his imagination.' Illustrations showed an obese Maori too tired to cultivate his land, another becoming enthusiastic only when food arrived (particularly shark), or lying on the ground while ragged boys tried to decide whether he was drunk or just asleep. In one story a proud father told a white farmer that his 'piccaninny' would soon be one of 'th' ora-pracks [All Blacks] eh, poss!'.

The book touched on most of the themes that would be prevalent in the future. Maori politicians were ridiculed, their concerns about land deprivation were dismissed and their interest in food and alcohol was drawn large. 'Some of the Maori members could be very entertaining, especially after a supper of muttonbirds and beer at Bellamys,' said one writer. 'Notable among them was Wi Pere, from the Hau Hau territory. There had been an angry debate on a Maori Land Bill. Wi Pere thought he smelt bare-faced robbery of native rights, which had been guaranteed under the much-abused Treaty of Waitangi. He wound up a fiery speech by threatening every European trespasser on those rights with a bullet.

'Then he almost paralysed the House by shouting, "And to hell with the damned pakeha". Barclay, the Maori interpreter, paused, doubting whether he should translate the violent denunciation, but he did. The Speaker let it go, but called the patriot to order, and the House took no notice.'[3]

The anonymous writer said that members of parliament rarely paid any attention 'when one of the Maori representatives arose on his legs. Of the picturesque Maori group of that period, Wi Pere, Hone Heke, Henare Kaihau and Tame Parata have long since set sail in the long canoe. They were all hard-doers, but jolly good company'.[4]

The ways in which Maori wore European clothing was a stock joke. A writer, Akarana, described a young woman 'in a black sealskin coat, quite modern' then added 'what is not so modern is the plaid shawl in which a tiny tamahine is wrapped upon the young woman's back ... She is smoking a pipe and set rakishly upon her coarse bobbed locks is a man's old felt-hat'.[5]

Akarana added, that Maori would never change, that the 'veneer of civilisation does not go down very deep – the pagan's in the grain in mankind. The primitive love of ease and comfort will always keep Henare and Mere fairly close to the standards of their forefathers. Mere may wrap herself up in smart fur coats, but never will she squeeze her stout brown body into smart rubber corsets, and while there is a man's sweater or an old felt-hat to supply warmth and comfort she is not going in for ninon and the cloche [silk dress and fancy hat]'.[6]

Another story tells how Tai is taken to court for not paying the dog tax. He travels at government expense, is put up at a pub where he has a good time: 'Prenty kai, prenty everyt'ing, te good soft bed, too, but I no pay. Kapai te Govmint.' When he can't pay his fine either he is sent to 'te boob' for one month, where he is given 'crean clothes, prenty kai, nice bath, prenty branket on te bed – by kripe! It te fine place'. As this is a far better life than he is used to he decides to not pay the dog tax next year: 'No proomin' fear, my oat', no!'[7]

No story showed an understanding of Maori history, culture, language, or why the characters were almost always poor. Maori were always the butt of the joke. Some of the stories were common to other countries but transplanted to New Zealand. For Maori, it was possible to read Irishman, Scotsman or Jew.

The education system compounded the general ignorance by not teaching New Zealand history, making it almost impossible for citizens to gain any idea of the country's troubled past or of the policies that created the modern Maori. After the wars over land stopped in the 1860s myths were fashioned about how well everyone got on with one another. Lies were told, and believed by most people. Maori had the same legal rights as all other citizens. They had equal opportunities for education and jobs. No colour bar existed.

The history of Maori–Pakeha relations was either rewritten in the form of fairy stories or not mentioned, thereby rendering it invisible. Maori were noble savages, or great fighters, who had to give way to a higher civilisation. They were then re-cast as colourful nobodies – happy layabouts, some of whom were great rugby players – who had no significant place in New Zealand society. Good chums though, as William Pember Reeves noted in his book, *The Long White Cloud*, published in 1898: 'The average colonist regards a Mongolian [Chinese] with repulsion, and looks on an Australian black as very near to a wild beast; but he likes the Maori, and treats them in many respects as an equal.'[8]

Myth-making was easy because the victors were writing the history and most non-Maori were, at the time, very new settlers. Assisted immigration schemes from the 1870s attracted hundreds of thousands to New Zealand where they settled on land acquired from Maori through Land Court manipulation, confiscation, forced sales and direct purchase at bargain-basement prices. In the first thirty years of the twentieth century about 200,000 new settlers arrived, three times more than the total Maori population in 1926.

Lillian Kenworthy's relatives had come to New Zealand as part of these waves of occupation. They knew nothing of the country's past. Their main aim was, literally, to carve a living out of the bush or dig a living out of the gumfields. All they knew about Maori came from observing those they saw around them – a tiny minority much poorer even than themselves. While Sir George Grey, a former governor, saw visions of a great, pure-blooded nation of Anglo-Saxons dominating the South Pacific, settlers struggled to survive in one of the most isolated countries in the world, 12,000 miles from Home.

Government policies over the previous forty or fifty years were aimed at creating a 'White' New Zealand by restricting immigrants who could be labelled coloured, such as Indians and Chinese. Race purity was the proudly expressed ideal.

Grey, when he was prime minister in the 1870s, said colonials could not allow 'a mixed breed of civilisation' to spring up in New Zealand. An Anglo-Saxon race holding a dominant position in the South Pacific would, on the other hand, bring peace, harmony, prosperity 'such as no former age of the world has known'. No place was seen for Maori or half-breeds, mongrels. Or, for that matter, foreigners like the Dalmatian gumdiggers, who were ranked even lower than Maori.[9]

One man, Lionel Terry, was so obsessed by the need for racial purity that he deliberately shot and killed an old Chinese in Wellington in 1905, believing that by so doing he was holding the 'Yellow Peril' at bay. An early advocate of apartheid, Terry wanted all Maori shipped to off-shore islands. (He was sent to a psychiatric hospital, dying there forty-seven years later.)

In this intolerant environment Lillian's marriage in 1921 to Graham Latimer senior, when he was twenty-one, was scandalous. Public opinion could overlook, if not condone, marriage between a Pakeha man and a Maori woman. She was seen as trying to rise up the social scale and was often described as being of high rank among her own people, a 'princess'. But a Pakeha woman marrying a Maori was plunging into degradation.

Many who were opposed to such marriages, of either sort, said they could, perhaps, understand the personal physical attraction but argued that the mixed-breed children would have a terrible life because nobody would accept them. So, the argument went, races must be kept apart not because we wanted it but because of the innate racial prejudice of everybody else.

Both the Latimer and Kenworthy families opposed the marriage. Lillian's father Joe and mother Pearl were more understanding though not happy and gave her all the support they could but some of her sisters would not speak to her for years: they felt she had shamed them. Latimer says he can still recall the pain his mother felt when her sisters would drive past her house at Pamapuria on the way to Kaitaia and not call in to see her.

Lillian's Maori in-laws were at first equally displeased. They had hoped for a much more suitable match for their son. They held high status in local hapu and in the Anglican congregation. Latimer's grandfather had been the first chairman of the local council set up under the Maori Councils Act 1900 to provide some measure of self-government for Maori, and was a widely respected kaumatua.

The birth of six children eased family tensions. The children knew nothing of hostilities between Catholic and Anglican, Maori and Pakeha, newcomer and tangata whenua. They were not aware that labels could be and were applied to people. In the official and common usage of the time they were all termed half-castes but they thought of themselves as Frank and Joe and Graham and May and Julia and Lloyd, and that those around them were Mum and Dad and Grandma and Grandad and Uncle Frank and all the rest.

Both families had to adjust to the idea that their grandchildren, nieces, nephews, and cousins were of mixed ethnic, cultural and racial ancestry. The Maori side had received one earlier infusion of English blood, the Latimer who had settled in the Hokianga Harbour, south of Kaitaia, in the nineteenth century. This man, a trader, had lived with Graham's great grandmother, from Te Hapua (near Cape Reinga), but never married her. She had seven children and named them all Latimer, though some had different fathers. One of her sons, Graham Latimer's grandfather, survived to be an Anglican laypreacher, with features combining English and Maori characteristics.

Latimer's upbringing as more Pakeha than Maori was, however, not determined by bloodlines but by his parents' determination to keep him alive. The gumfields were a dangerous environment. Disease was endemic in Maori settlements, sanitation was poor and the infant death rate was high. The influenza epidemic of 1918–1919 killed at least five times more Maori than non-Maori. Graham's parents knew from personal experience that going to hui and tangi often led to infection, to re-infection, epidemics and deaths – followed by more tangi.

Prime Minister Gordon Coates visited the area in 1927 and described Te Kao, just north of the Latimer's camp, as one of the most desperately poor communities he had ever seen.[10] Coates knew what he was talking about. He was one of few politicians with any understanding of or sympathy for Maori, and he was the only prime minister who could speak their language. In the Kaipara, his home area, Coates was aware of grinding poverty, and Te Kao was possibly worse.

Graham's mother and father were intensely conscious of health dangers. They saw death all around them. Two of Lillian's brothers had died while still young and she worried about her children while they lived in the camp (1921 to 1930). Tuberculosis – consumption – and other chest complaints, with dysentery, were the main killers. Though the northern winters were relatively mild Lillian rubbed the children down with cod liver oil, and sewed woollen chest pads saturated with camphorated oil into their clothing, in spite of anguished protests and mocking from others. Latimer: 'We smelled like fish. She was a very, very good mother.' They all survived.

The Latimer family had, therefore, only fleeting contact with Maori settlements and took little part in Maori community activities. Their squatter camp of corrugated iron and lean-to shacks sheltered many nationalities but the Latimers were the only Maori who lived there permanently. The camp itself was more hygienic than many permanent settlements. Houses were spread over a wide area. People gave themselves space, and disposed of their personal and household waste without endangering others. The Latimers had their own well and latrine.

This separation from Maori village life was made more complete when Lillian and Graham Latimer decided to send their children to general public schools (about half of all Maori children attended these by the 1930s) rather than to special native schools, which were also publicly funded. They thought the main school system had higher educational standards.

Latimer's father, an eloquent speaker of Maori, refused to teach his children, or recount cultural traditions or whakapapa, thus creating another barrier with the Maori community. Frank, Graham's eldest brother, said in an interview for this book that Maori was not spoken in their home, or around it.

Like many other Maori of the time their father wanted them to speak English, English, English, as Sir Apirana Ngata (then a member of parliament) advocated. That was the language of the future, of economics, of literature, and of the majority population. Their parents wanted them to be completely comfortable in English. They did not want the children to be bilingual.

Contact with the general community increased when the family moved to the small farm near Kaitaia owned by Latimer's Maori grandfather. They left a shack with an earth floor, and moved into a solid farmhouse. Their first beds were planks nailed to the wall, with mattresses of manuka leaves.

While the shift resulted from necessity it also meant the children could attend Kaitaia Primary School (later converted to a district high school, and college). Latimer enjoyed his school years, and did not see them as racial experiences. Joe confirms this impression. He was not aware of any prejudice or discrimination.

It was at Kaitaia Primary School, however, that Graham had the first direct experience of racial discrimination that identified him to others as Maori. This occurred in 1937 when he was about eleven. He knew nothing of it at the time. His father told him years later.

Some school committee members did not want Latimers sitting next to their children because they were Maori and, therefore, by definition, a health risk. The principal, Gair, responded in the most personal and final way. In a clear declaration of principle to the whole community he placed Graham next to his own son, George. The boys sat together for two years in a two-seat desk with a lift-up lid and became good friends. There is no record of any head-lice or other bugs being passed on and no committee member raised the issue again.

George Gair, who later became a cabinet minister in Robert Muldoon's National government in the 1970s and early 1980s, confirms the incident: 'My father wanted to accommodate Graham's father's wishes [to have his children at the school] and he defused a conflict with the school committee by putting me next to Graham in class. In this way Graham's father had achieved his objective and my father made it impossible for the school committee to go public with its opposition.'[11]

Almost thirty years later they met again, both aged thirty-nine, both National Party candidates. Graham contested the unwinnable seat of Northern Maori, held by his Labour friend Matiu Rata. George Gair was gifted the North Shore seat, went on to senior cabinet posts and later became high commissioner in London and mayor of North Shore. He had also gone to Japan, just after Latimer left, in the J Force second relief draft as a journalist with the Army Education Service.

Gair says that he was unaware at the time of his father's reason for sitting him next to Graham. When Graham told him about it later he questioned his father, then retired. 'He confirmed that it was true but I doubt he would ever have told me of this had it not been raised by someone else.'[12]

This incident reveals more than just the prejudice of some school committee members. What is important is that few people knew about it and it was never a public issue. If Gair had been asked later in life whether there was any anti-Maori feeling in his school days he would almost certainly have said no. He enjoyed his time in Kaitaia and has happy memories of playing rugby with Latimer.

Many people at that time would not have been aware of overt racism. Most, if asked, would have repeated the standard response. Race relations were good, not like in Australia where Aborigines were being treated as inferiors. No, in this country everyone was equal before the law: New Zealand was a model to the rest of the world.

The reality, however, was quite different. Maori were not seen as a threat and could easily be patronised. Almost all of their best land had been lost to incoming settlers. They were discriminated against in employment (the last to be hired, the first to be fired), in hospitals (some refused to accept them as patients), in pubs (they were banned from some bars), in accommodation (they found it hard to rent desirable homes), and in the courts (least represented, most often convicted).

Before leaving school Latimer cannot remember much conscious personal feeling about being Maori – or being anything else. It was not a subject for discussion. He just was. Few people agonised about being Maori or not. He and his brothers and sisters were fully accepted by their classmates as classmates. They were fit, agile, good-looking and popular; dedicated rugby players and basketballers.

While the young Latimers had very little experience of racial prejudice their father was well aware of it. Frank remembered his father being called a lazy black bastard but could not be certain, because he was so young at the time, whether it was said with contempt or as rough humour.

The children were conscious of differences, but did not necessarily see them as signs of racial discrimination. The Princess Theatre, Kaitaia's only cinema, was loosely segregated: most Maori sat left of the centre aisle, non-Maori on the right. Emily remembers Pukekohe's one cinema in the 1940s as having Maori downstairs, non-Maori in the gallery. In both places, however, segregation was not total. Maori and Pakeha friends sat together in Kaitaia. Emily and some of her Maori fellow-workers sat upstairs, because they objected to the behaviour of some noisy Maori downstairs.

By the time Latimer went to Japan he knew he was regarded as Maori because of his mixed racial background, because of his colour. Though he enlisted in the Maori Battalion D Squadron he could just as easily have joined Maori enlisted in the main force. Some men did not want to be in D Squadron because they lacked sufficient knowledge of language or culture. As Latimer's father was a recruitment officer for the Maori Battalion it was the natural place for him. While in Japan, Latimer worked as part of a team with members of other companies. The Maori squadron was not segregated or treated differently.

At that time, the standing of Maori in the community was as high as it had ever been. Before the war many people had regarded them with indifference or amusement. Attitudes changed after 1939. The Maori Battalion was legendary in the Second New Zealand Expeditionary Force. Its soldiers were all volunteers. They took part in the deadliest fighting in North Africa and Italy. General Freyberg and their German enemies acclaimed them as brave and intrepid. News stories stressed their ferocity in battle and their tendency to take few prisoners. They performed the haka. They looked different. They *were* different.

The Battalion, the twenty-eighth, received more publicity than most and their exploits were used to bolster the war effort. Children raised money for a mobile canteen. The Maori Battalion song was, for a time, sung everywhere: 'Maori Battalion! march to victory, Maori Battalion! staunch and true, Maori Battalion! march to glory. Take the honour of your people with you.'

The country that had patronised Maori for a century and denied them full civil rights then admired them. Maori had been transformed into brave brothers fighting for God, King and country. New Zealand troops had the highest casualty rate in the Commonwealth and Maori suffered severely. Graham's brother Frank was badly wounded. Emily lost two brothers in the fighting in North Africa.

This war record, a revival of the old fighting tradition, encouraged Maori to take pride not only in their men but also in their race. It showed itself in the 1943 census. Before then intermarriage had resulted in fewer people describing themselves as Maori but in that year the trend was reversed. Maori numbers rose suddenly, defying the laws of biology.

Latimer had personal experience of this new feeling. In 1943, then seventeen, he was in the Territorial Army and had spent some months driving his recruiting officer father all round Northland. He met more Maori than at any time in his life till then and visited more marae and Maori communities. He could see and feel the pride.

This was partly the result of the work of Paraire Paikea, the Northern Maori MP then coordinating the Maori War Effort Organisation, a man whose ideas were to have a strong impact on Latimer. Paikea had been creating local committees to take more control of policies and services relating to Maori. In Northland, his electorate secretary, Kemp Nathan, later to be Latimer's mentor, encouraged Maori to support his work.

Paikea, with Ngata and the other Maori MPs, saw the success of the Maori Battalion and Maori participation in the other services as a way of winning full citizenship. The blood spilt on foreign battlefields was part of the very high price that had to be paid for equality for all Maori, he believed.

New Zealand was proud of its Maori people. Nancy Taylor, author of *The New Zealand People at War: The Home Front*, said the 'high fighting qualities of the Maori Battalion, every man a volunteer, shone bright in the darkest places. It kindled appreciation in pakeha bosoms, gave élan and confidence to the Maori'.[13]

This was a very different reaction to Maori participation in the First World War. Little was then said about the bravery of the Maori Pioneer Battalion. Instead, one of the best-known soldiers was Private Henare Tikitanu, a fictional creation of the Reverend Fussell, Vicar of Waiuku, author of *Letters From Private Henare Tikitanu*.

Henare was the prototype Maori clown. 'Hooray! Hooray! Hooray! My korry te Poneke people werry glad to see Henare Tikitanu in te noo uniform. Me te big bug now, te rangitira – and I go to Parani (France) and help Englan' kick out te Sherman poaka (pig). Then make a finish and come back te big Maori sheneral – that me – py korry yeh! I tink all the pakeha gell want me then – but no plumin fear – Henare bring home te big fat Merikana millinare – plenty money, my wurra yeh! You bet.'[14]

In this one paragraph Fussell displayed his Maori soldier as an illiterate, boastful, stupid, greedy, male chauvinist pig. The book's cover included a sketch of the great Tainui chief, Rewi Maniopoto. Fussell produced a second series of letters and donated the profits from the sale of both booklets to the Blind Soldiers' Fund.

This sort of publication was not possible in the Second World War. Not only had New Zealand grown up a little in the intervening twenty-odd years, but documentary films, newsreels and the need for patriotic propaganda had created a new climate. Maori, during the war, were fashionable and admired.

But not enough, apparently, to give them membership of the famous Kiwi Concert Party. According to the late Basil Potter, former director of Wellington Polytechnic, Maori felt they had been slighted when they saw the all-white concert party. Were none of them talented enough to win a place, to sing and dance with their Pakeha brothers?[15]

When Latimer returned from Japan he spent little time wondering about his identity, or thinking of himself as Maori or Pakeha or New Zealander. He wanted what most young men then wanted: a steady job, marriage, a family, a home, a car, and a good time. Long term, he still wanted to be a farmer.

He shared the common cultural experiences of most young New Zealand men. He had attended public schools, played rugby and other sports, listened to the same radio programmes as his Maori and Pakeha mates, sung the same songs, been to the same dances, learned to smoke cigarettes and to drink alcohol, to play billiards and cards, and go out with girls. He went through the national rite of passage of young men of his time by trying to make old cars and trucks run for another mile.

He was a New Zealander, circa 1947, though more independent and non-conformist than most. He was also, as someone of Maori ancestry, becoming part of a public debate – the place of Maori in New Zealand society. He was, whether he liked it or not, becoming part of what politicians called the 'Maori Problem'.

While Maori remained isolated in rural areas they could be ignored. When, like Latimer, they were forced to find work in cities, encouraged by the government, social and racial relations changed, challenging the oft-repeated myth that New Zealand was an example to the world in the way peoples of different races and cultures could live together in harmony.

This was the new world Latimer encountered in 1947, a world full of mixed and conflicting signals.

As a Maori and former serviceman he had more rights; for example, he could buy alcohol and drink it away from licensed premises. By 1948 all Maori were given this right, something that had been denied them for more than a century. As one policeman commented at the time, the greatest waster of a Pakeha had been able to buy as much liquor as he wanted but a decent Maori could not even take home a bottle of beer for his dinner. 'It's a slur on the Maori at this stage of his history and a definite hindrance to helping him "stand on his own feet".'[16]

Walter Nash, then deputy prime minister, said that 'the Maori is good enough, strong enough and able enough to stand on his own feet and he will not reach the heights we would like to see him reach so long as he is placed in a protected position'.[17] Nash saw the denial of liquor-purchasing rights as a misplaced effort to protect Maori.

In practice the ban had given no protection. Instead it had led to excessive drinking in pubs, drunkenness in the streets, and the use of sly-groggers. Maori were sold alcohol adulterated with methylated spirits, flavoured with raspberry cordial, a lethal concoction. They gained a reputation for not being able to handle their liquor and for being violent drunks.

Latimer knew all about this. In the 1930s, bootleg wine ('Dally' plonk or vino) was sold in Kaitaia by Croatians and consumed in bulk by Maori. Frank Latimer remembered a boy telling him once that his father was 'sick' in the main street. Frank found his father, drunk, offering to fight people, and took him home – a shaming experience that was not repeated.

Graham Latimer also remembers this. 'My father never drank to excess from that time onward. He was a reserved man, concerned about the way other people regarded him. He'd work hard six days a week but every Sunday he'd dress formally, with a collar and tie, and go to church.'

Latimer and all other Maori soon found that the law change did not immediately mean the end of racial discrimination in hotels. Some publicans barred them from lounges and private bars by expressly excluding them or by discouraging them from entering. Service was denied. The reason given: some Maori patrons were rough and rowdy. Therefore, the argument went, all Maori were socially unacceptable.

He also found that while he was in Japan the demeaning word 'native' had been removed from the Native Affairs Department and replaced with 'Maori', as a mark of respect. He soon realised that a name change did not mean a mind change. One senior National MP, Stan Goosman, said Maori would always be natives to him.[18]

Latimer and other Maori were given the same benefits as non-Maori returned servicemen, in marked contrast to those from the First World War. These benefits included paid training in various trades and occupations. Frank Latimer, badly wounded in Italy, took advantage of these to train as a teacher, but believed veterans (Pakeha and Maori) were not well treated by successive governments. Joe decided to train as a carpenter, and later became a watersider. Graham preferred to go straight to work. Some of the gloss of being in the

Battalion and being part of the war effort faded rapidly. The urban shift had resulted in growing friction. Closer contact did not produce harmony. Competition for jobs and housing sharpened latent prejudice. As memories of shared experiences of the war years receded so did sympathy for Maori aspirations.

Henare (later Sir Henare) Ngata, Sir Apirana's son, commented on this at an Australian and New Zealand Army Corps (Anzac) Day ceremony in 1948: 'Now that the war is over many of us are lapsing into our old careless habits. Bonds which united Maori and Pakeha are not quite as strong in peace as they were in war. Little misunderstandings and prejudices, born largely of ignorance, are rearing their heads. They should have been forgotten, but some of them have not quite been forgotten …'[19]

Latimer also realised that he had become a member of an ethnic group being labelled trouble-makers and criminals. Magistrates commented adversely on the behaviour of young Maori offenders as a racial group. Newspapers consistently described them, but not others, in racial terms. Some told them they were a disgrace to their people and said they should be sent back to the country districts they came from – 'back to the mat' was the popular expression.

A senior magistrate, JH Luxford, said Maori themselves were becoming race-conscious and that a race question, for which he believed there was no justification or need, might arise. 'We have tried to preserve in the Maori his language and customs and also tried to make him stand up and take the impact of ordinary life with all its implications and complexities,' he said. 'We have maintained many restrictions for the native race and yet given it many privileges. We have now come to the parting of the ways, where we have to decide whether the Maori is to be kept in his pa or be allowed to work side by side with the European for the common good …'[20]

He added: 'There has been an influx of thousands of Maoris into Auckland of recent years. Many have gone to live in the poorest of the buildings of the city. Whatever the cause, the result has been that the Maori is fast becoming the major branch of the criminal class as unfortunately figures show and prove.' Luxford, an oft-quoted magistrate, said that the Maori was a good chap but was getting out of step.[21]

Latimer was one of those good chaps. He had, however, never noticed any special efforts to preserve Maori language and customs. He knew also that it was the wartime government itself that had actively encouraged the Maori 'influx'. And he had no doubts about why Maori lived in the poorest parts of the city. Nor did he believe that it was up to Mr Luxford or the government to send him back to the pa he had never lived in, or to *allow* him to work side by side with Europeans for the common good. He simply wanted to earn a living, like other people.

He was aware that newspapers were busily contributing to the perception that Maori were a problem which had to be solved – and, at the same time, were reviving the comic stereotypes of the past.

When the *New Zealand Herald* cartoonist, Minhinnick, made fun of a suggestion by Peter Fraser that Celts and Maori could have come from the same caucasian stock, he presented Maori as fools. One was shown half-naked, with tongue and eyes protruding, wearing a kilt and sporran and a tam-o-shanter, carrying a placard saying the Ngapuhis are coming, hurrah! hurrah! Another, equally fat, carried a placard saying 'Tis a great day for the Arawas, py korry.'[22]

Rugby was another flashpoint. Latimer returned to Auckland just in time to see how Maori rugby players were becoming part of the race relations debate – an irritant between New Zealand and South Africa. He and his family were rugby-mad. He had grown up believing rugby was the game of games and that being an All Black was one of life's pinnacles. (He was intensely embarrassed twenty years later when newspaper reports said he had been an All Black.) He had no objection to the great Waka Nathan being called the Black Panther. He did not see rugby as a political or a racial issue.

He took it for granted that Maori should be eligible to play for the All Blacks wherever they went, even in South Africa, then despised internationally for its apartheid policies. The New Zealand Rugby Football Union was, however, having none of that. Only white players could go because that was what the Springboks wanted. The Union was not going to embarrass the other great rugby nation by selecting Maori on merit.

Publicly, its spokesmen claimed in 1947 and 1948 that the Union's main concern was for the feelings of Maori players. If Maori were chosen they could have difficulty getting access to transport and being admitted to hotels. They could be snubbed socially and, possibly, be insulted in the streets. The Union said it wanted to spare the players humiliation and avoid controversy.

The ban on Maori players had been in place since 1928 when Nepia was told Maori were not eligible to play in South Africa. In 1939 no Maori were chosen for trials for a tour planned for the following year (not held because of the war). Everard Jackson, one of the best players of the time, went to Wellington to take part in the Possibles versus Probables game. He was told to go home: no Maori were going to South Africa. (His son, Syd, later charged the Union in the 1960s, 1970s and 1980s with hypocrisy, cowardice and dishonesty when it continued the same policy.)

By 1948 the climate was changing. Major-General Sir Howard Kippenberger, then president of the New Zealand Returned Servicemen's Association, argued that if Maori were able to fight for their country they should not be discriminated against in sport. The tour to South Africa went ahead, without Maori.

Latimer was hurt and disappointed, as were many Maori. His father had been convinced that the actions of the Battalion and other Maori in the armed services had earned all Maori the right to be treated equally. Now here was the Rugby Union again selecting its players on colour, pandering to the racial prejudices of the white ruling minority in another country. Had the sacrifices of war been for nothing?

Latimer disagreed with the views of a spokesman for the Maori Rugby Football Board that Maori would not be greatly concerned if their players could not go to South Africa, because they had their own tours. Ned Parata, a rugby administrator, said as early as 1946 that Maori 'understood' the position in that country and the problems its government faced with a 'mixed population'.[23] Latimer rejected that argument. He 'understood' the reasons given but did not believe they justified excluding Maori players.

For Rugby Union officials the public reaction of people like Kippenberger and some Maori was the first sign that their view of racial discrimination in sport was not unanimously supported. They had no hesitation in dismissing it, continuing to be encouraged by the game's massive popularity and, later, by the warm welcome given to the 1956 Springbok team.

For Latimer and other Maori the issue was simply deferred, a time bomb which was to explode again and again till it divided the whole country emotionally and tragically in 1981.

Over the next few years Latimer's experiences reinforced his Maori identity. Regardless of how he saw himself, he was seen by others as Maori, first by the overwhelming white majority in Auckland and then by the Uri-o-Hau hapu of Ngati Whatua in the Kaipara Harbour.

In the Far North most people considered him Maori but, because of the small communities he lived in, they also saw him as a person, someone from a respected family, who joined in with social activities and was not really that different from everyone else. In the city, however, he was surrounded by strangers, and was very much in a minority in appearance. Only about one-in-five Maori, out of a total Maori population of just over 100,000, then lived in urban areas. In an overwhelmingly Pakeha environment Latimer was Maori.

He also had a lot to learn about city living. Before he went to Japan his experiences had been mainly confined to Papakura military camp, with excursions into Auckland. Emily, however, was much more at ease. She joined basketball and tennis teams, went to films, dances, and to beaches in groups. She wrote five letters to Graham in Japan. 'That's how I first started to know him, through letters,' she says.

She lived in the centre of Auckland. 'It was a good life for me.' She had many friends and, coincidentally, met older people from the Kaipara Harbour, relatives of families they were to be closely linked with socially and politically in the future – the Paikeas and the Marsdens. She can't remember any discrimination against her as a Maori.

Graham and Emily married in 1948 despite the opposition of both families, mostly on religious grounds. Latimer, an Anglican, was prepared to convert to Roman Catholicism and began taking instruction from a priest. The process was so lengthy they decided to marry in the Auckland Registry Office, thus repeating the same offence committed by Latimer's parents, marrying outside their denomination and their iwi.

Neither family wanted their children to marry outside their own iwi. When Graham Latimer reminded his father that he had done much the same thing his father said not so – he had married a Pakeha, a different case altogether.

After the wedding, a priest called on them and blessed the marriage, probably at the request of Emily's mother. Emily became an Anglican some years later when Graham and the children were receiving communion, and she felt she would also like to take part. She talked to an older brother who told her to do what she felt was right for her.

In Auckland, the Latimers shared the same problems as other Maori in finding a place to live. They were, till their first baby arrived, both working, but for very low wages, Emily as a laundress in the Auckland Hospital, and Graham in labouring or machinist jobs. Like other low-paid workers, they were forced to take the cheapest accommodation they could find. Even that was not easy.

Maori, as with the Irish early in the century, were not welcomed by many landlords, who considered them to be not good tenants. They had reason to be cautious. Some young Maori, unused to city life and with no family responsibilities, occasionally skipped without paying rent. Others left their quarters dirty and damaged. One Maori landlady who had decided to take Maori only soon changed her mind because of the way she was treated. Instead, she favoured Dalmatians – far more honest and reliable she thought.

Most Maori were good tenants but were suspect because of bad behaviour by the few. They were also the most visible, because of skin colour (few people from the Pacific Islands then lived in Auckland). Once a stereotype had been created it applied to all.

The Latimers had found a flat in Hobson Street. It was small, cramped and dark but served their purpose. They considered themselves lucky. Some landlords did not want people with pets or children because of the damage they caused and the noise they made. And the Latimers had children, first Amy in 1949 and then Rayna in 1950.

Peter Fraser's Labour government was then trying to provide better housing for Maori. More state houses were built in cities but little help was given to those in rural areas, where many lived in overcrowded, substandard and often unhygienic dwellings.

These problems worsened as rural Maori became poorer and fled to cities in greater numbers. Latimer was wryly amused forty years later at a Billy T James cartoon by Chris Slane. It showed Billy, with wife and four children, standing in front of a 'Flat to Rent' sign, being told by a smiling Pakeha: 'Welcome!! Of course you can have the flat.' The cartoon was part of a series entitled: Scenes we're NOT likely to see.[24]

Latimer had no trouble finding a job at the unskilled lower end of the work force, where most Maori gained employment. Labour was still in short supply. There was no unemployment. Objections had even been raised to sending men to Japan – because it reduced the number of workers in New Zealand.

At first, all he wanted was a temporary job to meet expenses. He had saved money from his army days but wanted to keep as much as he could for a home or as a deposit on the farm he still wanted to own.

For just over a year he worked for a bottle collection agency, finding and recycling beer bottles, and then as a shoe machinist. At this time, in 1948, he decided to work for New Zealand Railways, one of the biggest employers in the country, with about 35,000 staff. Railways was seen generally as a secure place to work, not necessarily all that exciting but offering the prospect of forty years unbroken service and a gold watch at the end. Latimer started at the bottom, sweeping the Auckland station platforms, and then quickly went on to clerical and administrative positions.

In that same year his father and mother also moved to Auckland, with their younger children. His brothers Frank and Joe were already living there. Latimer's father had been a social worker in Kaitaia for the Department of Maori Affairs after the war ended, but saw little future for the family in the Far North. Their small farm could not support them all and he and Lillian did not want their children to leave home without help. So they joined the exodus to Auckland, then with a population of close to 300,000.

A little later Graham and Emily used the Railways job to move back into rural areas, finally settling in the early 1950s at Kaiwaka in the Kaipara district with Graham as stationmaster. They were still not far from Auckland so contact with his family members could be maintained easily, though it was further for Emily to reach her Bay of Plenty whanau.

For the first time in ten years both were back in a district with a significant Maori community, though still a poor minority. They were welcomed warmly by Pakeha because they were so active in sports but more cautiously by Maori. They were an unknown quantity.

For Latimer, part of the larger Ngapuhi iwi, Kaiwaka was an area of great historic significance. Just over 125 years earlier Hongi Hika, the Ngapuhi war chief, had almost wiped out Ngati Whatua in a battle near Kaiwaka by using muskets. The Uri-o-Hau hapu, among whom Latimer had come to live, suffered significant losses, and took more than a century to recover fully. By chance this was the place that Latimer was first drawn into Maori community life and Te Uri-o-Hau, the people who encouraged him to become their spokesman.

His Maori ancestry had not till then distinguished him in any special way from most New Zealanders. 'My Maori side was mostly a blank,' he said later.

Latimer found it easy to mesh in with the local community. The Kaipara Harbour was a wonderful fishing ground (he remembers how he and Joe caught almost 100 flounders in an hour in the 1950s). From his Kaitaia period he knew how small-town New Zealand handled its affairs. He knew how people with very little money but lots of energy spent their lives.

Latimer's father was delighted with his son's move to the Kaipara and gave him specific advice about how to behave. He was to take no part in any activities that involved Ngati Whatua hapu. His father said that, as newcomers, he and Emily should not push themselves forward, should not meddle in their affairs. If local people wanted their involvement, said his father, they will ask you.

This suited Latimer perfectly. He had no desire to become involved in Maori or marae activities. He had plenty to do already.

He and Emily spent all their time with their growing family (by then they had four children), with work for the Railways and with sport. He joined the local rugby team, made up mostly of Pakeha.

Latimer remembers the moment his relationship with Te Uri-o-Hau changed. He walked into a hotel after a rugby match and met Kemp Nathan, a local farmer with an interesting past and a sense of humour. Latimer: 'After my second year of playing for Kaiwaka I played against Oneroa and during one of our many encounters I scored three tries against the Maori team. While I was elated I also felt somewhat disappointed because I scored these tries against my own race. However, sport being what it was in those days, one soon forgot those emotions and we joined the usual social function held in the Mangawhai Hotel. It was there I met a very respected man in the Maori community and in the settlement – Kemp Nathan.

'While having the odd drink with a man named Jack Murphy I was still mindful of the fact that I was an outsider in another tribe. Then Murphy cut me to the quick by saying, "I suppose you think you're a king because you played for a European team and scored three tries against your own people."

'I was shocked that he should raise the very thoughts that had entered my mind earlier on. He went on to say that you could make all the contributions you liked in society but unless you made a contribution to your own people then as far as Maoridom was concerned you were non-existent.

'I went home and for some time I thought about what he'd said. Then, by good fortune, Father Fisher, the Anglican minister, asked me to go to church. He'd previously been a minister at St Thomas's in Auckland, where my father had been one of the vestrymen. As a result of this I got to know Kemp and his mother, Jessie, and other members of the Nathan family. That same afternoon Kemp suggested the two of us should get to know each other better, and to work together.'

That was also the day Nathan nominated Latimer to be secretary of the building committee for St Mary's Church, Kaiwaka. 'I remembered what my father had told me, and realised I was being asked to become part of the community, and that if I accepted there was no turning back. I had to go all the way. I suppose I made that pledge to myself at that particular time although it is hard to recollect, but I do know that suddenly I found that there was a new challenge ahead of me, a challenge of fitting myself back into my own race.'

In time, he came to see this as a wider challenge of working for the church, of trying to improve the conditions of Maori as a people, and 'reconverting myself back from just another human being in society to becoming a responsible Maori in Maori society'.

Kemp Nathan, a Te Uri-o-Hau kaumatua of the Ngati Whatua iwi, had deliberately moved into his life. Nathan had been private secretary to Paraire Paikea when he was member of parliament for Northern Maori from 1938 to 1943, and he was familiar with the world of politics. Latimer says that Nathan nudged him awake, telling him that now he was mature he should stop playing children's games, that he should join in the long struggle of Maori for survival.

When interviewed about his past by reporters Latimer always describes Nathan as his mentor. He still talks of him with a slight air of bemusement. Nathan took him out of his relaxed life as a minor Railways functionary and local sportsman and pushed him into a national arena of Maori politics, and confrontation with governments and their officials.

Latimer says he had not gone in search of his Maori past or expressed any wish to become a politician. Nathan, his mother Jessie, and other elders, thought he was, potentially, their man. Jessie Nathan, a powerful kuia, told Latimer she thought he might be able to do the job her two sons had not been able to do. She thought he had the stability needed for the long haul and that Emily was a supportive partner. She added that she believed he was strong enough to resist the temptation to be 'sidelined by women'.

Nathan confirmed this much later when Latimer was offered the leadership of the Maori Council. Latimer asked Kemp why he had not continued the work he had started with Paikea. Nathan said the final decision had been his mother's. Jessie considered her own son was too 'jocular' a man, not serious enough for what she had in mind. She decided that Latimer, not yet thirty, was more dependable, solid, tenacious, practical and toughminded. And he had many more years ahead of him. Latimer: 'Jessie Nathan was a remarkable woman, a much more powerful personality than Dame Whina Cooper. When she stood to speak all the men sat down.'

Kemp Nathan acted, from that time on till he died in the 1980s, as Latimer's mentor. Latimer says he was one of the most intelligent people he has ever known, with a tremendous sense of history and a vision for the future. 'He saw fifteen and twenty years ahead. You had to be wide awake when he spoke.'

Latimer's father knew Nathan – who had also been a welfare officer with the Department of Maori Affairs – and actively helped him to transform his son into an iwi spokesman. Latimer senior was then a respected watersider in Auckland. He was an active unionist and Labour Party supporter though he had earlier worked within the National Party's Maori wing. He had also maintained strong links with his Ngati Kahu whanau and hapu.

He had become a leading member of Auckland's Maori minority. With others, he helped to create a Maori community centre for the increasing number of rural refugees. He worked closely with Whina Cooper. They were relatives: his grandfather and Whina's had been brought up as brothers in the Hokianga. In 1951, the year before Graham and Emily moved to Kaiwaka, Whina Cooper became the first president of the New Zealand Maori Women's Welfare League, set up by the Department of Maori Affairs, and began her long climb to national prominence.

Latimer senior wanted his son to learn about his Maori heritage from Nathan and to take more personal responsibilities within his own wider family, his Latimer whanau. He formally asked him if he would accept and share these with him. Frank and Joe, as first and second sons, could have been expected to take such a role but they no longer lived in Northland, no longer had close contact with Maori communities, and had no special interest in family land issues in the Far North. Neither could speak Maori, though in later life Frank learned to speak a little and could understand more.

Latimer has clear memories of his father's request, and the long talks which followed over the next two days. He recalls the importance attached to it: he was being asked to take on a distinctive Maori role in a cultural context with which he was not familiar and in which he was certainly not fully comfortable. And, that it was a lifetime commitment.

He says he thought about it seriously and finally said yes, without fully understanding what it meant. For the first time he began to look at his whakapapa more carefully, to find out where he came from and to whom he was related.

Latimer says Nathan formed a close relationship with him: 'He was almost like a father. He continued to teach and to advise me in things Maori, in church matters, but above all in human values. I began to grow up in a new world.' He had brief moments of doubt about what was actually happening. 'Sometimes I wondered if he was having me on, because at that particular time I happened to be the only Maori with a car. It appeared to me that every time he wanted to go somewhere it was important that I should be there too.'

Nathan was a uniquely qualified teacher. He had a deep knowledge of the past. He knew precisely how his Uri-o-Hau hapu lost almost all its land in the first sixty years after the Treaty of Waitangi was signed and had been devastated by disease and poverty, reaching their lowest number, about 300, by the beginning of the twentieth century.

The Methodist Church, to which most belonged, had not been interested in helping them get their land back. The powerful missionary, William Gittos, deliberately persuaded them to sell. He called on them in the name of God to give up all aspects of their evil communal life and urged them to become individuals dedicated to Christianity. Shortly after the death of Gittos Te Uri-o-Hau rejected his vision of their future and converted to the newly established Ratana faith, almost en masse, in the late 1920s.

Nathan, because of his work with Paikea, also had a deep and direct knowledge of the Ratana Movement, its efforts to have the Treaty of Waitangi recognised, and of the politics involved. Before becoming an MP, Paikea had been Ratana's personal secretary and chief executive of the Movement.

Nathan taught Latimer about Wireumu Tahupotiki Ratana's life and the movement he started in 1918, and about Paikea's vision of Maori organisations taking greater control of activities that related to Maori alone. Paikea, formerly a Methodist minister, had helped Ratana to form a political alliance with the Labour Party in the 1920s and early 1930s. In 1936 he had become the paid secretary of the Maori Advisory Council which linked the Ratana Movement to Labour.

The deal was simple: Ratana would run Labour–Ratana candidates in the four Maori seats. Labour, when it had the chance, would try to improve Maori housing, health, education and employment. And, support moves to ratify the Treaty.

The alliance produced immediate results. Eruera Tirikatene took the Southern Maori seat in 1932. Paikea stood for the Northern Maori seat three times before beating Tau Henare in 1938, the first election to be held by secret ballot. (The Labour government had, at Ratana's request, given this fundamental right in 1937, sixty years after all other citizens had received it.) By 1943, even Sir Apirana Ngata, then National, was replaced by a Ratana MP.

The Maori War Effort Organisation established by the four MPs slowed suddenly after Paikea died of tuberculosis in 1943, and Native Affairs Department officials, mostly non-Maori, regained their former power.

Nathan took part in these events, working mainly in the Kaipara, but often visiting Wellington. He met the most important public servants and politicians of the day, particularly Peter Fraser, prime minister from 1940 to 1949. He knew Fraser sympathised strongly with Maori but was limited in what he could do by the hostility or indifference of many Labour politicians, Party members, voters, and bureaucrats.

In the Kaipara during the 1950s Nathan was the only person with a deep practical knowledge of national politics, of how decisions were made in Wellington, and of the backroom deals made to get policies through Cabinet. He shared much of this with Latimer, knowing that he could not fully understand till he had personal experience. Latimer says he realised later that Nathan had been looking for someone to be the recipient of his knowledge, and had picked him.

Nathan also introduced him to the Treaty and the ways it had been systematically breached since 1840. He told Latimer how Te Uri-o-Hau had attended the first national meeting of Maori in 1860, called by Governor Gore Browne, to persuade them to support government pressure on Tainui and Taranaki to sell their lands. At that meeting, he said, they were told they were children, minors, who could not be given votes because they could not even speak English. Trust us, said Gore Browne and his officials.

Latimer said Nathan was opening up a new world. He admits that he knew virtually nothing about the Treaty: 'It wasn't going to help me get a job.' Nathan was well aware that Latimer was ignorant of Maori politics and that his background was not traditionally Maori.

Neither was Emily's, though she had much more involvement with Maori communities. She was not taught Maori. 'Nobody was allowed to speak Maori in the house,' she says. She still does not speak the language though she can understand quite a bit. Neither she nor Graham taught their own children and the children do not speak it today.

After being adopted by the Nathans, Latimer went through an exhausting induction process. He visited almost all Ngati Whatua marae, went to many hui and tangi, meeting the men and women who were initiating him into the hapu and iwi. He absorbed the issues, felt the anger at past grievances and came to understand something of the collective determination to provide an economic and social base for the iwi. Nathan urged him to stand up and speak (in English) and then refused to take any responsibility for mistakes he made because of his limited experience. 'It was his way of teaching me,' says Latimer. 'Total immersion. Sink or swim.'

He tried to overcome his ignorance of Maori by absorbing the language, and the protocol, by osmosis, listening, watching and practising. He had no formal lessons. Later he read the Bible in Maori and built up his vocabulary and improved his grammar. Te Uri-o-Hau were satisfied that he was making an effort. He still maintains that his elders were far more concerned that he learn how to represent their interests than to speak Maori well.

In later years some critics pointed to Latimer's lack of a strong Maori background, his lack of knowledge of traditional customs and of the kawa of the marae and said he was, therefore, unqualified to be a leader of Maori. A leader, they said, has to be immersed in Maori culture. He was colonised.

Latimer says that was not the way Ngati Whatua elders saw him. He had never put himself forward, had never thought of taking a leading role in Maori community affairs or prepared himself for it. He had not been chosen as a boy or young man to assume whanau, hapu or iwi responsibilities, as had some other leaders, such as Apirana Ngata of Ngati Porou, or Robert Mahuta of Tainui, and had made no attempt to speak for the people.

During the next few years Latimer continued to work for New Zealand Railways, played as much sport as he could, became a Maori warden, went to more hui, learnt about Bastion Point and the forced land sales of the nineteenth and twentieth centuries, became a sports administrator, along with Emily, and earned his place as iwi spokesman. On one occasion the Railways offered him a promotion from tiny Kaiwaka to the city of Hamilton, a big step ahead. Kemp Nathan and other elders persuaded him to stay.

In 1961, when he was firmly embedded in the Kaipara, Te Uri-o-Hau chose him as its candidate for a Department of Maori Affairs dairy farm. He left his safe job and with Emily and the children began the daunting task of converting marginal land at Tinopai on the Kaipara Harbour into a productive unit. This was his chance to be a farmer but included in the price was an unspoken but permanent commitment to Ngati Whatua.

From that time he was, he says, in the context of things Maori, a Maori for Ngati Whatua, and then, from 1962, for the whole north, Tai Tokerau, as a member of the District Maori Council. Two years later, when he was one of the north's three representatives on the New Zealand Maori Council, he was given the shared responsibility for trying to speak for all Maori on major issues.

More than twenty-five years later, in the 1980s, he spelt out to a resource planning tribunal in the Far North precisely who he was: 'a direct descendant of Tu Moana by the following genealogy …'.[25] He then named his ancestors and said: 'That really makes me the spokesman for Te Paatu and Ngati Kahu. My father was the welfare officer for Mangonui County Area, his father in turn was the first Land Court Officer and Maori Interpreter in the Mangonui County, and my father's grandfather was one of the first ordained

Ministers of the Anglican Church to preach in the Ngati Kahu area. 'Therefore my roots are firmly established in Ngati Kahu.

'My mother was Lillian Edith Kenworthy. Her parents and grandparents were some of the early settlers in the Mangonui County. They settled in the gumfields and later played their part in helping the overall development of the Mangonui County.

'My grandfather, Joseph Kenworthy, was of Irish descent, and my grandmother, who was Pearl Priestley, was of Irish and Scottish descent.'[26]

Latimer has great respect for his Anglo-Saxon–Celt ancestry. When he visited his Scottish homeland he felt deep emotional ties. 'This,' he says, 'is part of where I come from and made me what I am today.' His mother always urged him not to forget who he was, Maori and Pakeha, and to not 'take sides' because that would mean he would have to treat some people as enemies. His father told him that 'God put us all here and God will take us away'. That, he said, was all you need to know: 'We are all children of God.'

He sees, however, that in the context of New Zealand, the greatest demands on his time, energy and loyalty come from Maori. So, he says, he is a Maori. And he believes that he does not have to do anything to prove it.

He is intensely aware of the confusion that exists today about who is Maori. One leader from Wanganui, Archie Taiaroa, says there is a very simple test for anyone in doubt: just look into the mirror.

Knowledge of the Maori language is no longer any sort of test. Between 80 per cent and 90 per cent of those who claim Maori ancestry do not speak te reo. Knowledge of marae protocol has become more widespread among non-Maori as well as Maori, but familiarity with the kawa of a particular marae is possibly not as great as in the past when Maori lived in rural areas. About 130,000 people with Maori ancestry cannot identify their hapu or iwi.

The number of those claiming Maori ancestry has risen rapidly. In 2001 it stood at almost 600,000 (in a total population of 3.8 million) though only about two-thirds classified themselves at the census as Maori. Just over half of the Maori who register to vote go on the Maori electoral roll. More than 40,000 people claiming some

Maori ancestry live in Australia, most of them seemingly settled there permanently. That equals the total Maori population of New Zealand at the end of the nineteenth century.[27]

Latimer believes people have to decide for themselves who they are. That could mean they identify with different parts of their ancestry on different occasions. Some could register on the Maori electoral roll, thus signalling clearly that they are Maori. Others could go on the general roll because they believe that is the best way to help their favoured political party to gain power. Those who know their whakapapa can register on one or more hapu beneficiary rolls, and thus have a chance to take part in hapu affairs, such as Waitangi Tribunal claims, or the management of conservation estates.

He believes that the word Maori now has many meanings, divisions and colours; that there is no simple, easy definition. He is also well aware that the news media use the word in headlines and stories as though it has one meaning only, that all Maori are alike, that all want the same things, that they all hold the same views.

His brothers and sisters have never been as actively involved in Maori affairs as he has. Joe says he never felt disadvantaged because of his Maori ancestry, and is proud of it. He is scornful of 'money' Maori, people who use their Maori descent to get special benefits. Frank, who died in 1998, believed it was not sensible to keep on emphasising differences between Maori and Pakeha. Unnecessary divisions were created.

Their mother, Lillian, made her own declaration about who she was shortly before her death in 1984. She told the family that she had been a Maori for them, the children, all her life, but she wanted to die a Pakeha. She was given a traditional tangi but was not buried in the Maori section of the Mangere cemetery. Instead, she was buried in the general section next to a grand-daughter.

CHAPTER FOUR

Becoming a National Leader
1956–1987

Once you've been elected, you move from the more or less normal to a larger than life world. You soon learn that you will become a caricature of your former self. Your survival depends on your success in projecting an image more favourable to your halo than your warts. Get further up the pole, and you find that the demands of the party leaders are legion. You have to be *driven* to want to do this.

– David Lange, former prime minister (1984–1989), commenting on being a politician; *Sunday Star-Times*, 7 August 1994

Leadership positions in Maori society come as a result of serving the people, learning to know the needs of the marae, gaining experience and knowledge in Maori lore, and being accepted and promoted by the people themselves. Mana cannot be attained by self-promotion.

– Sir Graham Latimer, 11 June 1996

Maori society has always recognised two types of leader, one who gets authority from his whakapapa [lineage] and the other who is recognised for his achievements. [Sir] Graham does not have high whakapapa status but he's had spectacular successes and has earned his position.

– Wira Gardiner, former chief executive officer, Te Puni Kokiri (Ministry of Maori Development), 1993

IN 1969, THIRTEEN YEARS AFTER GRAHAM LATIMER BECAME A SPOKESMAN for Ngati Whatua, he was called to De Brett's Hotel in Wellington by Sir Turi Carroll, the first president of the New Zealand Maori Council. Carroll told him he was to become vice-president and then, after a few more years, president.

Sir Turi was about to resign because of age (he was seventy-nine), and he was to be replaced by the vice-president, Dr Pei Te Hurinui Jones (who was seventy-one). Neither Carroll nor Jones pretended that any democratic election process was involved in what they were doing – though votes would be required to formalise the decisions. These two, with other senior kaumatua, had chosen the 43-year-old Latimer to be the Maori Council's leader after the briefest of apprenticeships.

Latimer says he was not asked his opinion but gave it anyway. He appreciated the honour but he was not ready. His knowledge and experience were too limited. He was not fluent in Maori. He didn't have the mana or the support. There were many more worthy councillors. He was too young.

Sir Turi told him that the decision had already been made. They had the support of enough councillors. Latimer would be nominated by John Bennett, of Ngati Kahungunu, and would be supported by Ngati Porou, Tainui and his own Ngapuhi iwi as well as Ngati Whatua. He could improve his language skills over time. He would gain experience in the job and be ready to take over the presidency when Pei Jones decided to resign. They had chosen him, in part, precisely because he was young and had the one essential thing they lacked, time. He would have to earn mana by his actions.

The Maori Council was not then highly respected by politicians or by some Maori, and it had no national public presence. It had not been able to prevent the National government from passing the Maori Affairs Amendment Act in 1967 which would lead to the loss of more Maori customary land – a move that even the conservative Sir Turi damned as confiscation.

The position of the Treaty was still in limbo. Keith Holyoake's government would not concede that it was an issue for debate. When the National Development Conference was held in 1969 to look at economic and social issues the Maori Council was not invited to take part. When visiting dignitaries were welcomed the Council was not asked to send representatives.

The council was then made up of thirty-three members: three representatives of each of the eleven rurally based district councils. It did not represent urban Maori, or women, or the young. Its electoral base was rural district councils, ensuring that most members would be elderly males. Nor, because members were elected regionally, did it represent iwi. Many also saw it as a tool of government, set up by the National Party to support its own policies.

Many Maori concluded that a body which was snubbed and rejected by the government that created it, had no power or authority, and was never going to be able to force the majority population to confront the injustices inflicted on the Maori minority.

The mood in New Zealand was also changing. The 1960s was a period of mass protest against the Vietnam War and of rising anger and frustration at the New Zealand Rugby Football Union's racial policies favouring South Africa. Racial tensions in cities were growing with the influx of Maori. Some young Maori adopted the rhetoric of the black liberation movement in the United States, and were impatient with the lack of progress in New Zealand. Action, not talk, was the slogan.

The country was prosperous, with full employment except for a blip in 1967. Young people had greater freedom than ever. The availability of the contraceptive pill was changing attitudes toward sex, morality and family size. Television, pop music and films widened cultural experiences and brought values from other countries into every home. The 'six o'clock swill' caused by the early closing of bars ended in 1967 and led to new drinking patterns. Travel to Australia, Europe and Asia was becoming easy.

Books were written about the problems faced by rural Maori trying to adapt to city life. Noel Hilliard's *Maori Girl*, based partly on the experiences of his wife, became commonly known and was widely used as a New Zealand school text.[1] An American scholar, David Ausubel, published *Maori Youth*,[2] and *The Fern and the Tiki*,[3] both denting the myth that New Zealand had full racial equality, loved Maori and treated them decently.

Latimer's initial response to Sir Turi was valid: he was unprepared and unqualified. He had been elected to the New Zealand Maori Council by the Tai Tokerau District Maori Council five years earlier but still had only limited experience of national Maori politics. His formal education had not improved since he left school at fourteen.

He was a struggling farmer with a heavy mortgage and needed to spend all his time at home. He was a National Party member in a council made up mostly of Labour supporters.

What the older leaders saw was Latimer's potential as a leader of a national Maori body. He carried no baggage from the past. His lack of a strong iwi base was an advantage; he did not have to re-fight old battles or push any particular iwi issues. He had already proved he was committed to remedying past injustices. He was hardworking. While he was not an experienced public speaker in English or Maori he was seen as direct, honest and straight-forward in expressing his opinions. He had the capacity to learn.

He also had personal experience of the rapid and unsettling urbanisation of the Maori people. He knew what it was like to be poor in a city and then to return to the rural Maori heartland. He spanned both worlds. He did not describe himself as bicultural; he always accepted his multicultural, multi-ethnic ancestry. He had no difficulty supporting one of the Maori Council's main aims, promoting harmony and understanding between Maori and Pakeha – he was both.

For these reasons, his most senior colleagues decided, within a relatively short period, to make him president and hoped he would be able to shape the Council into a national assembly with both the will and the authority to help Maori to gain full citizenship rights.

When Latimer joined the Council in 1964 older members had taken the time to explain to him the bitter story of land losses through court action, confiscation and enforced sales. They educated him on Treaty breaches from memory banks that were much more valuable than any official archive – gave him details of a history he had only recently realised existed.

His first meetings had been a sustained culture shock. He had to absorb the main features of a strange environment and work out appropriate responses to the distinguished kaumatua he was meeting. Their names echoed the history of their peoples. They represented most of the great whanau and hapu of the past and present, linking the Council with efforts made over the previous 100 years to attract the attention of governments.

Latimer says he was awed by the intensity of commitment he found. Councillors saw themselves as speaking directly and personally for their tupuna (ancestors). Their fight for Maori rights was based on the injustices of the past and the continuing abuse of the Maori minority by the Pakeha majority. They rejected the idea that they would all be assimilated into one happy, golden racial mix. They wanted to be free to decide their own future, a freedom all other New Zealand citizens had.

He says the elders tested him, put him through an apprenticeship to see how he would respond. He earned respect, slowly. Sir Henare Ngata recalls that in Latimer's first years he said little, but then emerged as lively and energetic. 'He was always very direct, honest, spoke his mind,' said Sir Henare at his home in Gisborne when interviewed for this book. 'He was not devious or manipulative.'[4]

Latimer: 'Soon after I went to my first meeting in Wellington some of the older councillors, Dick Stirling, Mat Te Hau and others, helped me to understand what was going on, told me who was who, and showed me how I could contribute. They wanted to know all about me, what I was doing, and what jobs I'd had.'

They also wanted to know what he believed in. He told them about Kemp Nathan and Paraire Paikea, his father's encouragement, and the way he had been co-opted by Ngati Whatua. Some who knew and admired all three men asked why he had chosen to join the National Party. Latimer: 'I can remember my father laying down the law one day, it must have been in the late 1950s or early 1960s. He told me in the most definite way that I must, just must, support Labour. My immediate reaction was to go out and join the National Party.'

Barry Gustafson, in his history of the National Party, says that Latimer was originally attracted to it because of its emphasis on self-determination and self-sufficiency, and also because of early, unhappy experiences with the union movement. He says Latimer was called out on strike when he worked for the New Zealand Railways, that his family suffered as a result because union officials claimed there were no funds for the relief of strikers' families. Yet, says Gustafson, 'a few months later the union gave a huge donation, reputedly 10,000 pounds, to the Labour Party to help fund the 1949 election campaign'.[5]

Latimer has explained his National Party allegiance in different ways. While it was partly a reaction to his father's pressure to support Labour he also had little respect for Maori Labour MPs in the 1950s. He thought they had not achieved much and that one or two were just coasting along.

Latimer joined National when he became a farmer, encouraged by his friends in Federated Farmers. In addition, because his family was mostly Labour it made sense to have at least one member in the other camp, so they had the possibility of some influence some of the time. He said publicly, when he became Maori Council president in 1973, that 'just because I am a member of the National Party does not mean I support National policies. One must use the best available channels to get points of view across. I thought the National Party was the best channel'.

(In hindsight he believes he made the right decision, that he did have some influence on National Party policy, particularly on Treaty issues. He points to its manifesto before the 1990 election that recognised the Treaty as New Zealand's founding document. He believes that he shares credit, with other Maori members, for that change of public stance by a party with a long history of indifference to Maori interests.)

Party membership was a sensitive issue when he joined the Council. Sir Turi, also a National Party member, said councillors must not offend the government. They could not afford to give even the slightest appearance of support for any political party (particularly Labour) or a movement like Ratana. He felt the Council's future was fragile and did not need enemies in high places.

This approach was common sense. If it was to make any progress the Council had to cooperate with the National government, which was in power for the Council's first ten years. At the same time it had to work as closely as possible with the four Labour Maori MPs, who suspected that the Council was just a tool of the National Party.

Latimer did not believe that party politics was ever an issue in Council policy and strategies. The Council was above politics. He would happily work with any politician who took Maori concerns seriously. He agreed that the Council had to stay out of party politics if it was to become a national voice for Maori.

Latimer: 'I met Mat Rata at this time [early 1960s]. We both came out of the Far North and had a similar background. He was about eight years younger but he'd gone through that same Depression period. He'd been a trade union official and was a strong Labour supporter – just like my father. He won the Northern Maori seat as Ratana in 1963 and came to talk to us soon afterward. He was never enthusiastic about the Council. He always felt it was competing with the Maori MPs for influence, and it was. But personally we got on well.'

Latimer's lack of a formal education was not an obstacle to becoming president. Instead, his basic education, and rural experiences during the Depression, strengthened his appeal to those who believed he was a potential leader. He was still connected to his roots, still linked with the day-to-day concerns of Maori.

After he became vice-president and then president some critics had drawn attention to his minimal schooling. They said he had little skill in preparing submissions, or writing reports and letters – and was sometimes ungrammatical in speech and overly colloquial, rough round the edges. Ngata, an accountant and the Council's expert on land issues, did not agree. He was not even aware that Latimer had only a primary school education. From Latimer's grasp of the main points being discussed, Ngata assumed that he was well-educated. He admired the skill with which he chaired meetings.

Dr Ranginui Walker, former professor of Maori studies at the University of Auckland and one of Latimer's most persistent critics, regards his limited contact with New Zealand's education system in the 1930s as a positive advantage. 'It saved his mind from being fucked up.'[6]

Wira Gardiner, a former chief executive officer of Te Puni Kokiri, says that educational qualifications are not important for leadership in Maori society if a person has other qualities. 'Sir Graham had those attributes and these were recognised when he was asked to take a leadership position. His rise since he was about thirty has been spectacular.'[7]

Latimer says his Kaipara kaumatua were not interested in school qualifications. They taught him to concentrate on what was important and not to try to read everything or to remember everything. When he went to his first hui he began taking notes on a small pad. He was told to stop. Latimer: 'No, don't do that, they said. You'll miss all the important stuff. Listen. Think. Remember. And I did. I put away the pad and began to concentrate on what was being said.' He used the same approach at Maori Council meetings, impressing Ngata with what seemed like a remarkable memory.

At that time his lack of a full secondary education was typical of both Maori and non-Maori New Zealanders. Until 1944, when the school leaving age was raised to fifteen, only a minority went to secondary school.

Few books were available at school and the only one he remembers at home was the Bible. Books were too expensive. His father helped his children to read by buying comics, full of written stories at that time. He also bought newspapers, such as the *Northern Age* from Kaitaia, but few magazines.

Latimer has never felt disadvantaged. His family, and the Far North environment, gave him, he believes, a rich education. Both parents encouraged learning. His father played games, particularly those involving numbers, with all the children. Grandfather Joe Kenworthy was skilled at finding gum deposits, able to read the lie of the land where great kauri had fallen hundreds of years before. He was equally competent at fishing, and built his own smoke-house. He also taught the young Graham to play billiards, and how to keep the green table felt in fine condition with a specially designed hot iron.

Latimer: 'Almost all Maori lived in the country. Men went into farming and forestry and general labouring jobs. Up to 1936 you could leave school at twelve if you passed the Proficiency examination. Or thirteen, if you didn't. Young people grew up early, left home if they could get a job, and looked after themselves.' (Until the law was changed in 1934 they could marry when they were twelve. The age was then raised to fourteen.)

Since then everything has changed. 'In the last forty years Maori have become city people,' he says. 'They need an education to suit them for here and now but still allow them to be as Maori as they want, though that's not what they've been getting.' He insists that the current school system is not the only or the most effective way of providing learning opportunities. Schools for many Maori have, he says, been rigid places with little freedom for children, including non-Maori, to develop: 'Today, in the year 2002, the system fails many Maori.'

Latimer still does not read widely (he says he never has the time) and does not rely on written words. He depends instead on things he has seen and heard, and on his thinking about them. He does not hesitate to ask people whom he believes are better informed and more experienced than he is to share their knowledge.

Speculation about whether he could have been a more effective leader if he had been more formally educated does not interest him. He did not choose to be born in a wasteland or to be the son of parents who had little money. He did not choose to go to small schools with very few educational resources and with no traditions of excellence, or high academic achievement. And, as Dr Walker has said, his lack of time at school could have been a distinct advantage.

Latimer believes that if he had gone to St Stephens College in Auckland, attended briefly by his father, or completed a full secondary education like his older brothers, his whole life would have been different. His choices of occupation and future would have been much greater and he would never have been president of the Maori Council.

When Sir Turi and the others told him he was to be vice-president they acted in a calculated way to strengthen the Council by choosing someone who was young and tough enough to learn, to serve, to survive. The older ones also knew they reflected an earlier time and that a new type of leader was needed.

Their choice had been limited. Many potential leaders died in the Second World War and others had not returned to their rural communities. Some of the most able had gone into the Department of Maori Affairs as welfare officers and were, therefore, not able to be chosen – they were government servants

Half of all Maori were, in the mid-1960s, under the age of fifteen, and the number of men – and they were thinking only of men – who could be leaders, and had the necessary commitment and attributes, was tiny. When Latimer was forty in 1966 he was one of just over 900 Maori males of that age. The number of non-Maori males at this time was over 16,000. Maori men aged forty were outnumbered about eighteen-to-one.

Others were not willing or free to be chosen. Outstanding councillors like Henare Ngata would certainly have had a prior claim. But he was fully involved with Ngati Porou affairs. He was willing to give his experience to the Council, particularly on issues related to land, but could not give the time the presidency would require. He strongly supported Latimer as a future leader but his first loyalty was to his iwi. Other councillors had much more experience than Latimer but for reasons similar to Ngata's or because of age or ill-health felt they could not embark on the sort of struggle that lay ahead.

Latimer had one additional essential qualification: he was self-employed. The president had to be free to attend meetings at any time they were called, had to be able to meet government officials, local-body staff, lawyers, advisers, and had to attend hui all over the country. Anyone working for an employer, no matter how supportive, could not be always available to represent the Council. Latimer's occupation, farmer, allowed him time, at his own expense, to take the position.

The old men were not doing him a favour. In 1969 the Council had no political power and existed only on sufferance. If it survived it would be because of its own efforts and at its own cost. Some councillors had not even been sure that it would survive its first three-year term of office.

The National government had set up the Maori Council under the Maori Welfare Act 1962 hoping to use it as a counterbalance to Labour's four Maori seats. Holyoake and Ralph Hanan, then (Pakeha) minister of Maori affairs, had, however, almost immediately realised their mistake. The Council was not going to win votes, and was showing every sign of being a nuisance. While Maori votes for Labour declined in 1960, because it would not support the 'No Maori No Tour' rugby protest, no more votes had gone to National.

The Maori Council, from its first meeting, did not live up to the National government's expectations. It did not support Hanan, and was far too independent, immediately raising the Treaty of Waitangi as an issue.

Latimer was told by councillors who had attended the first Council meeting in 1962 that Hanan, who came from Invercargill, had almost proudly admitted he knew nothing about Maori when he reluctantly accepted the position of minister. He believed, however, that he knew all about their current problems because he had read and re-read the 1960 Hunn Report on the Department of Maori Affairs.[8] He had, he said, made it his bible, and Jack Hunn, the new (Pakeha) secretary for Maori affairs, his expert on all things Maori.

Hanan was also absolutely certain about what he wanted councillors to do. He hoped they would elect Sir Turi as president, and appoint Department of Maori Affairs officer Norman (later Sir Norman) Perry as secretary, to keep the 'show on the rails a bit'. Latimer: 'Hanan wanted to control the Council from the very beginning. He wanted to wipe out every legal distinction between Maori and the general community. He wanted to change the adoption laws, and to alienate more Maori land. His policy was assimilation of the Maori. He thought this was inevitable anyway. He wanted to make all New Zealanders the same.'

Hunn, also, had little sympathy for Maori aspirations. He was more interested in restructuring the Department of Maori Affairs to make it tidier, and to transfer many of its functions, such as housing, to mainstream agencies. He began the movement, which reached its full force in the 1980s and the 1990s, to devolve the Department out of existence.

The Maori Council was ignored. The government did not provide it with funds to carry out its statutory duties. It was given no budget in its first year of operation (1962–1963). In 1965 the Council received a grant of 800 pounds from the Maori Purposes Fund Board: still not enough to set up an office, pay expenses or hire staff. Councillors were told to rely on the resources of the Department of Maori Affairs – which had insufficient resources to carry out its own functions.

For Latimer, this was history repeating itself. His Latimer grandfather had been elected to the Far North District Maori Council set up under the Maori Councils Act 1900 to provide some limited form of local self-government. Sir James Carroll, who became the first Maori minister of native affairs, had promoted the Act, hoping it would lead to the preservation and social and economic advancement of Maori at a time when many people still expected them to become extinct.

Latimer's grandfather had welcomed the establishment of district councils and had then watched them wither and die for lack of funds. Richard John Seddon's Liberal government provided no budget, saying that money for the councils could come out of the newly formed Health Department – which also had insufficient resources to carry out its own functions.

The district councils were set up to fail. This was a view shared by Apirana Ngata, Maui Pomare, and Peter Buck, leaders of the Maori renaissance of the early twentieth century. Ngata accused the National government of neglect and indifference[9] and Buck said that the government might just as well let Maori die out if it was not willing to spend some money on health, one of the new Council's main responsibilities.[10]

So it was with the New Zealand Maori Council. Latimer: 'From 1962 onward we were not given the funds we needed. We weren't asking for much. Maoridom didn't set up the Council. It was established by an Act of Parliament. We shouldn't have had to ask for anything. What other government body is set up and then expected to pay for itself by running raffles to keep going? At first we didn't even have a typewriter.'

Councillors understood what was happening. Maori issues had low priority with both political parties. Indeed, Hunn suggested casually at the first meeting of the New Zealand Maori Council in 1962 that Hanan's lack of knowledge about Maori was possibly the reason for his selection as minister of Maori affairs. Hunn, a career public servant, was aware of Maori need for help. However, based on his refusal to fund the New Zealand Maori Council and comments he made to his colleagues, it is probable that he had no intention of creating a strong Council as a competitor for his own department (Maori Affairs).

Form II, Kaitaia District High School, 1939. Graham Latimer is second from the left in the back row *(detail below)*.

Pearl Kenworthy, Graham's maternal grandmother

Joseph Kenworthy, Graham's maternal grandfather

Emily Moore (later Latimer) with the Franklin Representative Basketball Team, 1945. *Back row:* Mrs Te Kawa (referee), M Foy, P Silva, O King. *Front row:* M King, E Moore, J Cronin (captain), B Jones, J Ferguson.

Trooper Graham Latimer and Trooper Kino Beazley, 1946

Maori Unit, J Force, 1946

Kemp Nathan, Graham Latimer's mentor from the Kaipara

The North Auckland Rugby Union Maori Advisory Board, 1959.
Back row: W Welsh, JW Isaacs, P Birch.
Front row: G Latimer, WP Barclay, L Davis.

Maori had no political clout. Hunn's 1960 report had demonstrated the huge gap in standards between Maori and non-Maori but there was no political mileage in trying to do anything about it. Maori were moving into cities and becoming an urban people. In 1945 about 75 per cent of all Maori lived in rural areas.[11] By 1976, 75 per cent of Maori were living in urban areas.[12] They were not, however, a political force, a pressure group.

The single race issue in the 1960s which caused a public outcry was the exclusion of Maori from rugby teams playing in South Africa. Anger had been building slowly for ten or fifteen years, becoming stronger with each Springbok game. The fundamental issue was, however, less about Maori than about race and human rights. Television had vividly revealed to the whole world the true nature of apartheid. Playing games with a racist country whose politicians were also seen as murderers was gradually becoming unfashionable.

While rugby issues gave Maori a heightened public profile, there was no significant spin-off into action on the Hunn Report recommendations for better education, housing, health and employment.

Latimer was not forced to accept the vice-presidency, but if he refused his usefulness on the Council would have ended. He would have been seen as someone not fully committed, with no future as a leading councillor. He said later that he did not believe he had a real choice.

It was a difficult time for the Latimers. Their involvement with the Tai Tokerau District Maori Council and then the New Zealand Maori Council came at a heavy price. They could not afford the time and the loss of income involved. Unlike Sir Turi they had no iwi behind them, no financial resources and no family to call on.

They were developing their dairy farm on poor, acidic soil at Tinopai, Kaipara Harbour, an area once covered with kauri forests. The first timber workers and settlers had burnt much of the forest to expose trees they wanted, and to prepare land quickly for cultivation – dense smoke clouds darkened the sky south towards Auckland for many years.

The Latimers had to restore the land by clearing the manuka scrub and by the heavy use of fertiliser. They had no capital, not much farm equipment, and little time. Working on Maori community issues drained their energies and diminished both farm and family.

They rose well before dawn most days and put long hours into milking their herd, repairing fences, and caring for their five children, and others they were looking after. When Latimer was going to be away at hui and other meetings he would try to prepare everything for Emily to work on her own. For years the children were too young to help. Latimer can remember just sitting down in the mud on a hillside and crying in fierce frustration. The children remember being without a father, often, and giving whatever help they could on the farm.

Emily has similar memories: 'Graham would set up the paddocks for me to do the milking, and I'd be crying while I was doing it. Bales of hay had to be carried over the mud for the cows. We had so little money that I would make blackberry jam, blackberry jam, all through the season. There was no honorarium in those days so we had to bear all the expenses ourselves. The farm mortgage slipped back.'

Getting to Council meetings in Wellington was a test of character and physical endurance. No travelling expenses were paid for many years. Latimer could not use the farm vehicle: Emily needed it. He hitched lifts out to State Highway 1 north of Wellsford and then caught a bus if he could or hitched to Auckland. On the long, slow overnight train trip to Wellington he would try to sleep in a hard-backed, upright seat. After what was usually a two-day meeting going well into the night he would repeat the journey back to Tinopai. The Wellington meetings, and those he and Emily attended in Northland, took many weeks out of their year.

In time they were able to improve the farm. They still had financial difficulties, however, and Department of Maori Affairs officers had to be brought in for budgetary advice and support. Jock McEwen, a former Department secretary, said that because Latimer spent so much time on Maori matters the 'farm went from bad to worse'.[13] It eventually became highly productive and successful but only because of hard discipline and heavy physical labour.

Latimer: 'We just worked endlessly. We were always tired. We had to make time for the children, went to parent–teacher association meetings and school and church working-bees. On Saturdays we'd try to get all the farm work done quickly so the kids could play sports, and Emily could play tennis with her club-mates. We were always short of money. That was when I gave up smoking, when I saw one day just how much of our weekly house budget went on my tobacco.' He had been a heavy smoker, starting when he was thirteen. (He still remembers the day he stopped: 4 June 1972.)

In addition, the Maori community was trying to set up a mussel-farming industry in the Kaipara Harbour as a way of expanding Te Uri-o-Hau's economic base, and Latimer was, in 1969, standing for Parliament against Matiu Rata. Emily was again taking on extra farm work, caring for foster children as well as her own, and helping to raise campaign funds while Latimer travelled all over Northland. (In that same year Emily was also the first woman to take part in Maori Council discussions though she was not a member: she went as a Tai Tokerau proxy.)

When, with Emily's support, Graham agreed to accept the vice-presidency — with the prospect of the presidency in the near future — he had a clear idea of what he was being asked to do, and of the personal and family costs involved. He had to continue to push the agenda already laid down over the previous 100 years. Latimer says: 'They gave me no advice on how to do this. They made it very plain that they were entrusting me with a mission that I would have to carry out in my own way.'

Kemp Nathan was more helpful. Though he told Latimer there was no guide book and that it was not possible to tell anyone how to become a leader, he had been deliberately teaching him the necessary skills during the previous sixteen years. Nathan had known many of the early leaders and had tried to understand what made them special. Latimer: 'He told me that the human being was the most fragile of all animals, that it was easy for people to be negative, to give up. He said I must not hurt people, even those who criticised me the most. I had to hold on to my sense of humour, always. And I had to learn when to walk away, to compromise.'

Latimer asked him how long he would be expected to stay in the job, how long would it take. Nathan replied: 'As long as your memory lasts.' He was there for life. People would expect him to work miracles, would criticise him for what he did or did not do, would expect favours, and would demand more than he could ever give. Leaders attracted gossip and rumour. The envious and small-minded would say they could do a better job. He could never expect any praise or applause.

So why take it on? For Nathan there was only one reason: Latimer had to be personally and permanently committed to the Council's aim – raising Maori to a position of equality with the rest of the community, wiping out their second-class citizen status, and helping them to achieve a much greater quality of life, as Maori and as citizens.

Nathan knew that the Latimers had seen the results of ill-health, stunted lives, poor housing and high crime rates. If they believed the Maori Council could do something about that as a statutory body representing all Maori then the presidency would be worth having.

Councillors had already shown Latimer how seriously they regarded the Act that set the Council up and the aims it had been given – to consider and discuss everything which seemed relevant to the social and economic advancement of the 'Maori race'. The Council was obliged to represent Maori opinion, to put proposals to the government, and to work as hard as possible to bring about parity between Maori and the rest of the community. The councillors also expected governments to respond, to engage in discussion, to consider their suggestions positively even if they did not agree with the Council.

Latimer knew that the Council had not, in its first few years, developed ways of connecting with the government that would allow it to be more effective than the four Maori MPs. 'There was no vision,' he says. 'They had an agenda all right. That was set down at their very first meeting, but they did not know how they were going to achieve it.'

That agenda was very specific. The Council wanted the Treaty recognised as New Zealand's founding document, wanted to stop further land alienation, and wanted governments to remedy the injustices arising from Treaty breaches. The councillors tried to create an economic base for Maori to improve health, housing and employment.

The councillors demanded better educational opportunities and a school system more relevant to Maori needs – they did not want to stop being Maori by being forced to become Pakeha. The Council rejected policies of integration and assimilation. Instead, it asked for more trained Maori language teachers, protection of the Maori language, more access to radio and television, and more respect for the language.

It promoted Maori culture and urged governments to establish policies that would preserve heritage taonga. It wanted the judicial and health systems to respect Maori burial customs. The councillors also saw themselves as protectors of the environment, and asked governments to adopt conservation policies against slashing and burning and polluting. The Council worried about the social and cultural pressures on Maori because of rapid urbanisation. Councillors wanted to reduce crime rates, and to change attitudes in the justice system, such as the hostility they saw in the police force to young Maori.

While councillors had identified all their main policies and priorities, they had no idea how to translate them into government policy. The Council held meetings with Hanan and his officials. The councillors commented on Bills before Parliament, and put forward proposals on a Bill of Rights that would recognise the Treaty. And they were comprehensively ignored.

Councillors were caught in a trap. If they demanded aggressively that the government act on their concerns they would be publicly rejected, squashed. If they adopted a softly-softly approach they would be condemned by Maori as creatures of government, state lackeys.

Latimer strongly supported the Council's aims, and had at first been surprised at the lack of response by National and Labour politicians. For him, the Council had high standing. Never before had such prominent leaders been brought together to speak for Maori and to share policy-making responsibilities with government. The Council, he felt, was like another parliament, not part of the executive branch of government but a debating chamber where answers could be sought to urgent problems.

While he knew that National was the party of farmers and people in business and was not naturally pro-Maori he was also aware it had produced election policies which meshed well with the Council's aims. As early as 1946 and 1949 National promised, for example, to make special efforts to improve Maori health and to ensure that more Maori doctors and nurses were trained.

Gustafson, in his Party history, says National 'promised to use the education system to maintain and promote the Maori language, history and culture; establish a university chair in Maori studies; foster Maori community centres; use a tribunal to settle outstanding Maori land disputes; establish financial aid to help Maoris develop their land; and extend the Maori language in broadcasting'.[14]

National had been in power from 1949 to 1957, and was again the government when the Maori Council was formed in 1962. It had not fulfilled any of its promises, though this was a period of full employment and reasonable prosperity. The Korean War, 1950–1953, had boosted the economy, overseas markets for agricultural exports were mostly favourable, and money was available to use for social policies.

In spite of National's record of indifference, Latimer and his fellow councillors had every reason to be optimistic. The Hunn Report had stressed the need for rapid action to halt the creation of a low-paid, unhealthy, unlawful minority, and Hanan, as minister, supported Hunn. However, while some improvements were made, the gap between Maori and the rest of the community remained great and was still an election issue in 2002.

Latimer's first task when he became the Council's third president, in 1973, was to learn how to use his authority. If he was going to lead the Council and, on occasions, try to speak for all Maori, then he had to create a completely new style, personal to himself and sharply different from the hapu- and iwi-based roles of the past. He had to make his own rules, knowing that at any time he could be voted out of office by a simple majority, or be removed from the Council if he lost the confidence of his own district council.

Apart from the embryo Council, no national Maori representative body existed. The only structures that could be used for collective efforts were iwi-based, through trust boards, land committees or marae groupings. The Maori Women's Welfare League, formed and funded by the Department of Maori Affairs, had no mandate to speak for all Maori even in its main area of activity, health. Dame Whina, the League's first president, had not then gained Mother of the Nation status.

The King Movement, which Latimer regarded highly, had authority in the Waikato but King Koroki, who died in 1966, had not been acknowledged by most Maori as more than a respected Tainui leader. Princess Te Puea, who had died in 1952, had a greater public presence and was admired for her personal achievements but was an iwi leader not a representative of the Maori people. Dame Te Atairangikaahu was still very young, and had not yet stamped her own mark on the Kingitanga.

The Ratana Movement was the only organisation that consciously tried to speak to and for all Maori as Maori. Ratana, who died in 1939, had been the only leader who took his religious, social and political messages straight to the people, wherever they were and whatever their hapu and iwi affiliations. The movement's scope was, however, limited because it was fundamentally religious in aim and had strict rules governing membership.

Four Maori MPs provided some representation for Maori but party rules reduced their independence and their ability to reflect pan-Maori opinion. None held the portfolio of minister of Maori affairs when Labour was in power. Eruera Tirikatene was associate-minister between 1957 to 1960 but was given little freedom to move by Walter Nash, then prime minister and minister of Maori affairs.

The Council was the only body that had the potential to be an effective force but, to succeed, it had to transcend iwi concerns and speak for Maori nationally. Some councillors were still focused on iwi rather than national issues and were there to pursue iwi rather than Maori aims. Latimer: 'They could get into an unholy row if they weren't careful. Tremendous tolerance had to be exercised. Sir Turi had a very hard job to get them to stop competing with each other and to start working together.'

Most councillors did not see themselves as Maori in the national sense being imposed on them by governments that wanted only one organisation to deal with on all things Maori. It was not, for them, a natural, traditional order. Some even objected to the new words being coined – such as Maoritanga (first used by a Maori, Sir James Carroll). They accepted they held many Maori characteristics in common but most saw themselves first as representing their particular iwi.

Latimer realised quite early that he had to become completely familiar with the bureaucracy, find his way round the labyrinth of Parliament buildings and to meet the politicians and officials he would have to work with over the following years. He met all the senior staff in the Department of Maori Affairs. Hunn had left by the time Latimer became a councillor in 1964, his place being taken by Jock McEwen, another career civil servant. Latimer: 'McEwen was a remarkable man. He spoke Maori as though he had been born to it. He was a scholar, a carver, and an expert in Maori custom. But even though he tried to help the Council he could never persuade any government, National or Labour, to give us the money we needed.'

Latimer admired some politicians, like Hanan, for their personal qualities even when he opposed their policies. He already knew and liked Duncan McIntyre, Hanan's successor from 1969. McIntyre had been a colonel in J Force for part of the time Latimer was in Japan. McIntyre was also one of the few Pakeha ministers of Maori affairs who had any knowledge of Maori issues and ways of life. He earned respect for his efforts even though he failed to persuade National cabinet colleagues to take Maori issues seriously.

Latimer came to know the four Labour Maori MPs very well, and did not experience any animosity because of his National Party membership, though this was occasionally raised as a public issue. Latimer: 'We all had the same aims and mostly the same policies. Tirikatene supported the Council though he thought it was 100 years too late – I can't disagree with that. Mat Rata pushed some of the Council's policies when he became minister from 1972 to 1975 – in particular, the idea of a Waitangi Tribunal.'

Latimer met Norman Kirk soon after Kirk became leader of the opposition in 1965 and liked and respected him as a person. He found Kirk more sympathetic to Maori aspirations than most politicians, possibly because Kirk's working-class background gave him a better understanding of the realities of under-class status. Latimer: 'I made a point of meeting him. That was a time when you could just go up to a leading politician. He wasn't surrounded by minders. I was tremendously impressed. He was a great man. And he really did have Maori interests at heart.'

Latimer was later to have close contact with Kirk when he was prime minister and Latimer was Council president. 'He would ask me for my opinion on many things, and on one occasion, he wanted me to talk with Mat [Rata] about some of his concerns relating to the way Mat was handling his Maori Affairs portfolio. The fact that I was a National Party member made absolutely no difference. Mat was highly indignant, but later saw the funny side when he had resigned from Labour [in 1979].'

He came to know Robert Muldoon when Muldoon was minister of finance in the 1960s, and respected him for his bluntness and his intelligence if not for his attitude toward Maori issues. Muldoon had previously had little contact with Maori. He had met very few during his schooldays and had no interest in them. His first involvement came with the occupation of Bastion Point in 1977 and this experience had left him feeling confused, uncertain and angry about who spoke for Maori and what the real agenda was.

Latimer invited Muldoon to meet the Maori Council, and, later invited David Lange, when he became leader of the opposition. Muldoon was out of his element, and told Latimer never to do such a thing to him again. Latimer: 'At that time the Council had very respected leaders like Sir Hepi Te Heuheu. Muldoon had no idea how to relate to him and to the other councillors. He was extremely nervous, actually trembled.'

He and Latimer related well on a one-to-one basis. They were both direct, tough-minded and shared the same political party background. They were also both outsiders.

After being elected president, Latimer returned to the Kaipara, arranged to pay off all his debts, and took short-term forestry jobs in addition to his farm work. 'This was just to get extra money,' he says, 'so that nobody could say the president of the New Zealand Maori Council owed anybody anything.' He remembered his mother's experience with the policeman–debt collector when he was four. 'Owing money was absolutely sinful.'

He was intensely conscious of the importance of appearance, of the perceptions people had of him and his position. It was a question of credibility. He had to be, and be seen to be, free of blemish – no debts, no drinking, no womanising. Kemp Nathan had told him that a leader had to 'keep his hands in his pockets and not in the till' and to 'keep his pants on'. Nathan was conscious of criticisms of some earlier leaders, who were said to have used their positions for personal advantage, to help their own relatives or their own iwi, and to chase after women.

Latimer says he followed this advice. 'You're always in the public eye, always being scrutinised. People are looking for mistakes, for flaws, and they'll drag you down if they can.' Over the years there had, he says, been plenty of opportunities to transgress. 'I can't, because Maoridom would have to pay.' As he gained authority as president, Latimer applied the same principles whenever he could to other councillors. Because Sir Turi had urged councillors to avoid giving the impression of political bias, Latimer told a few of his colleagues that they would have to change their personal behaviour in Wellington while attending Council meetings if they wished to remain. 'They were away from home. They were being invited out. They'd gained some status. And some were taking advantage of it.' For him, that meant that the Council lost some of its credibility.

Latimer says that the temptations facing Council members were similar to those for MPs. He has great sympathy for politician's wives. 'Their husbands lead a tense, artificial life and can forget their family responsibilities. A book should be written about the sacrifices made by spouses.'

He gradually developed his own style of leadership – significantly different from all others. He had to convince colleagues and collaborators inside and outside Maori communities to accept him for what he was and not to expect him to be cast in the traditional mould. At that time, he says, 'it wasn't completely acceptable to be of mixed blood. I couldn't claim leadership rights from a direct Maori inheritance'.

Latimer consciously studied his older colleagues and other leaders. 'Pei Te Hurinui Jones had tremendous knowledge of all things Maori. He was a great scholar. I had none of that. Sir Turi had been bought up Maori, had war experience, and was a businessman and a sportsman – people looked up to him for what he had done for Ngati Kahungunu. King Koroki was a humble, wise man with great power – mana just emanated from him. Sir James Henare served in the Maori Battalion, had gained a lot of experience in the Department of Maori Affairs and was a distinguished and highly respected kaumatua.'

His own background was completely different. 'I'm just not like them. I came out of a different world.' But, though he had come late to the main elements of traditional Maori culture, he felt he embodied in his own experience many of the characteristics of modern Maori. 'Culture doesn't stand still,' he says. 'It's changing all the time. What we can do is decide for ourselves what we want to keep and to adapt, so that we have a sense of our past and our present. Then we can look to the future.'

Partly because of his own experience growing up in the Far North, going to Japan, working for a large organisation like the New Zealand Railways, and being a struggling farmer, he valued personal independence and freedom. People, he says, have to 'stand on their own two feet and not be dependent on the state or anybody else'. He argued that without economic independence and security people could not be full citizens or hold on to their ethnic or racial inheritance.

Jock McEwen described Latimer as a 'maverick'. He said that he had a lot of energy, was independent, and was willing to put forward his own ideas. McEwen thought he derived strength from his firsthand, daily knowledge of how Maori lived: he was not an academic, protected by educational institutions and divorced from the harsh realities facing many Maori.[15]

John Booth, a former Maori Council secretary and a member of the former Department of Maori Affairs, felt Latimer was, from the very beginning, a bit irreverent, not overly respectful of tradition, willing to try new things, upsetting the old order – in some ways not unlike the mythical demigod, Maui, the prankster, the younger son who fished up the North Island, Te Ika-a-Maui. Booth admired his 'boldness' and his willingness to 'act unilaterally using his Council position, and then getting approval later'. Looking back from the 1990s, he said that 'if Graham hadn't been there the Council wouldn't have got things done'.[16]

Wira Gardiner, when he was chief executive officer of Te Puni Kokiri (1992–1995), noticed some of the same sort of behaviour in the early 1990s. He says that Latimer often appeared to be 'off-hand, humorous', not taking everything too seriously. His manner could sometimes be misunderstood or misinterpreted – that he lacked interest in what was being discussed. Gardiner said that was not the case. He was always serious but he refused to be ponderous and heavy.[17]

When Latimer became president of the Council in 1973 he felt he was ready. Four years earlier the vice-presidency had frightened him. He was on probation. The following years had, however, been full of crises. The Council's composition changed when the first women joined. Academics like Dr Pat Hohepa, from Ngapuhi, and Dr Ranginui Walker from Whakatohea, Emily's iwi, were bringing a new edge to meetings. So was Titewhai Harawira, a relative of Latimer's.

Professor Hohepa, now chairman of the Maori Language Commission, says that Latimer found the presidency 'a tough, lonely, hurting job'. Hohepa, who was a councillor in the early 1970s, knows him well. 'It was not something a person would keep doing for personal advantage. If he wanted that he would have resigned and made money for himself through farming and other business interests. I've had many stand-up arguments with him but I've never doubted his integrity or his commitment to Maori.'[18]

Right from the beginning of his presidency Latimer came under continuous attack. He decided that Kemp Nathan had been right. There is an open-hunting season on leaders and, unless they are looking for something other than fame or notoriety, being a target is not worth a day of anyone's time.

Latimer had also decided from the earliest years of his presidency that he would not defend himself or debate public issues through news media headlines. He believed television and newspapers trivialised serious and sensitive matters by homing in on personal and emotional details, for their sensational value. He responded briefly to questions when asked, would not get into personalities, and would not pursue red herrings. Besides, he said, many criticisms came from relatives. After all the fuss had died down they still had to get on together as a big family. 'You don't draw blood just for the benefit of the news media.'

This policy left the field open for those who would debate public issues. Walker (Emily's cousin) became a preferred, instant commentator on all things Maori from the 1970s onward, always ready to call on his experience as a councillor and a university academic. Titewhai Harawira became the voice of protest. Whina Cooper, particularly after she became a dame, represented the voice of moderation, all colours living in close harmony.

The bitterness surrounding everything touching South Africa sharpened divisions within the Council. Latimer was criticised because he, and in the 1970s a majority of the Council, refused to condemn rugby contacts with South Africa on behalf of all Maori. Latimer agreed with most councillors that these were issues that belonged to hapu and iwi and individual Maori. No single body could represent such diverse opinions and had no right to say that it did. (By 1980 he had changed his mind and, with the Council, opposed the 1981 Springbok tour.)

The status quo of the Council was also threatened by new pressure groups, fashioned on overseas models, which demanded radical changes. Urban Maori were partly represented through new district councils such as Auckland. Claims that blood would flow on the streets if injustices were not remedied were designed to put Maori on the national political agenda. The Council was fractured on urban–rural lines, divided into young and old, radical and conservative, and was still overwhelmingly male.

Latimer responded to the new pressures by compromising when he had to while still trying to retain his individual integrity. He also developed his own methods of chairing meetings and of acting on behalf of the Council. Pat Hohepa remembers that he did not run meetings 'in a formal boring way. He does all the routine stuff then concentrates on things that have to be done. He wanted lots of information, then decisions to act'.[19]

Latimer says he has always favoured consensus, hoping that major debates could end in a generally acceptable approach. 'You have to give everyone a chance to say what they think, otherwise you've failed them and yourself.' But, when there was no agreement, he did not hesitate to act on his own, without a mandate from colleagues. He believed that the demand for consensus could be used by opponents of a particular policy to stop all action. 'If we waited for everyone to agree we'd never have done anything.'

Walker strongly condemned what he called Latimer's autocratic management style.[20] He also claimed that Latimer was acting the part of a subaltern, a junior officer, within an alien political establishment, a servant to his colonial masters.[21]

Latimer denies this and says today that the accusation showed a complete ignorance of the political process. Politicians, Maori and Pakeha, understand that they cannot always get their way, because of circumstances, so they wait, try again, modify and disguise their policies, do each other favours. They use each other and they bide their time, enemies today, friends tomorrow.

Latimer knew that Maori politics cut across all social, economic, political and religious lines. Shared history, old friendships, family ties, iwi responsibilities, inherited obligations, Maori Battalion connections and the Anglican mafia all influenced decisions in ways not anticipated by party rules. Issues were not as clearcut as they seemed; hidden agendas and personal ambitions were often more important than the policies being discussed. This was political reality: it was not a morality play.

As Council president he deliberately worked closely with politicians of both major parties, Maori and Pakeha, soon realising the huge gap between what was said to him face-to-face, privately, and what was said publicly in Parliament or through the news media. He had the option of revealing such hypocrisy publicly, or trying to persuade politicians that their interests, and the national interest, lay in improving Maori standards of living, and acknowledging the significance of the Treaty.

He refused to burn bridges and to alienate the other actors. Latimer chose the unpopular strategy of persuasion, of repeated requests for support on specific policies. With the Council, he pushed for improvements to land laws, stronger economic initiatives, better health systems, greater scope for the Waitangi Tribunal, and the inclusion of Treaty clauses in various Bills. Though success was limited, he believed greater progress was being made than was apparent.

He worked behind the scenes. He endured the humiliation of pleading with minor civil servants in the Department of Maori Affairs for additional funds for the Council. In budget meetings he argued, for example, for two meetings each year rather than one, admitting that, yes, one would be cheaper, but two was the absolute minimum if they were to make informed submissions to government – that is, to go part way toward fulfilling their statutory obligations as set out in the 1962 Act. And could we rent an office perhaps, and even hire some secretarial help rather than having to rely on Maori Affairs staff?

He became a practical politician and gained a street-wise reputation for knowing how to get things done, who to talk to. At the same time he had to live with the subaltern accusation – the charge that he was selling out Maoridom by working within the established system, by doing what his colonial masters told him.

He listened to angry proposals to grab public attention, and to change attitudes. Whina Cooper demanded that he make changes to one law that she found particularly repulsive, and refused to accept his lame excuse that he did not have the power. He says she asked him what he was going to do about it. He suggested that something dramatic should be done, perhaps a land march from Te Hapua in the Far North to Parliament? He remembers she replied: 'Is that all?'

Latimer says he persuaded her that it would be the most effective way of getting the alienation of Maori land on the public agenda. When she asked who should lead it he said she should. 'Why me?' she asked humbly. Latimer said he was sure she did not want any other kuia or kaumatua to lead it, or a younger man. 'True.' That left her, alone, as a well-known national figure with the mana to do it. She was forced to agree. And did. (There are, it must be admitted, a number of other versions of the origin of the 1975 Land March and Dame Whina's involvement.)

He and Emily were acutely aware of how much the presidency

had changed their lives. Almost all their major family decisions were linked with the demands of the Council and the rhythm of its yearly cycle. They had, he says, no life they could call their own. Their time was taken up with endless meetings, locally, regionally and nationally. Latimer was also secretary to the Tai Tokerau District Maori Council from 1966, replaced by Emily when he became chairman in 1979. They were both involved in gathering information, in preparing policy options and in debate.

On a number of occasions he and Emily raised extra mortgages on their farm to keep the Council functioning till overdue government grants arrived – possibly the only example in New Zealand of private citizens keeping a statutory body alive.

Latimer's Anglican Church work was also time consuming but, he claims today, enjoyable compared with much of his other public activity. Sir Paul Reeves, the former governor-general, remembers the pleasure gained in making progress on church policies on the establishment of a Maori ministry and, later, on attitudes toward the Treaty. 'Graham,' he says, 'was very much a practical Christian, wanting to get things done.'[22]

Formal recognition of Latimer's work for Maori, particularly through the Council, came with three offers of honours in the 1970s. He turned two down because he considered other distinguished kaumatua deserved such honours more than he did. He finally accepted a knighthood in 1980.

Muldoon's government missed a rare opportunity when it did not simultaneously offer Emily the title of Dame, recognising the equal but different contribution of husband and wife. She had helped Graham to perform the task of secretary to the Tai Tokerau District Maori Council before taking over the job herself. She attended many hui and carried out much of the follow-up work. She helped to shape Latimer's stand on many issues and gave him a wider perspective than some other Maori leaders. 'Without her support,' he says, 'I could have done very little.'

Instead, she became a Lady, by virtue of her husband's KBE (Knight of the British Empire), not in her own right. Whina Cooper was the government's preferred Dame that year.

During the following years Latimer seriously considered resigning from the Council. Personal criticism drained his energy. He was challenged in the 1980s for the presidency by Dr Walker and Maanu Paul, of Rotorua, and survived by only one vote. Personal attacks continued. Both political parties patronised the Council and both kept it poor.

He says today that he received strong encouragement from people at local and regional levels to stay on. Latimer also says he has been strengthened, ever since he was a child, by a feeling that he was not alone, that he had spiritual support, a 'mate'. He was first conscious of a presence, a friend, when he was about seven. His parents had gone to a meeting and left him with neighbours at Pamapuria. He had decided to go home during the night. When his parents returned they were surprised to find him there alone, sleeping, and worried that he might be cold. 'No,' he said, 'my mate is sleeping with me, keeps me warm.'

Latimer has always felt supported, confident; never abandoned or alone. He does not claim a guardian angel and has no feeling that he is protected in any way. 'There is nothing specific, just a sense of a presence special to me. I can't say that God is with me but I have the feeling that I have spiritual support. I have a feeling of rightness – not righteousness.' He is very conscious of the past, of the people he has known, of his younger brother, Lloyd, who died of leukaemia, of his Council colleagues like the late Joe Karetai.

Latimer: 'I find this very difficult to put into words that can have meaning for anyone else. When I'm home, particularly at sunset, I "see" my tupuna, I feel their presence, as though they're not dead, but still with me as family, part of my daily life. I think about them a lot.'

He says that this consciousness, of being linked with the past and friends and relatives who have died, has forced him to 'meditate', and to think seriously about what he does. He does not believe that, because of this, his actions are always right and knows he makes mistakes. But, he believes he is trying to do the right thing, even when he takes risks and cannot be sure of the outcome.

This intangible sense of support, of not being alone, has given him confidence as a leader and helped him to remain with the Council even when disputes become angry, personal and painful. Also, Lady Emily persistently urged him to stay because of all the work they had done and the family sacrifices they had made. There was so much to do, and the Treaty had still not been recognised.

CHAPTER FIVE

The Treaty Legacy
1840–1987

It would be pretty safe to say that [in 1982] very few New Zealanders had heard of the Waitangi Tribunal. When the Attorney-General, Jim McLay, telephoned me at my home one Saturday morning … and asked me if I would accept appointment to the Tribunal, I had never heard of it either. I asked him what it was and he told me that it was a body set up under the Treaty of Waitangi Act 1975 to deal with any claims that arose under the Treaty.

He went on to say that it would sit only one or two days a year and that it wasn't likely to be an onerous task. What an understatement that turned out to be.

– Paul Temm QC, member of the Waitangi Tribunal, 1982–1985[1]

The truth is, of course, that many of the 'settlements' in the past have not been settlements at all. They have simply been the imposition of the will of the government of the day upon Maori people, who have taken the half-a-loaf that has been offered to them and have bided their time. An injustice is never settled when a superior power imposes a solution.

– Paul Temm, again, on Treaty settlements prior to 1975[2]

Although not generally enforceable by court proceedings the Treaty of Waitangi may also be called constitutional because it has moral force no less potent than Magna Carta; while its precise status continues to be debated the importance of its values is indisputable.

– Justice David Baragwanath, former president of the Law Commission (1997–2000)[3]

When Latimer first became involved in Maori struggles for recognition the Treaty was invisible, not a public issue. The Centennial celebrations of 1940 marking 100 years since the signing of the Treaty had come and gone without any interest being shown. Two large official volumes titled *Making New Zealand* had been published in series form on the history and achievements of the previous 100 years.[4] Many references were made to Maori from the earliest times but the Treaty was mentioned only briefly.

The main writer, G Bamford, said Maori believed they had 'certain grievances' over the way the Treaty had 'been interpreted by successive governments, or over the method whereby native lands have been sold without giving him what he takes to be fair compensation for their disposal'.[5] He saw this as no problem: ' ... all of these grievances [can be] settled amicably provided both European and Maori bring to them a sympathetic understanding, a sense of justice, and an ability to compromise'.[6]

The 1946 *New Zealand Official Yearbook* described everything significant about the country in 983 pages but made three references only to the Treaty. It is listed in a chronology of events, then in relation to land alienation, and finally referred to briefly in the section dealing with annexation in 1840. Its text is not given, just summarised inadequately.[7] The 1970 *New Zealand Official Yearbook* gave no official information about the Treaty in 1,170 pages.[8] A 1946 school textbook, *New Zealand Community*, by FG Spurdle, did not even mention the Treaty.[9]

Claims that governments had deliberately breached the Treaty surfaced in newspapers from time to time but generated little interest. The public was told in 1946–1947, for example, that a complete and final agreement with Tainui had been reached. Everybody was said to be happy with a 5,000 pound a year payment in perpetuity for the confiscation of 1.2 million acres in the 1860s.

Political commentators rarely mentioned the Treaty. Maori had no influence in Parliament or on government. The existence of four Maori seats was a side issue, usually referred to only briefly in relation to the dominance of the Labour Party from 1935 to 1949.

Latimer says today that he had been amazed by the history that Kemp Nathan unfolded for him in the Kaipara. He had not been aware of the Treaty's fundamental significance to Maori as the way of gaining citizenship rights. He had not known that courts had long rejected it as a legal 'nullity', having no force in law, or that governments denied it had any significance. All appeals by Maori to implement the promises made in its preamble and three articles had been rejected by Queen Victoria and her descendants, by the imperial governments in London and by settler majorities in New Zealand's Parliament.

He cannot recall his father mentioning it when he was young. His Pakeha grandparents had no interest in it, though they had been in the country for fifty or sixty years when he was born. His great-grandfather, James Kenworthy, had been born in Lancashire, arriving in New Zealand in 1864 – at the height of the land wars started by Governor Grey when he ordered the invasion of the Waikato. His grandmother's family, the Priestleys, had settled in Kawakawa, just north of Whangarei, in the 1870s.

Both families probably had no knowledge of the Treaty. It was not a subject for discussion. They may not have even heard of it. Few of the settlers who poured into the country in their hundreds of thousands in the early twentieth century knew about it. For most people, other than Maori, it had dropped into the black hole of history.

Latimer's Maori tupuna certainly knew of it but he can't recall any talk about it in his youth. His family was, however, strongly Anglican and this could well have been another impediment to his learning about the Treaty. The Church of England at that time had conservative views on most issues, kept out of party politics and held itself conspicuously above the social issues of the day as much as possible. It had a long history of involvement with Maori in the Far North, going back to the arrival of the first missionaries in the 1830s, but the Church favoured Maori assimilation into the Pakeha mainstream rather than the preservation of a distinct Maori identity.

The Ratana Movement, which arrived in the Far North about the time Latimer was born, was, however, actively promoting the Treaty and wanted it implemented. Ratana appealed to all Maori, across iwi lines, saying he came to unite them, with the Bible in one hand and the Treaty in the other. He wanted the Treaty made statutory so that its principles could be recognised in all laws relating to Maori.

The Labour Party leader at the time, Harry Holland, promised Ratana that lands properly belonging to Maori would be restored to them as part of Labour's programme of attending to their grievances.

The Anglican Church, encouraged by Sir Apirana Ngata, tried to counter Ratana's rapidly growing influence by establishing a Maori section with its own bishopric of Aotearoa. However, this was done so painfully, so slowly, and with so few resources that it did nothing to damage Ratana's appeal.

The young Latimer had no contact with the Ratana Movement. When Ratana's missionaries moved north his Maori grandfather did not welcome them but conceded that people had the right to choose their own faith. Today Latimer describes the situation then as a sort of armed neutrality.

(Tension between Anglican and Ratana continued for many years, even involving the dead. In the cemetery opposite Latimer's family home at Pamapuria a fence was erected separating the burial plots of the two creeds. It is not there now. In Te Kao, just north of Latimer's gumfields home, a meeting house was cut in half with axes about the time he was born, bitterly dividing local Maori into 'white' sheep and 'black' sheep.)

As a result of this discord, Latimer missed his first chance to become familiar with the Treaty's significance. In an attempt to avoid conflict, Ratana's followers walked up the coast, along Ninety Mile Beach. They by-passed the Kenworthy-Latimer squatter camp and went on toward Cape Reinga, through Te Kao and Te Hapua. There they won support from some local people and set up, first in Te Kao, the most northern Ratana temple, with its distinctive twin towers.

When Latimer joined the Maori Council in 1964 the Labour Party still had no Treaty policy even though this was a condition of Ratana support. All it promised in its 1963 election manifesto was that a future Labour government would make Waitangi Day New Zealand's national day, and a paid holiday. The manifesto promised to ensure that all laws affecting Maori 'as such' would allow individuals 'the right to feel and express their Maori identity should they so desire'. The Treaty did not interest National or Labour. Politicians from both parties said they were worried about Maori housing and education. Labour promised to set up a commission of inquiry for the 'purpose of clarifying' the economic and social problems Maori were having because of 'their Maori status'.

The Maori Council placed the Treaty on the agenda during its first year. Members wanted it ratified, to be recognised as part of the law of the land. They saw it not only as a symbol of the promises made in 1840 but as an 'effective protection for Maori rights'. Because ratification was impossible in the prevailing political climate they adopted a more indirect approach – to determine how the 'spirit' of the Treaty could be implemented through official policies.

Latimer first saw a facsimile of the Treaty when he became a Council member. He was left in no doubt about members' feelings: 'Sir Turi was determined that we would not back down on the issues that were important, and the Treaty was the first of those.'

During the year Latimer was elected (1964) the Council was asked to comment on a proposed Bill of Rights. Members followed tradition and repeated demands that the Treaty be acknowledged as the basis of the relationship between the Maori people and the government. The Treaty had not even been mentioned in the Bill's first draft.

Councillors wanted a formal declaration of the special status of Maori deriving from the Treaty, and asked for the equal citizenship rights that had been promised by the Crown in 1840. They also asked that a public holiday be declared to mark the Treaty's first signing, and that full civil rights be accorded to Maori.

They suggested that if a second parliamentary chamber should be set up to replace the old Legislative Council (abolished by a National government in 1950) Maori should have separate representation. They did not see this as separatism or a form of apartheid. Maori had always been deliberately kept separate by the majority population and had never been truly represented in Parliament. They had always been an ignored minority. A second chamber was seen as a chance to gain a true parliamentary voice.

Councillors also wanted Maori to receive services suited to their needs where those differed from the majority population – in recognition of their Maori cultural background.

A Bill of Rights was seen as a way to free Maori from racial discrimination. The councillors asked that an institute of race relations be set up to sponsor research and act as a clearing house for information. Latimer was well aware of attitudes toward Maori trying to get jobs, a good education, bank loans, or buying or renting homes, and even going into private lounges in hotels. He knew all about police harassment of young Maori and resented the way in which the justice system treated them.

The Council's recommendations to the select committee considering public submissions disappeared along with the Bill of Rights itself until it was revived in a new form twenty years later by Geoffrey Palmer when minister of justice and attorney-general in the Labour government in the 1980s.

Keith Holyoake, Ralph Hanan and almost all members of the National government simply could not understand why the Council persisted in raising an insignificant treaty for discussion. They did not reject it; they could see no reason even to think about it.

Latimer says that this was the pattern for the next twenty years. People were not talking past each other – they were not talking at all. Mentioning the Treaty was bad manners, talking about something indecent in polite society, an expression of ignorance. The Council believed it had no option but to continue to press National and Labour for action. Latimer said in 1968 that his Tai Tokerau people believed that the Maori Affairs Amendment Bill (to reduce Maori land ownership rights) was another Treaty breach. He protested to Hanan and his officials – to no effect. Five years later the Council listed at least thirteen Acts of Parliament that breached the Treaty in some way. In the following years the list got longer. The response remained the same – silence.

Progress was made when Labour came to power in 1972. Latimer, by that time Council vice-president, hoped that Matiu Rata would be able to convince his caucus colleagues that the Treaty had more than symbolic significance. Kirk was sympathetic to Maori aspirations but died (in 1974) before he was able to do much in this area.

Margaret Hayward, Kirk's private secretary, said in her *Diary of the Kirk Years*, that he communicated with Maori better than any other Pakeha she knew, that he relaxed completely in the 'warm, caring environment of a marae'. She says he would occasionally refer to himself as 'this Maori here', possibly because 'although white-skinned he tans easily and has what some regard as Maori features – a big belly, fairly thick lips and a broad nose'.[10]

Latimer had great respect for Kirk. 'He had a presence, an authority and a vision which made him a real leader. He was tough, astute, well-informed. New Zealand would have been a better place had he lived.'

Rata and the other three Maori MPs were vitally interested in the Treaty, but Rata soon lost influence and came to be seen as lightweight, the butt of sarcastic public jokes. Latimer rejects the gibes. He says Rata tried to do too much, without resources and without support. 'He didn't have the budget to do what he wanted and tried to go too fast. Some of his policies would have been accepted in the 1990s, not in the 1970s.' He was not surprised when Rata, feeling Labour undervalued him, resigned in 1979, and set up Mana Motuhake (and lost his Tai Tokerau seat to Dr Bruce Gregory).

The most significant step ahead during this period was Rata's decision, with Kirk's support, to set up the Waitangi Tribunal. Latimer was disappointed that it had no power to look into claims relating to incidents which took place before 1975 but was, however, willing to become one of its first three members.

The Tribunal was almost dropped. Muldoon's National Party won the general election that year and so had responsibility for establishing the Tribunal, which it had never wanted, seeing it as a potential nuisance, a sop to Maori demands.

Soon after it was set up in 1977, with virtually no support services, a conscious move was made to kill it. Duncan McIntyre, then minister of Maori affairs, was a sympathiser but the Tribunal came under the control of the minister of justice, Dan Riddiford, who was not. Latimer remembers receiving a telephone call asking him to see McIntyre next time he was in Wellington. 'When I met him he asked me if I would be willing to resign from the Tribunal,' says Latimer. 'This was a complete surprise. The Tribunal was just getting under way. I don't think that even one claim had been presented to us at that time.'

The other two non-Maori members, a judge and a lawyer, were told that it was unlikely that they would be re-appointed at the end of their term of office. If Latimer, a Maori and long-time National Party member, had been willing to resign, the government could have repealed the Act and dismantled the Tribunal before it could cause any trouble.

He refused immediately, telling McIntyre that such an act was more than his life was worth. The Council and Maori elders had invested so much energy and hope into getting a judicial body that could hear their Treaty claims that they would never forgive any leader who betrayed them in this way.

Without consent from Latimer, Riddiford decided not to go ahead with the plan, which he had wanted to implement without any public fuss. If Latimer refused to go quietly and the Maori Council mobilised political opposition it was not worth the effort. Instead, Eddie Durie, chief judge of the Maori Land Court, later became chairman. Then, when the distinguished lawyer Paul Temm became a member, the Tribunal, with Latimer, began to develop into an effective forum for Maori grievances. (But, says Durie today, almost without any resources: 'We had hardly any secretarial services. I had to take my own notes at hearings.'[11])

The level of public knowledge about the Treaty during the 1970s and early 1980s never rose above abysmal, and some of the books that referred to it probably did more harm than good. In 1975, an expensive production designed to appeal to 'both young and old' summarised the Treaty contract by saying the 'chiefs gave the land to the Queen to rule over, and in return they gave her some of the land for her own use and the first chance to buy land which they were keeping for themselves'.[12]

In this book, *Aotearoa, A History of New Zealand*, Olive Baldwin said that Queen Victoria 'didn't want to be bothered with these islands' but felt she should send Captain Hobson out to 'settle the arguing [over land] once and for all'.[13] Baldwin said that some of the chiefs 'did not want to sign the Treaty but one called Tamati Waka

Nene reminded them that before the white man came to New Zealand the Maori could not rule themselves without a lot of fighting and killing. If something different was tried perhaps there would be peace: so the chiefs stopped arguing and most signed the Treaty'.[14]

Helen Clark, speaking as prime minister in 2000, said that when she grew up in the Waikato in the 1960s and 1970s she was aware of Maori grievances only in a very general way. The Treaty, she confirms, was not on the political agenda. Paul Temm, before he was asked to be a member of the Tribunal, had never heard of it.[15]

Latimer believed that the Treaty was the key to achieving parity for Maori, but still had no idea how to persuade governments or the public to accept it or apply its spirit, its principles, to their problems.

Muldoon refused to help. He was well aware of the danger of losing votes if he was seen to be giving in to Maori demands but was willing to increase the Council's annual grant if it did not cost anything. He managed this, without adding to the Maori vote, by cutting an equal amount from the Department of Maori Affairs budget.

Muldoon did not support new policies to help Maori, strongly objected to te reo being taught in schools – it should be learned at home – and had no coherent policy on Maori issues. In 1974 he had demonstrated how little he knew of the Maori urban migration by saying that young offenders should be prohibited from living in cities and sent back into the rural areas to live with their extended families, echoing suggestions made by magistrates as early as the mid-1940s. He also said that Pacific Islanders who committed crimes should be deported.[16]

Muldoon was responsible for the worst outbreaks of civil disorder the country had ever experienced by using racially divisive tactics during the 1981 Springbok tour for his own political advantage.

In 1983, Latimer and the Maori Council had another chance to re-state their Treaty aim clearly and strongly when a new Maori Affairs Bill was being discussed. They wanted all laws on Maori matters to begin with a preamble acknowledging the Treaty as the foundation for that legislation.

The councillors conceded that the Treaty could seem, to some, to be a quaint relic of a past time, with no current meaning. Not so for them. The Treaty, signed by their ancestors, carried their mana. It was a trust, a charter and an inheritance passed on to each generation. It was tapu, sacred. Councillors had a duty to keep faith with their people by seeking redress for past injustice.

For Latimer, this had also become a personal and an iwi kaupapa. Because the first signing had taken place at Waitangi, northern iwi had a special interest in the Treaty, a guardianship role. In addition, Latimer saw it as his and the Council's main source of power. As president, his aim was constant, embedded in a contract he believed to be sacred. Like his ancestors he wanted the other partner, the Crown, to carry out its promises.

But the Crown was never a stable entity. It was represented by a series of governments, ministers and policies changing with the whims of fickle electorates and given power by the majority non-Maori population. Since he joined the Council, Latimer had tried to reach agreements with two National and two Labour prime ministers, and three National ministers of Maori affairs and one Labour minister – all with very different personalities, abilities, agendas, policies, and levels of ignorance and knowledge.

The Council's Treaty declaration sank into the files of the Department of Maori Affairs. Latimer was not surprised when no response came from Muldoon's government. Neither the Council nor the Labour Party's four Maori MPs had any leverage. The Maori population was increasing quickly but it was still not an organised pressure group. Maori differed from one another ethnically, racially, politically and culturally, as did the non-Maori population, and they could not make or shape governments or policies.

Some Maori opted for direct action. As children of the television age and students with knowledge of African American dissent in the United States, they disrupted Waitangi Day ceremonies and occupied disputed land – protesting always in front of news cameras to gain the widest possible impact. At first some Maori damned the Treaty as a fraud. Others wanted it ratified, while some said, for dramatic effect, that they wanted to drive Pakeha into the sea. They were all exponents of the politics of embarrassment: make governments look bad or silly and they would cave in.

The inevitable public backlash reinforced the view of most politicians that no votes were ever won by seeming to support Maori causes. Racial harmony was a fragile flower and Maori urbanisation revealed a nasty underbelly of racism. In 1979, Bill Rowling, then leader of the opposition, said without argument that Maori were still regarded by many people as second-class citizens.

Latimer hoped that David Lange's 1984 election victory for Labour, with Koro Wetere as minister of Maori affairs, would produce a better climate for Treaty debates. He was wrong. Wetere and Geoffrey Palmer, then minister of justice, were able to extend the Waitangi Tribunal's scope for considering grievances dating from 1840, but the Tribunal still only had the power to make recommendations to government. And it was seriously underfunded, as it still is in 2002.

Sir Douglas Graham, then Justice spokesman for National, and Winston Peters, then a National backbencher, strongly opposed the extension. They warned that it would encourage Maori extremists, produce a flow of new claims for compensation worth many millions of dollars, and create a massive Pakeha reaction. They were wrong. These politicians were just trying to scare the public. They knew that the Waitangi Tribunal had no power to force governments to redress past injustices. When the backlash did come it was in 1987 in relation to the Court of Appeal establishing Treaty of Waitangi jurisprudence in the courts of New Zealand under the State-Owned Enterprises Act, not in response to the recommendations of the Waitangi Tribunal.

Latimer was unhappy about the attitude of Peters toward the Treaty and toward Maori. He suspected his motives and his sincerity. Peters was a new, smarter version of politician who knew the value of headlines and publicity. His ancestry (Maori father, Pakeha mother), similar to Latimer's, gave Peters credibility when he publicised scandals about Maori. Because he was seen as Maori, Peters believed he could not be accused of being racist.

Latimer appreciated the efforts made by Wetere and Palmer. He liked Palmer as a person: 'He was always clear and direct. He was open. You knew his position. He was worth arguing with. He was somebody. He wasn't afraid to confront his own colleagues. When he was in opposition he'd promised to extend the Tribunal's scope. And that was exactly what he did when he got power. He had to push it through caucus. There was a lot of opposition. In the finish it was supported reluctantly on his assurance that it wouldn't create any upheavals.'

Palmer also respected Latimer. He was aware that there was 'some natural suspicion' because of his National Party connections, 'a degree of nervousness'. Palmer says that, contrary to these fears, Latimer had always presented arguments for Maori in a balanced and reasonable way, and was 'never a source of embarrassment'.[17]

Latimer had high hopes of Wetere. Kirk had had more confidence in Wetere than in Rata, and believed he would have been more effective in winning caucus support for Maori initiatives. Kirk, however, never had the chance to make Wetere minister of Maori affairs. Labour's policy of allowing caucus to vote for those it wanted as ministers stopped him from choosing Wetere. He was not on the list. Rata was.

Latimer had less confidence in Lange's commitment to Maori. He invited Lange, as leader of the opposition, to meet the Maori Council in 1983. Lange was friendly, witty and articulate, but did not seem, to Latimer, to be engaged. Latimer remembers that he began by apologising that he knew little about the Council or its work and so could speak in only a faltering way. And falter he did, says Latimer: 'He said that recent census data *apparently* showed Maori were socially and economically disadvantaged.' He was optimistic, however, Latimer remembers, that things were getting better because of the work of kohanga reo and actions being taken by the Department of Maori Affairs.

Latimer says that Lange acknowledged that the country's poor economic performance as a whole put more stress on Maori than anybody else. He made no reference to the Treaty.

Latimer and his fellow councillors were not encouraged. All reports issued in the previous twenty-three years proved beyond any possible doubt that Maori were disadvantaged in every way this could be measured. The gaps were real. Lange was talking, however, only about apparent disadvantages and recent statistics.

Nor was Lange's confidence in Muldoon's government and the Department of Maori Affairs shared by councillors. National had no

Maori policy other than supporting the status quo. The Department of Maori Affairs was not only permanently underfunded, its loyalty was to its minister, not to Maori. National kept the Council in a state of poverty. It provided no grant during its first year of government in spite of promises by Ralph Hanan. District councils were expected to levy members to keep a statutory body alive, and were given permission to hold raffles. Small grants, totalling $5,000 to $10,000 were given during the 1960s and 1970s – still completely inadequate.

National also had no interest in the Treaty. Muldoon spent more well-publicised time with Maori gangs than with the Council. Latimer felt that Lange knew little of their concerns and was uncomfortable with Maori except at a superficial level. Intellectually Lange sympathised but found it difficult to relate to the councillors as people – no meeting of minds. He seemed to lack interest in promoting Maori initiatives.

After Lange left the Council meeting Latimer was not only disappointed, he also believed Lange had not even realised that the Council was a statutory body, with responsibilities it shared with the government. 'Lange was talking to us as though we were just another community group. He was not what we expected a political leader to be. Most councillors were Labour supporters, and here was a man they hoped would soon be prime minister talking to us without any understanding of what we were on about.'

Latimer had little to do with Lange after 1985. He says he was not surprised when Lange failed to support Wetere and his Department of Maori Affairs when they were attacked by Peters over what was called the Maori Loans Affair. This was a failed attempt by the Department of Maori Affairs to raise funds for Maori development from overseas sources without Cabinet approval. Instead, Lange was angry and embarrassed. Moves by Maori to bring about change became even less popular within the Labour government.

Wetere disagrees with Latimer's view of Lange. He admits that Lange did not support him as he had hoped he would when he was under attack from Peters but says that Lange's backing for the Tribunal's extended powers to 1840 was crucial. 'We'd never have achieved that without his help.'[18]

Richard Prebble, then a Labour cabinet minister and now leader of the Association of Consumers and Taxpayers (ACT) Party, also disagrees with Latimer's view that Lange and the Labour Party were lukewarm in their support for Maori. 'Our biggest problem as a caucus,' he says, 'was knowing what Maori wanted. There was very little agreement among our own Maori MPs. They all seemed to have their own agendas. And Maori were divided on big issues like how important iwi were, and how much power should be devolved to them. Nobody spoke for Maori.'[19]

Palmer has made a similar point: 'Maori politics is much more complicated than Pakeha politics.' As a South Islander, he had, like Ralph Hanan before him, little experience of Maori. He had not realised how much effort went in to discussions all over the country to get some form of agreement, consensus. 'Lots of personal and tribal factors have to be taken into account.'[20]

Latimer agrees, today, that Maori were divided and it was difficult for parties to understand the complexity of Maori politics. 'Maori aren't a single group,' says Latimer. 'We're just as divided as the Pakeha world and it's a brave politician who can say definitely what Maori want.' He concedes that this created problems for mainstream parties who had little knowledge of a Maori world that existed, mostly, outside their experience.

Palmer continued to use his position as deputy prime minister and minister of justice to strengthen the importance of the Treaty. As a constitutional lawyer, he pushed for a Bill of Rights, and wanted to see the Treaty given more formal status. He suggested modestly that New Zealand's system of government needed improvement. A Bill of Rights, he said, could provide greater protection for the fundamental rights and freedoms vital to the survival of the country's democratic and multicultural society. Palmer went further and argued that no supreme law could be considered unless it contained appropriate recognition of Maori as tangata whenua and included the Treaty of Waitangi.

Latimer thought this was a huge step forward for any senior politician, but noted it was still not Labour Party policy. He was also worried that, unless the proposed Bill was indeed 'supreme' law, it could be changed by vote of Parliament. That could eliminate the Treaty from New Zealand's constitution entirely. (When the amended Bill of Rights finally became law in 1990 it did not include the Treaty, and was a statute, which can be changed by a parliamentary majority. The Treaty was, and still is, not an entrenched part of the constitution.)

Latimer was disappointed and hurt when he was dropped as a member from the expanded Waitangi Tribunal after it was given authority to hear claims from 1840. He had enjoyed the work and believed the Waitangi Tribunal would be much more effective in the future. He had wanted to be part of it.

Wetere also wanted him to be a member, and said so publicly at the time. He was defeated by his caucus and cabinet colleagues, some of whom had decided that Latimer's involvement with the National Party made him unacceptable. 'It was party politics,' said Wetere in an interview for this book.[21]

Chief Judge Eddie Durie told Latimer he also was disappointed and surprised at the decision and said he would have felt far more comfortable with him on the Tribunal. He particularly admired what he called Latimer's 'marriage of Maori wairua with pragmatic realities'. He thought, also, that it was dangerous to take on board an entirely new team, without rotating members to ensure a continuation of experience. 'Perhaps,' said Durie to Latimer, 'as an old campaigner you may not have expected anything different.'[22]

Within a year of Labour's victory in 1984, Latimer and other councillors were seriously worried about the new economic policies imposed by Roger Douglas and Richard Prebble. Deregulation, an open market, 'level playing fields', and sale of state assets were slogans with a menacing ring.

Maori saw nothing level about the playing field they happened to be on. As most Maori were in relatively unskilled jobs they had no bargaining power or economic leverage. Sale of state assets would also cost them jobs in a time of rising unemployment.

The Council was still not highly regarded by Maori as an active force for change. Donna Awatere, who became an ACT MP, was then angrily waving the Maori sovereignty flag. Waitangi became a battlefield on each February 6 anniversary of the signing of the Treaty. The

Department of Maori Affairs was an agent of the bureaucracy and Pakeha politicians. The Council competed with the Department for scarce resources and was torn by faction fights. It could not force any government, Labour or National, to bridge the huge social and economic divide between Maori and the rest of the community.

While the Council had many achievements to its credit, only one mattered: it had survived twenty-four years of poverty, indifference and hostility. Most of its main recommendations had been rejected by National (in power for most of the Council's life) and then by Labour.

In 1986, it was still, however, the only statutory body that represented Maori. It was recognised in law as a channel for the expression of Maori opinion. No other organisation could claim this. In hindsight, Latimer sees the Council as a force waiting for its time.

CHAPTER SIX

The Treaty Goes to Court
1987

> The [state-owned enterprise] case established Treaty of Waitangi jurisprudence so firmly and dramatically in the courts of New Zealand that they can now play something of the role of American courts, and that will assist in the protection of the minority to secure to them things which the legislature would not award them directly.
> – Sir Geoffrey Palmer, former prime minister, 1992[1]

> The Appeal Court decision on the State-Owned Enterprises Act and the Treaty in 1987 marked the beginning of a new and different era for New Zealand. All the real work on the outstanding issues for Maori was done after that.
> – Jim Bolger, former prime minister, 26 March 2002[2]

EARLY IN 1987, LATIMER WENT TO THE TANGI OF A MAORI COUNCIL member, Joe Karetai, on the West Coast (of the South Island). When he looked at his friend's face in the open coffin he remembered how Joe always greeted him at meetings: 'Hi laddie. How are you getting on with those fellows on the hill?'

Karetai, a distinguished Te Wai Pounamu kaumatua who had travelled to New York with the Te Maori exhibition in 1986, was, in Latimer's opinion, a gentleman, thoughtful, totally committed to the Council's work. 'He was always immaculately dressed, very well-spoken. Had a lovely sense of humour. I'd always felt close to him and he was always supportive.'

Karetai had died just as the State-Owned Enterprises Bill (1986) went through its last stages in Parliament. Richard Prebble, then state-owned enterprises (SOE) minister, wanted to change most state trading departments into corporations run on commercial principles for profit. The sale of billions of dollars of state assets, including land claimed by Maori, was planned. Karetai saw this as yet another attack by Pakeha governments, another massive land grab.

Latimer, and many other Maori leaders, objected strongly. So also did the Waitangi Tribunal. Part of those assets included Crown land under Treaty claims. If they were transferred to state-owned enterprises and then sold to private owners the Waitangi Tribunal would be unable even to make recommendations. Its sphere of action was confined to grievances between Maori and the Crown only. Private property was outside its range.

The Maori Council asked that nothing in the Act should be inconsistent with the 'principles of the Treaty of Waitangi'. Palmer believed these fears were genuine: 'I felt we had to act. It seemed to me quite reasonable that the State-Owned Enterprises Act ought not to have the effect of frustrating Maori claims, claims which the Government had so recently implemented legislation to allow to be heard.' He then said that when the legislation was in the Committee of the Whole [in the House of Representatives] he had two amendments drafted. One was section 9 as it appeared finally in the Act and the other was section 23, another protection clause.[3]

On his way to the tangi, Latimer read his copy of the Act and was surprised to see that the words similar to those the Council had requested had been included as section 9: 'Nothing in this Act shall permit the Crown to act in a manner that is inconsistent with the principles of the Treaty of Waitangi.' No 'principles' were defined in the Act and were potentially open to varying interpretations and challenges. He had not believed that the government would have been 'silly enough' to include them.

Looking into the coffin, Latimer re-played Joe Karetai's question in his mind. Just how was he getting on with those fellows on the hill, those politicians in the Beehive? The answer he gave was, he believes, spontaneous. He was getting on fine thanks Joe. He was going to stop them from implementing the Act till Maori interests were fully protected. How? By taking the government to court.

Latimer says that he does not want to present this response as a 'spiritual thing'. Everything at that moment just seemed to fall in place. For the previous four or five hours he had been wondering what the Council could do about the Act. Joe's question produced the decision that had been forming in the back of his mind. 'Yes, it was like a message. And I felt absolutely certain it was the right thing to do, and that we'd succeed. I was convinced – just by looking at him, no matter what anyone else said. The government had no right to sell what it did not own, though it's often done so in the past.'

Latimer: 'I left the tangi, didn't stop for a meal, and went straight back to Wellington. I tried to see Koro Wetere [then minister of Maori affairs] but couldn't get an appointment. I spoke to Denese Henare [another lawyer who advised the Council] and she thought a court injunction might just be successful.'

Others were equally worried, especially Ngati Te Ata and Tainui advocate, Nganeko Minhinnick. She spoke to Sian Elias, a lawyer with an interest in Treaty issues. Elias, in turn, discussed possible legal action with Latimer and David Baragwanath, then a senior counsel in Auckland who had not, till then, worked with the Maori Council.

What followed was a uniquely cooperative effort involving executive committee members of the Maori Council, Maori from other bodies, and members of the legal profession. Some of the country's most experienced lawyers contributed their time freely or at little cost because of the importance of the issues at stake.

Urgent action was needed: the Act was due to come into effect in May 1987. No full Council meeting was scheduled in the immediate future. Latimer discussed the options with Emily, Professor Whatarangi Winiata, Maanu Paul, and with Tai Tokerau elders. They agreed that an appeal to the courts was worth trying, as long as it would not cost a lot. The Council had no funds for going to court. Latimer: 'Quite a few of them had a distant look in their eyes. They thought it was a very long shot.' Latimer and Emily then did what they had done before when the Council had no cash to meet expenses: they added another mortgage to their dairy farm. (They had, by this time, shifted from Tinopai to a bigger farm at Taipuha, still in the Kaipara.) For them, the gamble of going to court was intensely personal. Everything was staked on this one action.

They believed they had little choice. Unless the government was stopped Maori would lose huge land, forest and fisheries resources. The Council did not believe that another provision in the Act (clause 23) could effectively protect Maori interests.

Counsel preparing the case, particularly Sian Elias and David Baragwanath, worked intensively in the short period of time available to lodge an injunction. At the very last moment the application went to the Court of Appeal by way of the High Court, with the New Zealand Maori Council as first applicant and Latimer (named individually) as the second. They asked the Court to stop any transfer of Crown property to the new corporations until systems were in place to deal with Maori claims.

The Court declared unanimously that the principles of the Treaty of Waitangi over-rode everything else in the Act. All five judges wrote their own decisions and, though differing on a number of points, came to the same conclusion about section 9 and its significance.

Sir Robin Cooke, president of the Court of Appeal, said the Maori Council's case was 'perhaps as important for the future of our country as any that has come before a New Zealand court'.[4] He went on to say that the Treaty signified a partnership between races and added:

'For more than a century and a quarter after the Treaty [was signed], integration, amalgamation of the races, the assimilation of the Maori to the Pakeha, was the goal which in the main successive governments tended to pursue ... Now the emphasis is much more on the need to preserve Maoritanga, Maori land and communal life, a distinctive identity.'[5]

Cooke, and the four other judges, stressed that the Crown had a duty to be not merely passive but to give 'active protection' to the Maori people in the use of their land and waters to the fullest extent practicable.

He said the Court's two major conclusions were that the principles of the Treaty over-rode everything else in the Act, and that Treaty principles required both the 'Pakeha and Maori Treaty partners to act towards each other reasonably and with the utmost good faith'. Cooke said that such a duty was 'no light one. It is infinitely more than a formality. If a breach of the duty is demonstrated at any time, the duty of the Court will be to insist that it will be honoured…'.[6]

By this decision the Treaty was suddenly elevated to a position of great constitutional importance: Maori could, in future, seek redress in ways which no parliament or government up till that time had foreseen or been willing to give. By its unanimous decision the Court of Appeal changed everything. The government's assets-sale policy was stopped. New policies based on the Treaty, and on good faith, had to be worked out to respond fairly to long-standing Maori claims. Many legal precedents have since been discarded and other cases have ridden to success on the back of the 1987 decision. The Treaty was vested with real power and authority for the first time since Britain annexed New Zealand 147 years earlier.

Sir Geoffrey Palmer later described the case as among the most important ever to come before a New Zealand court, leading to irreversible changes in the way in which the Treaty would now be regarded as the country's founding constitutional document. Looking back in 2002, he said the decision was a 'seismic event'. The 'tectonic plates moved in law. Afterwards Maori always had a remedy in law'.[7]

He called it a 'watershed' case: 'Till 1987 the Maori dimension in New Zealand law was understated in New Zealand jurisprudence. After the Appeal Court decision it attained a position of equality. The case broke new ground and set precedents for the future. We are still feeling our way in looking at these issues.'[8] He said that the decision gave Maori faith in the legal system for the first time. 'Up till then all their past experiences, particularly the Prendergast ruling in the nineteenth century that the Treaty was a nullity, had made them very dispirited.' He conceded that if the decision had gone against the Council 'a great deal of land' would have gone out of the ambit of Maori control.[9]

Latimer was more than delighted by the Court's judgment. He had watched governments reject every Maori Council submission on the Treaty for twenty-three years, with not even one hour's discussion. He believed that the Court of Appeal had validated efforts made by all Maori for more than 100 years to have the Treaty recognised as a constitutional contract with current relevance.

In his opinion the Council had, by this first legal action, justified its existence completely. Politicians had patronised and marginalised it since 1962. Now, after being bitterly attacked for not forcing governments to respond to Maori demands for justice, the Council had changed the political landscape permanently. Arguments in the future would centre on *how* remedies would be provided, not on *whether* grievances were justified.

For Latimer, personally, the Council's success gave meaning to the work he had done since he was co-opted thirty-one years earlier in the Kaipara by Te Uri-o-Hau. From 1956, the biggest single ethical, political and economic issue that had monopolised his time had been the contract signed between representatives of a twenty-year-old Queen Victoria and Maori chiefs during a few months in 1840.

For the Ratana Movement, in particular, the decision had special significance. By 1930 more than 26,000 people had signed a Ratana petition asking that the Treaty 'be embodied in the Statute Book of the Dominion of New Zealand, of the Dominions of the British Commonwealth and of the British Government respectively, in order all may know that the Treaty of Waitangi is operative, also to preserve the ties of brotherhood between Pakeha and Maori for all time'.[10] Fifty-seven years later the Treaty became 'operative' and Ratana's vision was realised.

Palmer was amazed at both the decision and the explicit reasons given by all five judges. 'My intention was for [section 9] to announce that the Government did not by passage of the State-Owned Enterprises Act 1986 seek to frustrate or jeopardise Maori rights.'[11] He had not envisaged that the provision would have such a dramatic effect, making the Act inoperable till Maori were fully protected.

Palmer said at the time, and later, that he did not believe section 9 would cause any legal problems. He could not see how the Maori Council could win its case. 'The Crown's legal advice was that section 9 of the State-Owned Enterprises Act could not be read in the way contended by Maori ... Conventional statutory interpretation would dictate victory for the Crown, I thought. I was wrong and so was the Solicitor-General.'[12]

Politicians from both parties were furious. Some Labour members wanted to overturn the decision by passing new laws. Palmer admitted it was a great set-back to the government's policy and said there was 'loose talk among some Cabinet members that we should legislate it away'. He was totally opposed, saying such an action would have been violently unconstitutional.

Prebble was angry and denied all responsibility for section 9. He blamed Palmer: it was all his fault. Twelve years later in his book *I've Been Writing* Prebble said that the first he had heard of the section was when it was being attacked in Parliament by the National opposition. 'I raised the matter with Geoff, who assured me that he and his advisers were agreed that the clause was "harmless window dressing".' (In 1999 Sir Geoffrey disputed this recollection.) Prebble said in his book that he had told Palmer that it was always unwise to include a clause that could give a court licence for a very broad interpretation.[13]

Prebble still says that the SOE–Waitangi policy 'has no democratic or Parliamentary mandate'. It was, he said, 'an error of judgment by one man', meaning Palmer.[14]

In an interview for this book Prebble, now leader of ACT, admitted that Maori had never got anywhere till Latimer took the government to court. 'We were stopped completely,' he said. 'Our whole programme was paralysed and we would have to abandon our policy unless we could find a solution quickly.' He knew Latimer well through Anglican Church connections – Prebble's father was a minister and Latimer was a senior layman – and decided to talk with him directly, without lawyers present. In a shared taxi from Wellington airport they discussed the possibility of setting up what later became the Crown Forest Rental Trust.[15]

Jim Bolger, leader of the opposition in 1987, condemned Labour's 'mistake'. He said section 9 was hastily drafted. Speaking at the Wellington Divisional Conference of the National Party in 1988 he called it a 'political gesture on the Labour Government's part to allay the fears of the Maori people over the possible consequences of corporatisation on their land claims under the Treaty'.[16]

Bolger said there was little discussion and none at all that placed that section in the overall scope of the Act. It was a mistake. This was admitted, he said, when the solicitor-general submitted to the Court of Appeal that it was not the intention of Parliament to fetter the operations of state-owned enterprises in this way.

Latimer expected such opinions from Bolger. He believed him to be 'deeply conservative', a farmer who at that time was not sympathetic to Maori and who had very little understanding of Maori issues. Personally, however, they got along well with each other.

Bolger's views on section 9 were strongly supported by his colleagues, particularly by Doug Graham, the lawyer MP for Remuera.

Latimer did not agree that section 9 was simply Palmer's mistake or that it was a hastily drafted political gesture. He admitted that the lawmakers did not foresee the way in which the Court of Appeal would interpret it but he points to a number of earlier decisions that were already beginning to shape a new legal and moral response to the Treaty.

The Waitangi Tribunal had been given much greater scope to look at Treaty claims, and some of its decisions were clarifying the precise nature of the principles involved. More laws referred to Treaty rights, though they did not define them. In 1986, a High Court judge recognised the customary right of a Maori to take shellfish, basing the decision on section 88 of the Fisheries Act 1983. This was similar to section 9, insisting that nothing in the Fisheries Act 1983 would affect Maori fishing rights.

An earlier Waitangi Tribunal decision in 1983, when Latimer was a member, over Maori objections to the pollution of traditional fishing grounds by the outfall of untreated sewage and industrial waste from the Synfuels plant in Taranaki, had also emphasised the importance of the Treaty. Muldoon, then prime minister, had ignored the Tribunal's recommendations but was forced to backtrack by the fierce public reaction of Maori and the general community. Latimer's case to the Court of Appeal should be seen in this context. Gradually the Maori Council's strategy from 1964 of asking that the 'spirit of the Treaty' be accepted by governments was being reflected in new laws. Almost imperceptibly the 'spirit' of the Treaty was transformed into the equally undefinable 'principles' of the Treaty, helped by Waitangi Tribunal declarations.

Going to court in 1987 had seemed hopeless. The entire history of judicial responses was against Maori. Courts had always decided in favour of the government of the day, representing the majority interest. Why should it have been any different?

Why, then, did Latimer do it? 'We had nothing to lose,' he says. 'We decided to ask the highest court in the land to test the government's honesty of purpose, its good faith. If the government meant what it said in the Act then it would do everything in its power to ensure that Maori interests were protected. The government, as the Crown, was being judged by judges on the sincerity of its own words – for the first time ever. And five judges agreed with us, that the government should not implement the Act till it had worked out a fair and open method of handling our claims.

'We couldn't have done it unless the Waitangi Tribunal's scope had not already been extended back to 1840. We have Palmer and Wetere, both of them, to thank for their efforts in pushing that through the Labour caucus. And then section 9 gave us the chance we needed, the only chance we'd ever had. Of course we were going to take it. If we hadn't, the Council might as well have dissolved itself.'

Latimer was well aware that the Council's action and the Appeal Court's radical decision would be attacked and misunderstood. Some critics conceded, for example, that while progress had been made, the Court had also solidly re-affirmed the Crown's right of sovereignty over Maori – a right they dispute was given by the Treaty.

Others, such as Professor Walker, expressed surprise at Latimer's decision to go to court at all. He described it as an 'assertive attack on the Government' from a man whose position, he believed, had always been one of 'conservative accommodation to Pakeha power'. His rationalisation for this 'remarkable' change was that Latimer had been 'reclaimed and empowered by the revolutionary practice of the people' – referring to the protests and demonstrations of previous years.[17]

Latimer had never been a conservative on Treaty issues. He understood the anger and frustration of the demonstrators, as did many Maori, but did not agree that the methods they used had favourably changed public attitudes. Instead, he had been waiting for the chance to act with reasonable hope of success, a chance which came with the State-Owned Enterprises Act 1986.

Jim Bolger, looking back at the decision from the vantage point of 2002, believes he was right at the time to question the inclusion of section 9 because its implications had not been fully considered by anyone. 'But,' he now says, 'there was an inevitability about the way the Maori Council's concerns were balanced, finally, with the needs of society as a whole.'[18]

Bolger also believes that Latimer had picked the perfect time to act. 'The Council was the Maori interface with government. Sir Graham emerged as a national leader just when the time was right for change. He was able to take full advantage of that, and was extremely successful.' He says that national perspectives, at all levels, had been shifting for some years as the country developed its own character, and that included full recognition of the identity of its indigenous people. The National Party had gone on, in the late 1980s, to acknowledge the Treaty as the founding document of New Zealand. 'That would have been impossible even a few years earlier. It would not have been acceptable.'[19]

For Latimer, the following years were to be his most turbulent time as Council president. Great gains were made, but the backlash against the Treaty strained race relations and revealed a deepseated prejudice among a minority of the non-Maori population. The Treaty itself increased in importance and became embedded as part of New Zealand's constitution. Fifteen years after the Court of Appeal decision, about twenty-six statutes now contain specific references to the Treaty, similar to section 9.

Latimer became a full-time negotiator with government on behalf of Maori. He had to cease work on his farm, leaving it to Emily and hired hands. He became immersed in what seemed to be endless court cases, moving steadily toward winning greater control of Maori resources and developing the undefined principles of the Treaty.

But, just as he was beginning this new and much tougher political role, he and Emily made a side trip to London.

CHAPTER SEVEN

Tupuna Maori – Item 181
1988

Bonhams Auctioneers
Auction Item: Number 181
Date: 20 May 1988
Venue: Montpelier Galleries, Montpelier Street, London
The Property of Mrs Weller-Poley: A rare and important early nineteenth century Mokomokai Preserved Human Head.
181
    This rare Mokomokai Head dates from about 1820. It is in remarkable condition with original hair, eyebrows and eyelashes. The skin is in a very good state of preservation and bears authentic pre-mortem tattooing (Moko). The unfinished aspect of the Moko is particularly interesting, signifying that the head is probably that of a young warrior.
    Other noteworthy features of this head include early 19th century alterations, such as: the opening of the eyelids, the insertion of glass eyes and the reshaping of the lips.
    The head is mounted in a blue velvet collar stand and is contained within it's [sic] original glass dome. Probably taken in battle the warrior head would have been ritually preserved by a complex process which involved the removal of the brain and other fleshly organs, steaming and drying (Paki Paki Mahunga).
    The early date of the head, circa 1820, must establish the warrior as an important member of his tribe, for, at this date, the wearing of Moko was still restricted to the more prominent members of Maori Society.

EARLY IN 1988 LATIMER WAS ABSORBED IN URGENT NEGOTIATIONS WITH Labour ministers and their officials about the ways in which forests, fisheries and land, including wahi tapu, were to be protected following the Court of Appeal decision on state-owned enterprises.

At the same time, an Englishwoman, Nancy Weller-Poley, found her grandchild in the attic of her Suffolk country house combing the hair on the preserved head of a long-dead warrior from New Zealand. The head had been in the family since it was brought to England in the nineteenth century.

Weller-Poley thought the sight was 'gruesome'. She did not want the child to play with the head like a toy and she did not want it in the house: 'It was making its presence felt.' So she decided to auction it.[1]

On 4 May 1988 Latimer heard that in sixteen days Bonhams Auctioneers was to auction the tattooed head of a Maori warrior from New Zealand. He was angered by the firm's arrogance, by its belief that part of a human body was just a commodity, an item, number 181, in a catalogue. As a Maori, he was also offended because of the spiritual and cultural significance Maori give to a person's head.

He hoped the auction would be stopped but did not see what he could do. He had no time for personal involvement and was unaware of what action could be taken during the very short period before bidding began.

In England, a small voluntary group called Survival International had a very clear idea of what could be done. Their members had seen Bonhams advertisement and a feature article in London's *Sunday Times*. They wanted New Zealand's Department of Maori Affairs and the National Museum to stop the auction through the courts, and offered help.

Survival International supported the 'rights of threatened tribal peoples to survival, to self-determination and the use and ownership of their traditional lands'. Because it had no resources, other than information and intelligence, Survival International used publicity to alert others to dangers to indigenous groups so that action could be taken. Its president, Robin Hanbury-Tenison visited New Zealand later in 1988, and in the following year published a book, *Fragile Eden*, on his view of the dangers facing the planet.

The Board of the National Museum (Latimer was a member) could do nothing. Its policy was to negotiate quietly, without publicity, for the return of artifacts and human remains from overseas collections, public and private. Persuasion, through appeals to goodwill and human decency, was its preferred method. It never offered money: that would increase the value of the artifacts as commercial products. Nor did it have the resources needed to take legal action. This policy resulted in a slow, mostly invisible, recovery process involving museums, friendly diplomats, long-term loans, and promises that anything recovered would be available for study, or future research, if needed. Feelers, proposals, were always made delicately so museums did not feel exposed to greater demands for the return of stolen or doubtfully acquired treasures from other countries, other peoples.

Item 181 had already emerged explosively onto the public stage. Groups in Australia, Canada, Papua New Guinea and South America heard about the auction and expressed their anger, not just because of that one head, but at the principle of selling what they saw as the essence of human beings, of humanity, for profit. Nancy Weller-Poley's claim to own the head, because she owned a Maori treasure box (also up for auction), was held in contempt and flatly rejected.

The Department of Maori Affairs was also not strongly placed to act against Bonhams. Wetere and the Department were still embarrassed by the fallout from accusations over the Maori Loans Affair. Staff were, however, willing to give Latimer and the Maori Council advice on possible court action in New Zealand and Britain.

Because no Council meeting was scheduled, and no money was available to bring members together, Latimer, Professor Whatarangi Winiata and John Bennett, chairman of the Maori Education Foundation, looked at their options. Latimer: 'We were in a hard place. The Council didn't have any money to buy the head. Anyway, we were completely against the idea of buying back something that was ours, something human. Our view was that the auction was a degrading and deeply offensive desecration.'

They refused even to consider bidding for the head: that would have made them accomplices in an 'abhorrent' trade.

They could ask Weller-Poley to return the head in exchange for a gift that did not have the same tapu significance, though this seemed hopeless because she regarded the auction as a simple business transaction. Bonhams encouraged her to make a stand on principle, the right of ownership, the sanctity of private property, the right to make money by selling people parts.

Latimer: 'We finally decided to break new ground and get a legal injunction against the sale in a British court. We had more faith in the judicial system after our experience with the Court of Appeal the year before. We knew we had the moral high ground.'

The Department of Maori Affairs helped to prepare a request to the New Zealand High Court to make the president of the Maori Council the administrator of the estate of an un-named warrior, whose head was being held by Bonhams Auctioneers. The warrior was described as Tupuna Maori (Maori Ancestor), the equivalent of the American terms, John or Jane Doe, for an unknown person.

Latimer asked, in effect, to be made the legal guardian of the warrior's interests. He was immediately helped by lawyers, public servants, and by Dr Joan Metge, former associate professor of anthropology at Victoria University of Wellington, and Dr Hirini Mead, former head of Maori studies at Victoria University of Wellington.

Latimer was making history. No such request had ever gone to court in New Zealand. He had to prove that there was such a person as Tupuna Maori, that he had no known living relatives, that he had left no will, that he had no known debts or assets and that his tattoo indicated that he was formerly a native of this country. These legal requirements were matters of form and the proof was self-evident. The warrior's head was in a glass dome, on a blue velvet base, in London. His age was about 160. Nobody knew which part of New Zealand he had come from. And, Tupuna Maori certainly did not have any surviving documentation in the form of a will, or any obvious close relatives.

Latimer also had to show that he was a suitable person to be given letters of administration. He claimed that his position as president of the Maori Council gave him that right; and that the Council had the statutory obligation to protect and promote the interests of all Maori, and of Maori cultural traditions, which included the right to a proper burial.

He also said that he was a Ngapuhi rangatira and that the warrior could, possibly, have come from te Tai Tokerau, the north.

Dr Metge filed an affidavit with the High Court supporting Latimer's contention that, unless proper respect is accorded the dead then 'discontinuity is introduced, the social fabric is torn'. She said that a proverb quoted by Latimer stressed 'that the mokomokai is a person and must be accorded all the loving care and rituals that every deceased person is entitled to'.[2] Without burial the warrior's soul wandered endlessly. Dr Mead also gave strong support.

While the case was being prepared, opposition to the auction grew rapidly. The Maori Council and Survival International received strong support. Hanbury-Tenison wrote to Bonhams one week before the auction pointing out that common law 'imposes upon any person having a human body in their possession a duty to dispose of the body by burial, cremation or other lawful means'.[3] He said that law related to body parts and asked Bonhams to comply. Five days later Bonhams said no.

Bonhams staff were astonished at the public reaction. Why all this fuss? They were doing just what they had always done, legally and openly. They were selling an old head, in good condition, to anyone with enough money to buy it. It was an item of trade, a commodity, not a person.

Representatives of the auction house said if they had known the warrior's tribe that would have been a different matter. The head, over a long period of time, had, they said, acquired artifact status. They had treated it with respect, had cleaned it carefully and then 'tastefully displayed' it on a wooden platter under a glass dome. What more could they have done?

They added that no formal request to stop the auction had come from the New Zealand government and that they believed, on legal advice, that they had every right to sell the head on behalf of Weller-Poley. 'A sale by public auction is the fairest way of disposing of such an item.'

Bonhams also warned that there was a danger, if such sales were outlawed or made impossible due to public pressure, that other owners would sell 'under the counter'. 'This would play straight into the hands of those motivated by morbid interest and would deny museums of national collections any chance of acquisition.'[4]

Latimer's legal action, and the international uproar, challenged their beliefs and assumptions, which he described as obscene.

Yes, he said, the warrior did have relatives, about 400,000 of them, the Maori of New Zealand. Yes, he said, Tupuna Maori did have many people who cared enough to stop the indignities being heaped upon him, to want to return him to the earth with customary rituals. No, he was not an item, a number in a catalogue; he was still part of the spiritual legacy of a human being.

Maui Pomare, a member of the National Museum Board, was not happy with Latimer's intention to bury the head. Pomare had successfully recovered human remains and artifacts for many years by subterranean methods, and by promising that everything would be permanently available for research.

Newspaper articles had appeared in New Zealand from early May. The *Truth* weekly had enthusiastically displayed a large photo of the head, adding to the indignities. In England a Bonham's staff member was photographed posed beside the head in its glass dome.

Pomare said publicity about the auction, and the anger it generated, was jeopardising delicate negotiations. He was afraid a market was being created for Maori artifacts, inflating their cash value and driving them onto the black market. He said little publicly at the time, but later commented that he thought Latimer was wrong to 'go it alone'. He liked and respected him as a person and as Council president, but said that he should have involved the National Museum and considered its tapu vault as the head's final resting place.

Latimer says he had briefly considered that possibility. He was familiar with the vault, a temperature-controlled concrete room under the National Museum on its commanding site just above the Basin Reserve in Wellington. Latimer: 'I didn't want to place him there. It was very solemn but cold and impersonal. I wanted to put him in the earth, near other Maori, in a natural setting. Dust to dust. I felt that he would be more comfortable with us.'

On the morning of 19 May 1988, one day before the auction, Justice Greig heard in Wellington the application for administration rights. In a formal deposition Latimer said it was for one limited purpose only, 'of according the deceased a proper burial according to Maori law and custom, and to prevent as far as possible further indignity being visited upon him ...'.[5]

Justice Greig had read through the argument the night before and granted the application immediately. He said there could be 'little if any dissent from the proposition that the sale and purchase of human remains for gain and for the purposes of curiosity is abhorrent to New Zealanders and, I hope, to any civilized person. There is a macabre circumstance to the proposed transaction which has some of the attributes of necrophily'.[6]

He added that Latimer's application was 'plainly quite extraordinary and, I think, totally unprecedented. Certainly no case has been referred to me which has any similarity at all'.[7]

A few hours later all formalities had been completed and Latimer was the legal guardian of Tupuna Maori. The day before, he had forewarned the High Court of Justice (Chancery Division), London, that his application was being heard and, if successful, he would immediately ask the British High Court to stop the auction. He had also written to the British government asking it to stop the sale: 'The remains of our dead, and of this man in particular, are our greatest treasures.'

On receiving notification of the decision by the New Zealand Court the British High Court stopped the auction of the head, allowing it to be retained by Nancy Weller-Poley but not to be publicly displayed.

The other items she had on sale were bought for over three times the expected price because of all the publicity. Bonhams said later it had received one clandestine offer of 20,000 pounds (NZ$60,000) for the head from an anonymous overseas bidder.

Latimer took no further court action. Bonhams and Weller-Poley wanted no more abuse. Negotiations over the next six weeks resulted in an exchange of prisoners: the head would be returned and a non-tapu gift, a greenstone mere, would be presented in a formal ceremony in the New Zealand High Commission in London.

For Maori, and other indigenous people, this auction was a test case, the culmination of years of protest. Latimer: 'Our taonga [treasures] have been desecrated ever since 1840 in spite of the protection we were formally offered in the Treaty and all the promises made to us.' He mentioned one of the very earliest incidents in the north, when a Ngapuhi hapu had destroyed a store in which skulls, stolen from a wahi tapu, had been kept and were left lying on the floor. Governor Hobson made no effort to find those responsible for the desecration but punished the hapu for the damage done to the store (nobody was hurt) by confiscating about 6,000 acres.

The defeat of the Bonhams sale was not confined to this one auction. As a direct result of the adverse reaction from different countries it decided to stop all dealing in human remains. So also did Christies, the other major auction house in Britain, and all other companies that till then had auctioned bits of people.

Christies had followed the case of Tupuna Maori with intense interest. At the time it was planning to auction thirty-five shrunken heads, mostly from South America. It asked Survival International to state precisely what it was objecting to: heads only, mummies, bones? Hanbury-Tenison responded by saying everything human. Do the honourable thing. Stop selling pieces of people. Set an example. And Christies did.

Bernard Levin, a world-famous English writer and columnist, helped to change the attitudes of auction houses by linking their actions with those of Nazis who used the skins of Holocaust victims for lampshades. The issue, he said, was ethical, not legal. It was all about imagination, about understanding the essence of humanity.

His article was headlined 'Foul deeds of desecration' and was accompanied by a drawing of a preserved head (not Tupuna Maori) on a wooden stand. Instead of moko the head was tattooed with pound sterling signs.

Levin said to the sellers, auctioneers and buyers of human remains: 'If a human head is to you a toy, an ornament or another acquisition for your *cabinet de voyeur* it does not mean that you are wicked but it does mean that there is something missing in your makeup'. Imagination, he said, was the missing ingredient, the ability to imagine the Maori warrior as formerly a person who laughed, cried, got wet in the rain, and was just like us. Anyone without that ability was less than human and would not be able to tell the difference between a lampshade made from human skin and any other piece of furniture.

He rejected Bonhams's claim that the age of the head had any relevance. Profaning 'the dead has no statute of limitations ...'. He praised the Maori Council for its court action and its clear affirmation of the essence of humanity regardless of age.[8]

Latimer had one more duty to perform. Because he had been appointed by the High Court to be the guardian of Tupuna Maori he had to go to London for the ceremony. He said later that he was not the right person. 'There were many elders who were far more appropriate than I was. I've always considered myself an apprentice. The older people have a deep knowledge of our traditional culture. They would have been better companions for the warrior.'

He had no choice. He was the nominated guardian, and whoever went would have to pay their own way. No travel grant was offered by the New Zealand government and the Maori Council had no money for the trip. Unlike the much-publicised journey by Tau Henare, when he was minister of Maori affairs in the coalition government of 1997–1999, no funds were available for the return of taonga.

Latimer says he prayed for guidance. He was then living on his farm in Taipuha, at Kaipara Harbour. 'I went into the bush, walked in the salt water, tried to get a proper feeling for what I was doing. I spent a lot of time talking with my father [he had died twenty-three years earlier]. This was a tapu experience. I had to do it right. I can't explain what I was feeling.'

He and Emily flew to London at their own expense. By the time they arrived they were exhausted, there had been no time for any stopover, but went straight into meetings. They met Nancy Weller-Poley the day before the ceremony to explain what was going to happen and to get to know her, to introduce some lightness and humanity into what had been a tense and angry two months. She had been represented as the villain, resistant initially to any compromise, interested only in money rather than a reciprocal gift.

Nobody knew what to expect. Weller-Poley was nervous, uncertain how to relate to a Maori rangatira who had taken her to court and publicly labelled her behaviour as abhorrent. All three were surprised at what happened. Emily: 'I liked her. She was tall, very well dressed, very impressive, but nervous. She wanted, finally, to do the right thing and didn't know how we would feel about her.'

Weller-Poley had visited New Zealand and had been to the Riccarton horse races. She and the Latimers found they shared what Latimer described as a common 'vice': horse-racing. By the end of the meeting they all relaxed.

Tupuna Maori was returned to Maori at the London High Commission. The head had been placed in a specially made, sealed casket, covered with a feather cloak. Archdeacon the Very Reverend Kingi Ihaka, who was in London for a church conference, conducted the ceremony, reciting pre-Christian incantations as a mark of respect for the warrior's spiritual traditions. Emily led the karanga, joined by a number of Maori women then living in London.

Ihaka told Weller-Poley that she was giving the head back to the whole nation, not just a single group. 'This is a fantastic gesture on your part and will give tremendous mana to people belonging to various indigenous races.' She was given a valuable greenstone mere, carved especially for the occasion, and was happy that her world was returning to normal. She was moved by the rituals and the intensity of emotion felt by those taking part.[9]

Ihaka knew the Latimers well. They were part of the Anglican community and Latimer had been born only a few miles away from Ihaka's home at Te Kao on the Aupouri Peninsula.

Ihaka was not entirely comfortable with the ceremony. It was not Christian, and there were no precedents for what they were doing. He saw that Latimer was visibly affected by the experience, and worried that he was relating too closely to the warrior, developing an affinity with a man who had died so long before.

Latimer confirms this sense of kinship. 'I can't prove that he came from Tai Tokerau, that he was Ngapuhi, but I felt for him. I had an inner feeling that I wasn't treating the head as a stranger. There was a spiritual acknowledgement.'

Some years later, in the 1990s, the name Weller-Poley appeared in some old records of transactions in the north in the nineteenth century, so it is possible that it was Nancy's grandfather-in-law, the one supposed to have taken the head to England. That makes it possible that the sale could have taken place in Ngapuhi territory. As DNA testing continues, in the future, the possibility of determining Tupuna Maori's origin is increased. It is equally possible, however, that nobody would wish to open the casket, another intrusion – and Latimer was given guardianship rights solely for burial purposes.

The head had been brought back to New Zealand by the captain of an Air New Zealand flight. The Latimers had hoped to bring the casket back themselves but instead they greeted him in Auckland, where he was blessed.

The Latimers then went north to Whatuwhiwhi on the Karikari Peninsula and buried Tupuna Maori immediately in a wahi tapu, Te Potakapu, where people from all over the Far North, Ngati Kahu, Te Aupouri and Rarawa are interred. He rests halfway up a hill overlooking the broad sweep of Doubtless Bay. Latimer says that he had the feeling that the warrior had come so far, and waited so long, that he needed to be placed in the earth as soon as possible.

The casket was not opened and the head was not displayed from the time it was taken from Bonhams. Nobody at the local ceremony, attended by the largest number of kaumatua and kuia seen for many years, knew precisely what to do. Tupuna Maori was not newly deceased and they had no protocol for burying the remains of a person who died so long ago. They improvised, modifying the usual tangihanga rituals, to suit the occasion, hoping that the respect shown would meet the spiritual needs.

The Latimers remember the trip with pride and satisfaction. They both felt they were part of something that was extraordinary and spiritually fulfilling, apart from the influence it had on auction house policy toward human remains. Latimer says there is still one more thing to do: Tupuna Maori has yet to have a headstone placed over his grave.

In the years since Tupuna Maori's return, the speed with which mokomokai have been repatriated has increased. Museum directors and those holding private collections have been more prepared to accept the rights of iwi descendants over body parts. Public tolerance for displaying the dead has disappeared.

Maui Pomare, who did more than any other individual to find and bring mokomokai home, died in 1995. His cousin, Maui Dalvanius Prime, has made a personal commitment to continue his work, but with more willingness to use publicity.

The former minister of Maori affairs, Tau Henare, made a widely publicised journey to Europe in 1998 to take charge of mokomokai already about to return to New Zealand. His behaviour, and the expense of his trip (about $100,000), contrasted sharply with that of the Latimers ten years before, mostly at their own cost (they also lost $2,000 by theft from a restaurant). Henare's trip resulted in cartoons, editorials, letters and interviews that concentrated attention on him rather than on the bigger issue of government support for the repatriation of taonga.

Latimer believes that governments could do much more to preserve historic sites, including wahi tapu, and help iwi to regain part of their heritage held hostage overseas.

After the burial ceremony and his seven-day return journey to London, Latimer had a short rest on his farm in the Kaipara, and then flew to Wellington to continue the interrupted negotiations over state-owned land, forests and fisheries, and to face the anger of some members of the public who resented Maori and their new Treaty rights.

CHAPTER EIGHT

First Fruits and Backlash
1987–2001

> How much longer is this Maori nonsense to be tolerated? It is time Maoridom faced facts. The early Maori were immigrants – they drove the earlier inhabitants [possibly, Moriori?] off the land and settled where they pleased. They have never owned any land in this country and are not entitled to the ridiculous amounts of money they are demanding. If some compensation is approved, it should be the value of the land in the 1800s, not today's inflated value. I wonder how many of today's Maori would enjoy the living conditions of their ancestors?
> – Letter to the *New Zealand Herald*, 14 March 2000

> The trouble is that few of them [Waitangi Tribunal claimants] are actually ready. They can say it's the Crown's fault and they are frustrated and don't have enough money. But the fact is that, with a lot of these claims, there's no research available. Some of them haven't got much of an idea, frankly, of what the claim's about, I'm sorry to say. And then, of course, you've got endless problems of who is representing whom and overlapping claims … And that's not our fault. We're sitting here ready to go.
> – Doug Graham, Treaty negotiations minister
> (*Dominion*, 5 January 1996)

FOR LATIMER, THE FIRST FEW YEARS FOLLOWING THE 1987 COURT OF Appeal decision were ridiculously busy. The general principles laid down by the Court of Appeal were, most often, upheld, and Maori won a number of fundamentally important cases against the Crown.

Nationally, he was involved in almost all the test cases that defined the new Treaty relationship between Maori and Crown. In the

Tai Tokerau he and the Tai Tokerau Maori Trust Board bought the ailing Waitangi Hotel and tried to turn it into an economic and iwi base. Locally, in the Kaipara, he helped Te Uri-o-Hau to begin its reparations case for the Waitangi Tribunal.

Latimer also continued to help other organisations and groups working with and for Maori economic, educational and social development: Maori International, fisheries companies, the Northland Polytechnic, Maori wardens, the National Museum of New Zealand, the Anglican Synod, the Alcohol Advisory Council, to name a few.

The gains made after 1987, and the continuing support that courts have given Maori, resulted in a massive shift in attitude toward the Treaty and its constitutional importance. These gains give Maori and Pakeha groups and institutions a chance to evolve a system, over time, of positive self-determination for Maori – the sort of thing Latimer's grandfather hoped would emerge from the Maori Councils Act of 1900.

Te reo was made an official language in 1986, but court decisions subsequently gave it more support. Maori broadcasting and television rights have been recognised, though with great reluctance. The Treaty of Waitangi (State Enterprises) Act 1988 was passed and systems designed for settling Treaty claims through the Waitangi Tribunal and by direct negotiation with the Crown.

The Crown Forest Rental Trust was set up in 1989, with Latimer as chairman, giving claimants resources to research and present their cases to the Waitangi Tribunal. Decisions and reports from the Waitangi Tribunal revealed, often starkly and in abundant detail, the injustices of the past, and called for speedy resolution.

A fisheries settlement, the Sealord deal, was worked out in 1992, though its full implementation has been bogged down in legal argument among Maori groups. Latimer, one of the four Maori negotiators, argued that it was the first real chance to provide Maori with an economic base. One constant critic, Frank Haden, predicted in a *Sunday Star-Times* column in 1994 that Sealord would fail within two years. Its resources are, in 2002, estimated at about $1 billion.[1]

While not all the new initiatives for Maori were always precise, practical or completely efficient they were a quantum leap compared with what had gone before.

But with each advance came a backlash. As the Council promoted Maori social and economic interests in compliance with the first aim it was given in the Maori Welfare Act 1962, it met with ever greater difficulty in working for its second aim, promoting harmony with Pakeha.

Maori were criticised in the news media for being greedy, trying to get more than their fair share, living in the past, being a lot of whining bludgers, and for making outrageous claims that could not have been foreseen by those who drew up the Treaty in 1840.

Winston Peters said in 1988, that as a 'constitutional device', the Treaty 'may well have served its time'.[2] He spoke of it as a talisman of the past, said 'our aim must be to the present and the future' and called for a review, long overdue, of the Treaty's current relevance to New Zealand.[3] In the following year he claimed that Maori gangs were involved in the land-rights struggle: 'Clearly they have been involved for some time as para shock troops to militant demands by certain radicals.'[4] Some senior politicians in both major parties welcomed such attacks. They wanted to settle all Treaty claims quickly and cheaply and they used the retaliation against Maori and the Treaty to tell the Council and other groups that middle New Zealand was unsympathetic and did not want the government to respond generously.

News media gave wide and constant publicity to the most extreme claims, reported them superficially and often wrongly, and then printed angry responses from members of the public who said they were fed up with all this nonsense. Newspapers, television and talkback radio fed this frenzy because trouble, real or manufactured, is their business – more scandal, more readers, viewers, listeners, and more advertising, more profit.

Newspaper editorials were almost uniformly against the decision of the Court of Appeal and the importance it gave to the Treaty. Twelve years later the *Dominion* (2 June 1999) was still complaining about the 'genie well and truly freed from its bottle'. The editorial blamed Palmer's 'folly' and said that a 'sloppy law change' had enabled an 'activist Court of Appeal to make an unprecedented interpretation of the Treaty so that power shifted in this area from Parliament to the courts'.

Palmer says that within two years of the Court of Appeal decision a climate of political hostility had developed toward Maori. The Labour government had, he said, secured a reputation by 1989 of doing things for Maori but not for anyone else. At least one of his colleagues, Ralph Maxwell, under-secretary for agriculture and fisheries, called publicly for the Treaty to be scrapped. Others expressed their reservations in Cabinet but not elsewhere.

Latimer and his fellow councillors were disturbed by the ferocity of the responses and the ignorance shown about the legal decisions, the reasons for them, and about the Treaty.

In 1988, Latimer asked Wetere for funds to help the Maori Council mount a public education campaign on the Treaty. He wanted to try to provide more accurate and accessible information about what was happening, to promote an informed public debate, and to improve race relations – all requirements placed on the Maori Council by its foundation Act (the Maori Welfare Act) in 1962.

The answer was a flat no. A senior Maori legal officer in the Department of Maori Affairs wrote a curt reply for the minister: the Department had no budget allocation for such activity. No suggestion was made that perhaps next year some allocation could be made. If the Council wanted to do something it was on its own.

In 1989 Chris Laidlaw, then race relations conciliator, was equally concerned. In his 1999 memoirs, *Rights of Passage*, he said that just before Christmas that year he went to see Palmer, then prime minister, and asked for a new Treaty education programme to be set up under the wing of the Race Relations Office. Palmer 'was enthusiastic. He knew better than most people that the Maori–Pakeha divide was the greatest single challenge faced by New Zealand and promised to pursue this in the new year'. Laidlaw proposed a nominal budget of about $1 million.[5]

Next year the economy was in trouble, little money was available and Labour was defeated. Undaunted, Laidlaw put the same idea to Doug Graham, the new minister of justice and of Treaty negotiations.

He was again unsuccessful. 'Terrific idea old chap but don't ask for more money.' From that time onward there was virtually no support, said Laidlaw, for Treaty education as a major priority.[6] Latimer agrees. He found that some senior officials in Te Puni Kokiri, the new Ministry of Maori Development, which had replaced the Department of Maori Affairs, were equally unenthusiastic. As civil servants they were obliged to support their minister, initially Peters, then Doug Kidd, John Luxton and Tau Henare. Some officials reflected the hostility expressed by their political masters to the Council – which had forced elected governments, through the courts, to negotiate with Maori on Treaty issues; while other officials still saw the Council as a competitor.

National's policy was even less favourable to Maori than Labour's. Claims were to be resolved as fast as possible, and cheaply. A time limit of ten years (1990–2000) was imposed. Prebble's ACT Party appealed even more directly to anti-Maori sentiment and attacked the Treaty and the claims process at every opportunity.

Two key figures emerged: Jim Bolger, the new prime minister, and Doug Graham. Latimer had maintained his good personal relationship with Bolger. They were both farmers. Neither was an academic. Practical and pragmatic, they wanted solutions. They spoke the same language, were long-time members of the same political party. Money was the main issue dividing them.

Latimer: 'I'd always thought Jim Bolger was a typical redneck. He had a terrible time with Peters, first when he was minister of Maori affairs and afterwards, when Peters was sacked [in 1991]. Mostly, he just wanted to get Treaty issues off the political agenda. He was always easy to talk with.'

Bolger was, however, quick to exploit public frustration with what seemed like never-ending demands from Maori. Exasperated and angry, he said in 1993 that he could not understand why Maori were not more grateful for what his government was doing for them in settling grievances.

Shortly after the Waitangi Day ceremonies Bolger said Maori should be 'thankful' for the progress being made in settling claims and should remember to say so. 'I believe that some of the Maori commentators are not doing their cause the justice it deserves when they forget that very simple word of thanks. I think it is important that New Zealand hears that word from time to time when legitimate claims are being genuinely addressed.'[7]

Paul East, then attorney-general, supported Bolger, saying 'public patience' was running out with Maori.[8] Other National MPs had already said the Treaty and the Waitangi Tribunal should be scrapped. Clem Simich, replacing Sir Robert Muldoon as Tamaki's MP in 1992, said in his maiden speech that the Treaty was a document from the 'dim past' and Maori should not use it as a 'walking stick'. He said that the 'fixation' on the Treaty and related issues was 'unfair, unjust and divisive'.[9]

Sir Douglas Graham, who looked back on this period in his 1997 book, *Trick or Treaty*, made only a very general reference to the state-owned enterprise case and did not mention his own opposition to the extension of the Treaty's authority back to 1840, or to section 9. He did, however, make a blunt statement about the power of the Pakeha majority over the Maori minority.[10]

In objecting to the Waitangi Tribunal having the right to order a government to take certain actions when it found in favour of Maori claims he said: 'Now, while on the face of it there appears something unfair in the government once again holding most of the cards and having the ability to decide the value of any compensation, the fact is that these matters are political issues of considerable importance.' He went on to say that only 'the government can decide how much can be afforded by the country. The courts cannot do this. Nor can Maori. Nor could an outside independent arbitrator'.[11]

Sir Douglas was reaffirming the traditional system, in which governments, reflecting the majority views of one racial or ethnic group, should perpetually have the power to impose their views on minorities. In short: Majority Rules OK. Those governments had, Sir Douglas admitted, been guilty of gross injustices in the past but, he maintained, there was no alternative in a democracy. Settlements were imposed and said to be final and binding but the Maori claimants had never agreed. He said nobody should be surprised when Maori emerged out of the past to bite everyone again.

Latimer says that the political dominance of the Pakeha majority over the Maori minority had led to deliberate oppression, deprivation of property, poverty, sickness and second-class citizen status. 'Yes, it was unfair. It still is. The government still holds most of the cards but not all. Since the Court of Appeal decision in 1987 the Treaty has been brought into the game, and all governments have been told they must act in good faith. To us, that means honestly and fairly.'

Doug Graham shared many of Bolger's opinions. As the government's chief negotiator with Maori he had, however, to wear a number of incompatible faces at the same time. He had to reassure claimants he was acting in good faith as Crown representative. Simultaneously, he told his National colleagues he was doing everything possible to ensure that very little money would be spent. To the public he admitted terrible wrongs had been done and wept sincerely, promising that lasting solutions would be found. He then blamed Maori for delaying what he said were reasonable settlements.

Doug Graham was forced to keep reinventing himself. In 1985 he had strongly opposed Labour's decision to allow the Waitangi Tribunal to consider claims going back to 1840. He said then that the answer to current problems was not to go back to 1840 and try to decide whether prejudice was involved, because that would cause greater division than ever. He feared the economic and social consequences of the move. Eight years later he seemed to have changed his mind. He then praised the decision to extend the Waitangi Tribunal's scope as 'bold'. When asked how he had felt about it in 1985 he said he 'couldn't remember', waving a hand in the air.[12]

Latimer says that the minister received a lot of credit for getting the Treaty process underway but doubts whether it was deserved. 'The only reason he was doing anything at all was because of court decisions. Many cabinet members were against giving anything to Maori under the Treaty. The Treasury wasn't interested in justice – just the smallest payout possible to make the Treaty go away. Officials who worked for Doug Graham's office delayed progress as much as they could.'

Sir Douglas admitted in his book, *Trick or Treaty*, that his government started to negotiate with Tainui before it had even developed its own policy: 'In retrospect it might have been better to have waited until the Government was really ready before starting the talks because it must have been very frustrating to Waikato to find I was unable to make any commitments for so long.'[13]

So it was with Ngai Tahu. Negotiations were broken off with the South Island iwi, which waited for years for the government to decide how little it would pay in reparations. Neither Tainui nor Ngai Tahu have happy memories of those times. In the end both iwi accepted what seemed to be the only settlement possible, not what they felt was justified. The negotiation process took place on an unequal playing field. The government, as the Crown, controlled the rules and determined the outcome. No referees.

Latimer knew the Treasury was juggling figures, trying to limit the size of the fund needed to meet all claims. The problem was not to decide how much, but how little. Maori could never be fully compensated for their losses. Doug Graham said in public statements that this was a complicated issue because it depended on what the country could afford.

The Treasury produced a range of figures but insisted that the decision was, finally, political, not financial. Latimer was aware that some politicians wanted to set aside as little as $250 million, even though the Sealord fisheries deal of 1992 alone would take most of that. Other figures he heard were $500 million and then $1 billion spread over ten years. This latter figure was, in fact, the sum Doug Graham suggested as early as August 1992.

This was, also, the figure National finally presented to Maori as a take-it-or-leave-it ultimatum late in 1994. No details were given on how it had been arrived at. Doug Graham later described it as a 'best guestimate' and as 'a stab in the dark'. But, he said, it had to be done. 'We could not set off down the path without any idea at all where it would lead and what it would cost.'[14]

Maori were outraged. All their claims were squeezed into one financial box of a predetermined size, and reparations were then to be worked out on a sliding scale by government officials. Rejection of this 'fiscal envelope' was total. Latimer was amazed at Doug Graham's determination to attend all the angry hui held round the country to tell him what he already knew from a representative

Waitangi Tribunal Chairman Eddie Durie, Bruce Robinson (Department of Maori Affairs), Sir Graham Latimer and Sir Henare Ngata (member of the New Zealand Maori Council throughout the early 1980s)

Sir Graham and Lady Emily Latimer, early 1980s

Sir Graham Latimer at Waitangi Day service, 1981
Northern Advocate, February 7 1981

Mr John Bennett and Sir Graham Latimer, right, Waitangi Day, 1981
Northern Advocate, February 7 1981

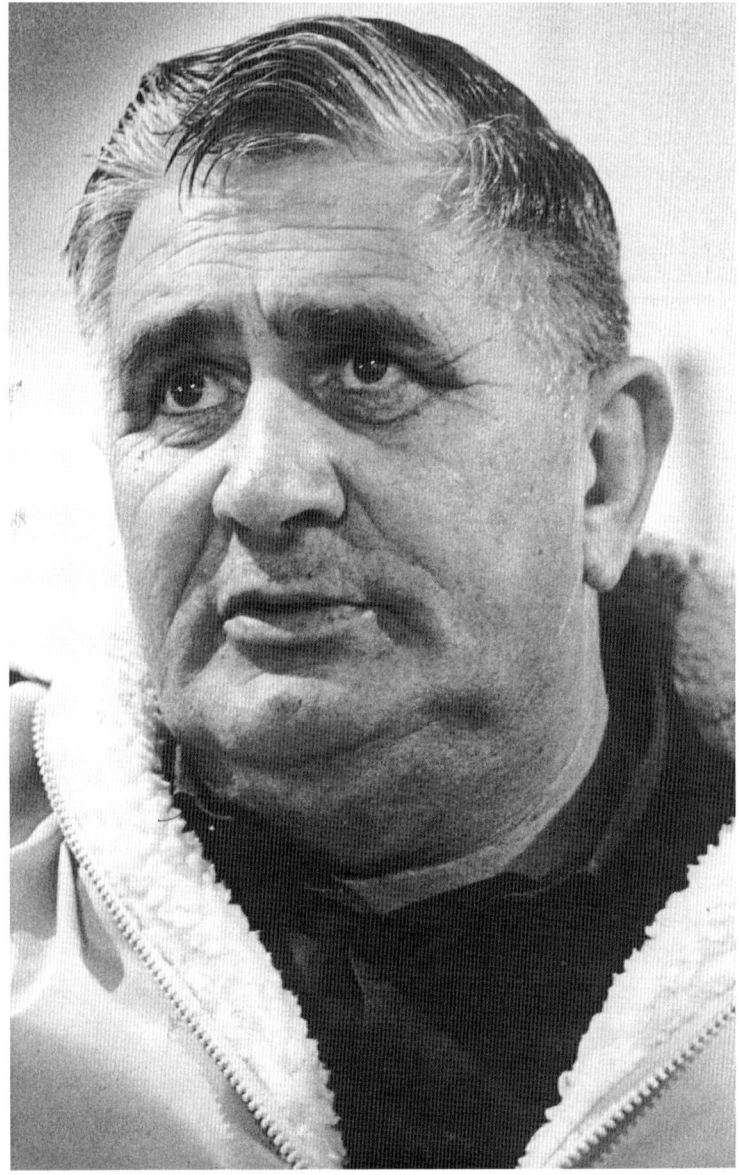

Sir Graham Latimer, 1988
Northern Advocate, October 4 1988

Still work to be done: Sir Graham Latimer, 1996
Northern Advocate, June 12 1996

Sir Graham Latimer at Houhora with Mount Camel in the background, 2000

Sir Graham and Lady Emily Latimer outside their home at Pamapuria, 2000

Sir Graham surveying his farm at Pamapuria, 2000

The generations meet: Sir Graham Latimer and Sir Edmund Hillary with some of their grandchildren

meeting of Maori leaders at least one year earlier. The cap was just not acceptable. Latimer: 'It was a pointless exercise but Doug has a romantic, emotional streak.'

Further negotiations were adversarial, angry and confrontational. The government had again reverted to its role as judge and jury in an attempt to limit the Court of Appeal 1987 ruling that it must act in good faith to protect Maori interests.

Laidlaw describes this strategy as a gigantic mistake, as bad a blunder as could be made: '... the product of the myopic, bean-counting mentality of a Treasury which never understood Maoridom and still doesn't.'[15] He did not understand how Doug Graham could have been convinced of its merits. 'The only realistic explanation is that he was simply outpointed by his considerably less visionary cabinet colleagues.'[16]

Latimer sees it differently. The minister's behaviour was quite consistent, he believes. Doug Graham had always agreed with his colleagues that a cap had to be imposed on Treaty claims. He had gone along with all the delays and the consequential frustration and bitterness while claiming publicly that the government was acting in good faith, yet knowing that it had not worked out its own policy.

Maori themselves were the problem, he argued righteously, because they couldn't make up their mind who represented them. They were always going to court over something or other, said the minister – who represented the Crown which had used courts for more than 100 years to deny claims, that had then been found to be justified.

In addition to these strategies, said Doug Graham, the government had to consider seriously public resistance to Treaty claims. In *Trick or Treaty* he said that one of the government's big problems was 'lack of public understanding of the issues'.[17] He said that 'most New Zealanders are aware of the claims but very few know the detail. How,' asked the minister who had refused to support a campaign to provide such details, 'could we better inform the public of the facts? The Tribunal had reported regularly on claims but not many people had read them'.[18]

Latimer says that it was Doug Graham himself who was unwilling, as early as 1991, to provide any funds to help the public to understand what was happening about the Treaty. The minister was a senior member of an administration that had consistently refused to give the Waitangi Tribunal more money for research or publicity.

The Waitangi Tribunal's reports are long and detailed, as they have to be if they are to be an authoritative record of New Zealand's past race relations, and the injustices of the last 140–150 years – injustices that Doug Graham acknowledged. The Waitangi Tribunal needed funds to publish short, simple summaries for general use on a much wider scale but was never given them.

Latimer believes it has been in the government's interest to keep the public ignorant – so that, in turn, it can force the cost of Treaty reparations down – to the cost of some out-of-date American fighter planes, for instance. He points to the $1 billion that Doug Graham's colleagues intended to pay for twenty-eight F-16 aircraft over one or two years and compares it with the $1 billion offered over ten years to Maori for the loss of many billions of dollars of land, forests and fisheries, taken unjustifiably by previous governments.

While Chris Laidlaw found it difficult to understand how someone he respected, like Doug Graham, could agree to a billion dollar fiscal envelope, Latimer has no such problem. Politicians and governments have been saying one thing and doing another ever since the Treaty was signed. Why expect them to change now?

In the preface to *Trick or Treaty*, Doug Graham says that one of the main reasons for writing the book was the 'urgent need now for material to help the public understand what is being done and what is at stake'.[19] He said he wrote the book for the average person who may not know a great deal about the subject but was keen to find out more.

If that is true then he failed. This short book of just over 100 pages was published by the Institute of Policy Studies, Victoria University of Wellington. The first print run was 1,000 copies, at a cost of $22 each. Two more editions were printed, each at 750 copies. His book would have reached only a tiny audience and tells much more about the minister and his justification for his party's policies than it does about Treaty history and current issues.

So also does Doug Graham's attitude soon afterward, in 1998, when he sharply criticised Taranaki iwi for not forming a united group to negotiate with government over land settlement issues. 'Don't blame us for delays. I can't help it that Maori can't get on with themselves, if they can't agree and won't talk to each other. I'm getting quite depressed about their inability to agree on anything. They are a litigious people.'[20]

In 1999, the minister had another chance to demonstrate his sincerity and help the public to learn more about the Treaty but he dismissed it angrily. An American Fulbright scholar, Kirsten Carlson, had carried out a survey that revealed, yet again, how ignorant many people were about Treaty issues. When Carlson suggested that the government develop an educational campaign to improve understanding Doug Graham refused. He said that taxpayers would be outraged if the government spent millions of dollars on advertising and other campaigns to explain why Maori land grievances were being settled.

He admitted that the level of ignorance was high but said that children, at least, now had a better knowledge because of the amount of work done in schools. A large number of older people knew little about the history of the Treaty and, he said, did not want to know. He thought the government has done a 'reasonable job' explaining why multi-million dollar payouts were necessary.[21]

Again, none of this surprised Latimer. Every attempt to engage the National government in a joint campaign to present Treaty issues to the public had failed. While Doug Graham and Bolger repeatedly warned they had to take full account of public feelings about the Treaty when fixing compensation they were determined to do nothing to improve understanding.

When Labour won the 1999 election, Te Puni Kokiri said in its briefing paper to government that 'many [people] have little understanding of the unique position of Maori ... and the ongoing meaning and value of the Treaty of Waitangi to successive governance'. Anti-Treaty sentiments and resistance to the expectations of the Maori people could lead to a deterioration in race relations, said the Ministry, repeating the warning given by the Maori Council over the preceding twelve years. Te Puni Kokiri proposed, again, an education strategy that aimed to foster understanding so that an informed public debate was possible.[22]

The Maori Council continued to argue for a better and more fair system. In 1999 it proposed that an independent judicial body chaired by two former governors-general be set up to oversee Treaty settlements. Maanu Paul, the Council's executive chairman, said the Western legal system did not allow the thief to set the terms of retribution or the level of restitution to the victim. 'The offender – the Government through the Office of Treaty Settlements – can no longer be allowed to determine the process of settlement.'[23]

Latimer welcomes the 1999 decision of the Labour minister in charge of Treaty negotiations, Margaret Wilson, to provide resources for a public education campaign on the Treaty.[24] He also believes that the government's intention to include Treaty principles in more of its proposed legislation, particularly on health, helps to entrench the Treaty within the country's constitutional framework.[25]

He knows, however, that this strategy is politically dangerous. It provides a focus for attack on Maori initiatives. Using terms like 'Closing the Gaps' outrages those who resent any action being taken to help Maori, and allows National and ACT leaders to pose as the voice of middle New Zealand.

He is also concerned that the Waitangi Tribunal is accepting too many minor claims. Long delays are being experienced, creating more frustration and doubts about the government's honesty of purpose. He argues for amalgamation of similar and overlapping claims so that negotiations can start with the government, on the basis of all the evidence that has already been supplied in overwhelming detail to the Waitangi Tribunal.

In an attempt to deflect criticism, Margaret Wilson has attempted to reassure the public that Treaty claims are not too expensive and that Maori are not getting too much, echoing National's fiscal envelope policy. Wilson says that just over $50 million has been paid out each year, on average, over the last ten years, a figure she describes as modest compared with government expenditure in other sectors.[26]

Latimer: 'So far, much of the rhetoric of the new government sounds good but we're not seeing much action. A Ministry of Justice report earlier in the year [2001] said that the ministry has still not been able to promote a coherent and comprehensive approach to handling relationships with Maoridom. Margaret Wilson says she is going to set up a specialist Treaty team but it hasn't happened yet.'

For Latimer, the constitutional status of the Treaty has always been the most important issue. He accepts that some politicians will continue to act in bad faith and do everything possible to delay settlements. He is unworried by campaigns to put a strict time limit on Treaty claims through their appeal to anti-Maori sentiment in the community. He believes that this is using the race card: whenever you want quick popularity declare an open season on all Maori.

The process of embedding the Treaty in the constitution is, Latimer believes, now unstoppable. Even the most conservative politicians accept that a series of historic legal decisions have changed the political scene permanently. Sir Geoffrey Palmer has also consistently favoured action on constitutional lines. 'In my view the constitutional change that is most likely to be beneficial and acceptable is to make the Treaty part of a basic constitutional document in New Zealand law which is part of our higher law.'[27]

Palmer went further in his 1997 book, *Bridled Power*, written with his son Matthew Palmer, now (2002) dean of the law school at Victoria University of Wellington. He asserted that the 'Treaty is a key source of the New Zealand Government's moral and political claim to legitimacy in governing the country. It may have some status in international law. It is referred to, and given specific legal effect, in a number of specific pieces of legislation. It is used by courts as an aid to interpretation of statutes. It is the basis on which the Waitangi Tribunal recommends, and in some cases can order, action by government. The Crown proclaims its intention to abide by the Treaty and to settle past breaches of it.'[28] The Palmers offered a possible draft of a written constitution (intended to be the Supreme Law) for discussion. In its introductory declaration they include the Treaty: 'The Maori, as tangata whenua o Aotearoa, and the Crown entered in 1840 into a solemn contract known as Te Tiriti o Waitangi or the Treaty of Waitangi, and it is desirable to recognise and affirm the Treaty as part of the Supreme Law of New Zealand.'[29]

Doug Graham publicly insisted on the need for justice and for an honourable settlement of disputes but, for example, refused to fund the Waitangi Tribunal adequately so that it could cope with the complex process of handling more than 800 claims. Latimer says that a massive shift in public attitudes has taken place since 1962, when the Maori Council was set up. He believes that this was made possible *only* by the Court decisions of 1987 and the following years. They, in turn, would not have been effective without the creation of the Waitangi Tribunal and the extension of its authority back to 1840.

He believes that Matiu Rata, Koro Wetere, and Geoffrey Palmer were the key figures in Parliament during those critical years, that the Ratana Movement's public commitment to the Treaty was crucial to their success, and that the Maori Council's strategy of promoting the spirit of the Treaty, rather than asking for ratification, had shown great political sense.

He says the Treaty is now so firmly a part of New Zealand society it will always be relevant. There can, in his opinion, be no simple end to the Treaty's significance when current cases before the Waitangi Tribunal are finally heard or agreement is reached by negotiation. 'That's past history. What we have to do now is look at the Treaty's implication for the present and the future.'

Latimer sees many obstacles ahead, including the bigotry reflected, and magnified, in the news media. He does not believe, however, that the front pages of daily newspapers or the first ten minutes of television news programmes are accurate or realistic snapshots of life in New Zealand. He points out that journalists and politicians show up in opinion polls as among the least respected people inthe community. 'Yet these are the people who tell us each day whatthe people of New Zealand think about the Treaty and Maori issues!'

He welcomed the initiative taken in April 2000 by the Institute for Policy Studies at Victoria University of Wellington to hold a conference to introduce constitutional issues for continuing debate. He was not surprised, however, by the angry assault on the conference launched by Wellington's *Evening Post* and *Dominion*. Both papers, owned by Independent Newspapers Limited (INL), attacked the conference relentlessly. An *Evening Post* editorial condemned it as elitist because its members were not representative of the total population – no plumbers, secretaries, florists or truck-drivers, for example.

The editor then published letters from incensed people, who complained they had been deliberately excluded while academics, judges and Maori radicals tried to change a constitution that was working very well thank you. Long articles were published pointing out how ridiculous the conference was before any papers had even been presented.

The *Evening Post* announced the conference with an inflammatory headline, saying that it was going to discuss the setting up of a separate Maori state. This possibility – put forward by one academic (Professor Raj Vasil) and not supported by conference members – heightened fears already held by some concerned citizens that Maori were, again, up to no good.

Latimer sees the newspaper's response as a revealing example of the way the media uses the Treaty to inflame the public. Any attempt to discuss the Treaty in a rational way (such as the Institute for Policy Studies conference) is criticised through the media as an attack on New Zealand's way of life by intellectuals and Maori radicals.

Latimer attended the conference and was pleased that the Treaty's significance was brought forward in such a public forum with more than 100 jurists, politicians, academics, community representatives and business people taking part. He did not expect any consensus to emerge – that was not the conference's purpose – but is satisfied that the Treaty is now such a prominent part of the debate on constitutional reform.

He considers that Sir Douglas's dismissal of the Treaty as 'quaint' reveals clearly the attitude of the previous government toward Maori claims. The Treaty had passed its use-by date; it should not be added to formal legislation. That view explained, he says, why Maori had so much trouble reaching agreement with the Crown. There was an absence of goodwill, of good faith, on the part of government negotiators. Their aim was not to achieve fair settlements; just to remove Treaty claims from the political agenda.

While Latimer's energy was focused mainly on the Treaty during the 1990s, he and the Maori Council were still trying to carry out the prime aims embodied in its 1962 Maori Welfare Act. The 1990s was a period of unprecedented political instability because of the introduction of the Mixed Member Proportional (MMP) electoral system. Shifting voting preferences led to mixed messages from MPs, slim majorities in Parliament, government by deals within deals, and the emergence of personality politics on a grand scale.

Though the National Party remained on the Treasury benches for nine years, its ability to implement its policies was sharply limited by public opinion, by lack of a clear mandate on important issues, splits within its own ranks (leading to Bolger's replacement by Jenny Shipley) and by the compromises needed to keep the support of its coalition partner, New Zealand First, and its leader the mercurial Winston Peters.

Latimer believed that MMP provided a chance to form a Maori political party that could hold the balance of power in the new political environment. The Maori Council even considered facilitating this opportunity, registering the name Aotearoa Party. It drafted a constitution and a set of very moderate objectives before deciding to not go ahead: such a move was clearly outside its functions as a statutory body.

Latimer strongly supported the expansion of Maori parliamentary seats, matching a rise in the number on the Maori electoral roll. He hoped that Maori MPs could shape themselves into a bloc or an informal caucus to support bipartisan laws promoting economic and social development. (The number of Maori seats is seven in 2002.)

The Council's future became a political issue when the Department of Maori Affairs was replaced by a Ministry of Maori Development (Te Puni Kokiri) in 1991. Latimer argued that a group of civil servants could never provide governments with a coherent view of Maori opinion. In the absence, he said, of an elected assembly for Maori, 'the Council is the only statutory body with enough authority and experience to do that'.

He asked the government to give the Maori Council stronger support services, an effective internal secretariat, and additional powers to develop Maori initiatives, such as economic enterprises, language programmes, and training for the unemployed. He believed that such an expanded body should also have the authority to monitor the ways in which other state agencies carried out their responsibilities to Maori in terms of their charters.

With other leaders he explored a range of alternatives, all with the common aim of securing for Maori greater control over their own affairs, including the transfer of resources from government to Maori groups and the creation of elected forums or assemblies able to represent regional and national opinions.

Latimer: 'So long as the main political parties and governments ignored Maori interests we had to look at ways we could influence national policies. We were not trying to create separate or racist parliamentary systems. We were trying to come *into* a political system that had deliberately excluded us, kept us separate and powerless.'

All suggestions were rejected. The Council itself was attacked and its future placed in doubt. Bolger accused it, rightly, of not being representative of Maori opinion but omitted to say that the Council's composition and structure was determined by a parliamentary statute, which it could not alter. Instead, he said that the lack of a unified voice was a problem for the government, because it preferred to speak only with a single group that could represent all Maori opinion.

This was as impossible, responded Latimer, as expecting all Pakeha opinions to be represented by one body. Latimer: 'Bolger was saying, in effect, that nothing could be done till all those claiming to speak for Maori had a formal, binding mandate on every issue. That was a tactic aimed at dividing us, and excusing delays in acting.'

Instead of supporting the Maori Council, the government decided to review it, to determine just how accountable it was: 'whether the outcomes it achieves reflect its statutory obligations'. Because the reciprocal duties and accountability of governments to the Council, and to Maori, were not part of the review the exercise was futile. Recommendations included the suggestion (to be ignored) that the Council be given more resources, and that it should draw up a strategic plan, and try to develop better relationships with goverment.

The Council continued to do what it had always done: keep itself alive on a minimal financial allocation from the state (not even enough to sustain an office) by relying on the voluntary efforts of thousands of supporters, and to use its statutory powers to represent all Maori in the courts. Latimer remains optimistic. The advances made over the last fifteen years are, he believes, all positive. Differences of opinion among Maori groups are to be expected, and can be worked out in time. The important change is that systems are in place to allow that to happen and that these are supported by the courts and accepted, however reluctantly, by most politicians and all parties.

CHAPTER NINE

Race Relations – a Minor Miracle
1926–2001

> As a Maori family growing up in suburbia in the 1950s we were called 'those hories', were always assumed to be dirty, uncouth and thieves by Pakeha neighbours and schoolmates. For generations our people have not cried 'gimme, gimme'. That started with Pakeha settlers, who when they couldn't steal our land, used the excuse of confiscation to get it. Many of our people are on welfare – a direct result of apartheid in education and the job market.
>
> Letter to the editor, New Truth, 15 January 1993

> She had just enough Maori blood in her to make her lazy.
>
> A Wellington secondary school teacher commenting in 1960
on an attractive student she liked but believed could do better
(she did: she became a model)

> How much Maori blood does someone need in them to qualify as a Maori and receive the benefits which are not available to us honkies? Some say you have to 'feel' Maori. If that's the case, then kia ora bro!
>
> Letter to the editor, Weekend Herald, 1 September 2001

> In my considered view the state of race relations is getting worse and the potential for it flaring up is heightened by the present climate.
>
> Dr Rajen Prasad, former race relations conciliator,
11 December 1997, Dominion

> The differences from our colonial past are being settled in the bedrooms of the nation.
>
> Professor Ranginui Walker, Metro, 2001
(referring to intermarriage: 'one of the most potent
ameliorating factors in race relations in New Zealand')

159

Hostile attitudes toward Maori by what, Latimer believes, is a relatively small minority hardened after 1987. Ignorance allied with prejudice produced a rabid response. Geoffrey Palmer commented on this strong reaction at the time, and later, saying in 1995: 'There is an unpleasant underside to the New Zealand psyche when questions of race are confronted. For much of the time the truth is disguised under an egalitarian exterior. We have achieved a fair measure of tolerance, but the situation is fragile.'[1]

Mike Moore, writing in 1987, also observed that 'there is still a lot of racism in New Zealand'.[2] As minister of tourism he had proposed spending $5,000 for a pilot scheme to pay for Maori and English signposts on the East Coast. Lobby groups opposed it fiercely. 'In reality,' said Moore, 'most were against it because it was Maori.'[3] He received this letter: 'We won the war, we beat them; they have no rights.' Moore gave up. 'A simple idea to make motoring more interesting, to educate Maoris, Pakehas and visitors, was stalled.'[4]

A detailed Massey University study published in 1989 showed that most New Zealanders wanted to limit claims under the Treaty or to abolish it altogether. Respondents favouring the National Party were less likely than those favouring Labour to support the campaign for greater Maori rights.

Researchers concluded that while a bit more 'support for Maori concerns is found with younger and better educated people, the important political truth is that in each political camp, at all ages, and at all education levels, even where they are most favourably disposed to Maori concerns, large absolute majorities continue to oppose special Maori land and fishing rights'. Most respondents believed Maori were already well treated.[5]

Treaty claims were damned as the grievance industry, and the Waitangi Tribunal was belittled as a gravy train express for lawyers and consultants who were robbing the taxpayer and dividing the nation. New right-wing groups with small memberships sprang up to speak for middle New Zealand and white rights. They argued that because today's citizens were not involved in past events they should not accept any responsibility. Angry politicians joined in.

Much of the hostility focused on Latimer as president of the Maori Council. Latimer: 'We were all surprised at the reaction. For the Council, the decision by the Court of Appeal in 1987 was tremendous because of the status it gave the Treaty. But we'd been asking for this for more than a century so it was part of a long struggle for us. We knew its history but the public didn't. It shocked a lot of people. They had the idea that we'd conned everyone and got something we didn't deserve. They knew none of the history.'

In the 1990s, race relations and the Treaty became staple scandal items in newspapers and on television. Enthusiastic coverage of every act of vandalism by protestors, of the annual spectacles orchestrated at Waitangi, and of claims to rivers, coastline and air waves all contributed to the impression of a world of Maori out of control.

Some newspapers appointed Maori affairs reporters, with varying degrees of knowledge and ignorance of their new field, and confidently expected and got excitement and sensation. Editors did not want fact-based stories: they wanted headlines. A study carried out by Massey University senior lecturer, Judy McGregor, found in 1992 that Maori journalists had a low opinion of the news media's performance when reporting Maori issues. The main reason: 'The pathology of reporting Maori news concentrates on "bad" news, with Maori people as a "problem".' The report concluded that an urgent reappraisal of what constitutes news about Maori is needed.[6]

Since then the media have given bad Maori news higher priority. Scandals and personalities are even more highly rated. Ken Mair and Titewhai Harawira were awarded demon status for their increasingly professional protests. A pub fight involving Maori and Pacific Islanders and some Pakeha was given billboard treatment as a 'Race War'.

Latimer: 'The news media has to take some responsibility for changes in attitudes toward the Treaty, and between Maori and Pakeha. In the past, newspapers would report an event but wouldn't necessarily splash it all over their front pages with huge headlines. They've now entered into a sort of partnership with the protestors, who say that they'll be at such and such a place at such and such a time. Come along with your cameras.'

Reports on Maori issues were, and still are, designed to outrage viewers and readers. Journalists traded on fear and loathing, and stimulated anger with headlines such as: Maori Claim the South Island, Maori Want Separate Parliament, and Kill a White. Syd Jackson told the *Sunday News* in 1995 that Pakeha could no longer rule and Maori would take the country back by 1 January 2000. The paper gave his threat a four-column headline, accompanied by a photograph of a suitably serious Syd. No follow-up story appeared on 1 January 2000.

Cartoonists during the 1990s ridiculed the Maori protest movement. Jim Hubbard showed a blindfolded, wild-haired Maori waving one hand in the air and, holding a revolver in his other hand, shooting himself in the foot (labelled Maori Grievances).[7] When the Waitangi Tribunal ruled that urban Maori groups can be described as iwi Tom Scott showed a city kid kitted out in trendy American clothes telling old fat-cat Maori drinking champagne and smoking cigars to 'shift along guys and pass the gravy …'.[8]

Latimer accepts that protestors share the blame for the angry image being generated, and has always had mixed feelings about them. He sympathises with their frustration, and says that to some extent protestors have been useful in discussions with governments. They make the Maori Council look reasonable and moderate when they ask for much the same thing: recognition of Maori rights and, in particular, making the Treaty part of the country's constitution.

At the same time, he is aware of the depth of anti-Maori feeling protestors generate among people who would reject any suggestion that they are personally racially biased. These people see protestors as rude, arrogant bullies, taking advantage of rights they hold as citizens to burn the country's flag, spit on the governor-general, throw things at Queen Elizabeth II, behead colonial statues, deface buildings, humiliate their own elders, reject marae protocol, and refuse to accept the authority of the courts while accepting state benefit payments.

Latimer is intensely conscious of the changes that have taken place in race relations in his lifetime. When he was born in 1926, for most people there weren't any. Less than forty years after his birth, when Latimer joined the Maori Council, race relations had been elevated to the status of a national problem.

In less than forty years after that, race relations had become one of New Zealand's three main media topics along with scandals and natural disasters.

In the 1920s the country's 63,000 Maori could have fitted into one city the size of Hastings today. Nine out of ten were scattered in very small communities in mostly isolated areas, except for some slightly bigger groupings in Rotorua, parts of the Waikato and Taranaki. They had only limited and fleeting contact with the Pakeha majority, about 1.4 million, mostly living in urban areas. They were outnumbered about twenty-three to one.[9]

Governments, officials and Maori leaders knew that the enforced confinement of Maori in rural areas was ending. They had not been living in isolation and poverty by choice but as the result of deliberate policies to populate New Zealand as quickly as possible with British migrants on Maori land. Because of rising numbers they could not be supported any longer, even in poverty, in country districts. Governments were told as early as the 1920s that unless Maori were to become permanently dependent on state handouts they had to go where they could find work, to towns and cities. Land development schemes initiated by Sir Apirana Ngata failed to hold Maori in their rural settlements.

By the end of the 1960s more than half of all Maori were solidly established in urban areas, with more coming each year. Maori and non-Maori New Zealanders were encountering each other closely for the first time en masse, and some found the experience unsettling and stressful. Maori, for an increasing number of citizens, were now the people next door or down the street, not out there somewhere.

One Thames hospital matron refused to accept Maori nurse trainees, complaining she had enough trouble with 'white' nurses. George Hogben, an early director-general of education, raised sex as an issue when considering whether Maori women should be trained as nurses: 'You have to take great care as to how you allow the women of one race to go among the people of another race where different ideas prevail as to the relations between the sexes, and until the ground is prepared for them you will have danger.' The matron of a Waikato sanatorium refused to accept Maori women as probationers until a small room or cottage could be provided for them because some 'white' nurses could object to sleeping in the same room.[10]

By 1961, when the Maori Council was being formed, about 200,000 people claimed Maori descent, one in every twelve in a total population of about 2.4 million. They were increasing at an annual rate of 4 per cent, still twice the national average. More than 100,000 were described in the Census as full Maori. Just over 50,000 were Maori–European, three-quarter and half-caste. Another 35,000 were Maori–European quarter-caste. The rate of intermarriage was increasing. By the mid-1950s one-in-three Maori children in urban areas had a European parent, compared with one-in-seven in rural areas.[11]

Latimer strongly supported the Maori Council's efforts to promote harmony between Maori and the general community. Latimer's experiences in the 1940s showed him that many city people were unprepared for what some saw as an influx of aliens. They did not understand that it was a forced exodus encouraged by their own government. To many it was an intrusion, an invasion. Those with Maori neighbours often found their large families noisy, and different – with friends calling at all hours, lots of visiting relatives overcrowding their homes, late-night parties.

Perceptions of Maori had been shaped for many years by publicity given to a few individuals, mostly entertainers, and by photographs of ceremonies on marae, children diving for coins at Rotorua, and by haka and concert parties. Few journalists covered Maori events. General books on New Zealand mentioned Maori briefly, mostly as picturesque artifacts.

Newspapers showed little interest except when scandals were involved. *Truth* criticised Sir Apirana Ngata vigorously in the early 1930s over the administration of his land development programmes and hoped that never again would a Maori be made minister of Maori affairs.[12]

Even earlier, the *New Zealand Herald* attacked the appointment of Sir Maui Pomare as minister of health and said when he lost the position: 'It is pleasing to see this important portfolio returning to one who represents a European constituency.' The *New Zealand Herald* declared its position on race just fourteen years before Latimer was born: 'There is no getting over the inherent detestation of the white races and especially of British people towards anything which savours of rule by coloured or native races.'[13]

There were exceptions. One journalist, Mel Taylor, won the Cowan Prize with a series in the *Auckland Star* in the 1950s about racial discrimination, singling out housing. Another journalist, Eric Ramsden, had close contacts with the King Movement in the Waikato, and helped to make Princess Te Puea known nationally. Both men had Maori wives and understood the situation that this group of people were experiencing.

Humorists and cartoonists did more than politicians or officials to shape racial perceptions. While few people read the Hunn Report on the state of Maori in 1960, many thousands laughed at the character named Hori, who came to represent one persistent stereotype of Maori.

Hori's adventures with the Pakeha coot up the street, his day at the races, arguments with his mother-in-law, consumption of beer, the size of his gut, and his attitude toward politicians began as articles in magazines and were then reprinted as cheap paperbacks, *The Half-Gallon Jar*, *Barrels of Fun*, *Flagon Fun*, and *Fill it up Again*.

The writer of the Hori stories was W Norman McCallum, a New Zealander of Scottish descent. He was a commercial traveller based in Auckland who claimed he had 'countless friends among the Maori people' and that his 'admiration of the First New Zealanders is unbounded'.[14] His stories were extremely popular, easy to read, cheap and accessible to a wide public.

Maori stereotype and average Pakeha met in the 1960s. The Hunn Report had said that New Zealand was two nations and that very rapid action was needed to close the gaps between them before the personal and social costs became too great.[15] Other studies added to the sense of urgency: positive discrimination was needed. Look at what happened in other countries when a minority felt disadvantaged and alienated.

Ralph Hanan, then minister of Maori affairs, responded by telling the Maori Council that it alone had the responsibility to do something about all this.

Latimer: 'Hanan told us that the future of Maoridom was in our hands. He said that progress from now on depended on our deliberations and the extent to which we could obtain "unanimity" on the problems of our time. This was completely unfair.'

Latimer despaired of Hanan's ignorance of things Maori and the lectures he delivered on what they should do. Once, Hanan pointed to the photographs on the walls of the meeting room – Carroll, Ngata, Buck, Pomare – and said there are your great leaders, emulate them and raise your people up. Councillors knew that those rangatira believed all previous governments had failed in their duties to Maori, had stolen their economic base, land, and rejected their requests for help in combating disease and ignorance – had, indeed, watched many Maori die. Hanan knew nothing of their struggles.

While Latimer's experiences, particularly in the Kaipara with Kemp Nathan and Te Uri-o-Hau, convinced him that the big issue was the survival of Maori as an ethnic group, he knew that Hanan wanted complete integration of Maori. All Maori should be like those in Southland, Hanan's home, where, he said, they were completely integrated.

Hanan acknowledged that there were pockets of what could be called racialism but believed race relations were good and getting better, citing the 'vast potential of goodwill that has been exhibited to the Maori people in the campaign to raise funds for the [Maori] Education Foundation'. (Maori trust monies that could have funded the Maori Council were redirected by Hanan to set up the Maori Education Fund.)

Latimer and his colleagues disagreed with Hanan on all fundamental issues. They opposed integration and assimilation (both meant the same in practice) and were determined to have the Treaty accepted. They did not agree that race relations were getting better (how could Hanan know?) and were painfully aware of the tensions that were growing as the mass flow into the cities continued. Their own families, their own children, were the ones who were suffering most from the painful adjustments they had to make.

Latimer: 'We knew it was no good just saying nice things about race relations. The issue was parity. You can't have a happy community when the minority feels oppressed by the majority, when families are sick, on low wages and live cramped together in poor houses.'

He felt personally committed to the cause. Harmony was not just desirable, like 'Mom and apple pie', but urgent and necessary if the community was to understand and support Maori aspirations to parity. Latimer: 'The old councillors were never anti-Pakeha. Most had Pakeha relatives. They all believed that they'd benefited in many ways from modern technology and new ideas. But they also knew that Maori had been cheated of the rights promised in the preamble to the Treaty and in the three articles. They believed Maori could never climb up from the bottom of the heap till they were treated as full citizens.'

Councillors knew from their own experience that many people, including Hanan, regarded Maori as second-class. At their first Council meeting in 1962 Hanan had urged them to not regard themselves as second-class. Maori could be as good as everybody else if they just caught up educationally, stopped trying to hold on to communal land and accepted there was one law for everybody. Hanan reassured them that they were as good as everyone else. They needed no such reassurance. Their problem was, they felt, with the attitudes of so many of their fellow-citizens, including their minister.

The Council's first task was to persuade governments and the public to recognise the existence of the problem – not the Maori problem but the problem of two peoples, two nations, learning to live together.

David Ausubel offended many when he said New Zealand was deceiving itself by hiding behind myths of racial harmony. He was fiercely criticised as an outsider who did not understand the special relationship that existed between Maori and Pakeha, and anyway, look what was happening in the United States: how could he find fault with New Zealand?

Ausubel's book, *The Fern and the Tiki*, gave the fullest and most damning summary of race relations to be published till that time (1965).[16] He included all the things omitted from the Hunn Report: details of discrimination in housing, employment, hotels, schools and community groups. During a year in New Zealand he observed anti-Maori behaviour and heard Maori described as bloody bastards, lazy layabouts, as people with no future unless they became fully Europeanised.

He agreed that race relations were not bad compared with other countries, but said that New Zealand's biggest problem in resolving racial difficulties was in admitting they even existed. He believed younger people were less prejudiced than their elders and saw that as the brightest hope for the future.

Latimer agrees that most people tended, in the 1960s, to look away, to minimise the problems involved in facing the difficulties of Pakeha and Maori co-existing in harmony. Few politicians shared this view. One who did, Duncan McIntyre, minister of Maori affairs after Hanan died in 1969, spoke openly about past mistakes, and paid a heavy price – he lost his Hastings seat at the next election in 1972 because he was seen as pro-Maori.

McIntyre said that the Pakeha majority had been at fault in not respecting Maori social and cultural institutions. While he blamed indifference rather than intolerance he accepted that the result was much the same. He acknowledged the tensions that accompanied Maori migration to cities but welcomed the high rate of intermarriage as reliable proof of a reasonably good state of race relations.[17]

Latimer believed that most people got on well as individuals. That had certainly been his and Emily's personal experience in Auckland in the late 1940s and in the Kaipara in the 1950s. He knew, however, that the country culture Maori brought with them did not always fit easily when Pakeha lived only a few feet away.

Many problems involved young Maori. At that time almost half of all Maori were under fifteen. They had little guidance from adults because there were so few of them, proportionately, and many had remained in their rural homes. Young Maori were adrift in an often hostile environment.[18] Councillors formally asked police to stop harassing them just because they were Maori, and stop picking up children without letting their parents know immediately. Efforts were made to get legal advice when Maori were charged with offences: most had no knowledge of court procedure and consequently had much higher conviction rates than those able to afford lawyers.

The Maori Council received little response to their requests for: police officers to be trained in Maori cultural practices; coroners to show respect for Maori burial customs; government agencies, developers and farmers to stop desecrating burial sites, wahi tapu; government support in regaining artifacts and body parts from overseas museums and collections; broadcasters to pronounce Maori words correctly; more teachers of Maori, and more Maori programmes when television started. Latimer: 'We wanted some sign of respect. There was hardly any response.'

The Council also asked Keith Holyoake's National government to fulfil its promise to conduct a review of race relations. When this was rejected the Council suggested that a Race Relations Institute be set up to carry out research into the nature of prejudice, and the way Maori children were taught in city schools.

Latimer: 'We didn't want a Race Relations Office, though National set one up later. We didn't want to concentrate on complaints, because that seemed to just make matters worse. We wanted to look into what caused racial tension. A lot of work had been done overseas and we hoped that with more knowledge, and better education, we could avoid many of the problems we saw elsewhere. And though we knew that everyone was not equal in New Zealand, we also knew that there was a lot of goodwill between Maori and Pakeha.'

McIntyre was, in 1971, confident that positive policies, affirmative action, would heal the divisions between the races, which then included migrants from the Pacific Islands. He saw little profit 'in the continuous shouting of slogans about the evils of the Pakeha to the Maori. We have had a good deal of this lately and I sense that it is provoking a reaction of the very type we would all wish to avoid'.[19]

While the Council continued to press for parity of respect, New Zealand's obsession with rugby, and desire to play the Springboks, became the ultimate race relations test case for the Council till 1980. This human rights issue also raised questions about the treatment of Maori in the past and the present. Indigenous rights became the new protest flag, transcending such practical issues as education, housing, unemployment and health.

Councillors were sharply divided. Rugby was a big part of Maori life. Players such as George Nepia had legendary status, admired by Maori and non-Maori. Titewhai Harawira was amazed when a Council meeting was suspended so members could listen to a rugby commentary. Latimer had played as long as he could and then became a coach and an administrator. He believed he reflected a substantial body of Maori opinion when he said that rugby was such an important part of 'our lives and the lives of our Pakeha brothers that we should do nothing to interfere in the success or progress of the sport'.

As the reality of apartheid became more apparent when sixty-nine people were massacred at Sharpeville, South Africa, in 1960, and when blacks were brutalised, tortured and murdered by police solely because of their race and colour, rugby ceased to be seen by many New Zealanders as sport. Instead it became a symbol of racial oppression and race hatred.

The 1970 All Black tour of South Africa polarised opinion. Maori team members were declared honorary whites by the South African government. Many anti-tour leaders received anonymous phone calls: they were nigger lovers. Before the team even reached South Africa the players, including Chris Laidlaw, were given a message by a lone ex-Dunedin woman in Perth. She was holding a placard: All Blacks last tour of South Africa. To ensure that this mother of five, Margaret Sundbourn, did not disturb the peace an Australian policeman stood on each side of her while other New Zealanders rebuked her with their own placards: Boo, Hiss, Hiss.

During the tour, the All Blacks saw coloured supporters viciously kicked and beaten by white spectators just because they cheered for the All Blacks. Unhindered by police, whites openly attacked men and boys on the field at the end of one game – confident they had every right to do so, as they did.

Latimer had no illusions about South Africa and strongly opposed apartheid but he also supported the National Party policy of 'bridge-building' – hoping that New Zealand's example, demonstrated through Maori–Pakeha rugby teams, could bring about change. Rugby players would see how people of different races could live together and take the message home and apply it there.

When he realised slowly during the 1970s that apartheid was not going to disappear as the result of gentle persuasion his views changed. The Maori Council had been repeatedly asked to condemn the tours but most members believed that each Maori District Council had the right to speak for itself.

Latimer was criticised for being too accommodating to the white establishment, being 'too white' himself, and putting rugby before principle. Finally, in 1980, the Council said no to Springbok tours. Latimer: 'We should have been wiser sooner.' When South African rugby players were welcomed on to the Poho-o-Rawiri marae at Gisborne he told them, as Maori Council president, that this would be the last time in New Zealand they would receive such a welcome till apartheid ended.

By this time racial politics and rugby had become a highly emotional issue, dividing families, communities, political parties and churches. In the 1975 general election Muldoon promised that a National government would greet Springboks with open arms, and then in 1981 he again used rugby to gain an electoral advantage over Labour at a heavy cost to the country and to its good race relations image.

Some angry Maori saw the Maori Council's attempts to promote harmony as giving in to the majority race and condemned the Council itself as unrepresentative of modern Maori opinion. Few people remembered or mentioned that a partnership had been established between the Maori Council and government by the Maori Welfare Act 1962. Promotion of harmony between the races was a joint aim and a joint effort. Politicians were obliged by statute to help as well. What statute was that, they asked?

Politicians were only facing reality: supporting Maori aspirations was a sure way to lose votes, while keeping Maori at a distance and even using the race card certainly did no harm and probably helped on election day. Latimer: 'Some politicians were anti-Maori but most weren't. They knew, however, that even a small group of people who hold very strong views on an emotional issue such as race can have a very big effect on public opinion. And on winning and losing elections.'

National politicians had good reason to hesitate when thinking of implementing policies favourable to Maori. In the 1946 election

Sidney Holland (later, Sir Sidney) made a strong pitch for Maori support, saying National had no desire to absorb the Maori race into Pakeha customs and culture. 'We want them to retain their own culture,' he said. The Party recognised the right of Maori to equal participation in all the benefits and advantages that were available to Pakeha.[20]

In spite of this public policy, many National MPs said that the sooner all Maori were integrated the better. There was little sympathy for Maori and some MPs were happy to use insulting expressions about Maori as a put-down. A former prime minister, John Marshall, said in his memoirs: 'Our people used to say [that Peter Fraser] was "as cunning as a Maori dog", and there was an element of truth in that charge.'[21]

Keith Holyoake, following Holland as National's leader, had no deep interest in or understanding of Maori culture or history, and no special sympathy for Maori concerns. He also held some unscientific opinions on racial genetics. Sir Robert Jones says that in the 1970s Holyoake told him about his theory of the natural inferiority of dark-skinned races, which he attributed to a 'genetic inability to organise themselves'. Jones said that sort of opinion 'was common in National Party ranks'.[22]

Latimer, as a member of the National Party, was well aware of its anti-Maori stand. McIntyre had told him that the Afrikaans-dominated government in South Africa could not have been less sympathetic to Maori Council proposals than his own Cabinet in Wellington. Nothing personal. Maori issues generated no votes. Latimer stayed because he believed he would have more influence inside the Party than outside.

Labour was more sympathetic but it was out of power during the Council's first ten years. Even though leaders like Norman Kirk supported Maori initiatives some Labour MPs were unsympathetic. They had elections to win and believed a solid core of voters was anti-Maori.

Some of these MPs were prejudiced, reflecting earlier colonial views of superiority toward Maori, Asians and foreigners generally. Others thought no special provisions should be made for Maori for anything, because everyone had equal opportunities. Some saw them as competition on the labour market, people who were willing to take less-than-standard wages. Some resented the way their own neighbourhoods were changing, by lower house values, and by what they viewed as increasing aggression by young Maori. Racial insults were not all one way. The American word, honky, for whites, was increasingly used to match nigger.

When National lost the 1972 election, party leaders deliberately identified some new Labour ministers for attack, those they considered soft targets. Rosters of up to four MPs at a time were allocated to each minister. Two of these were Matiu Rata and Whetu Tirikatene-Sullivan (Southern Maori). Echoing the contempt for Maori MPs in Pat Lawlor's *Maori Tales* the story went round that Rata's happiest five years were those he spent in standard two.[23] Billboards went up around Wellington: 'Mat Rata reads comics.' And then: 'No he doesn't. He just looks at the pictures.' Muldoon had absorbed the message of McIntyre's defeat in Hastings. National voters had seen him as pro-Maori because of what he tried to do for Maori, though with very little success. Just seeming to be supportive was enough to lose the seat. Instead, Muldoon took a tough line on race issues. He said Maori youngsters who got into trouble in the cities should be sent back to the country, echoing magistrates from the 1940s.[24] In the 1975 election he appealed directly to racial prejudice by attacking Pacific Islands overstayers – but not those from Britain.

The Council took every opportunity to lobby politicians to accept what was becoming real, that Maori were a political force that had to be heard. The Maori population continued to grow and by 1990 about nine in every ten lived in urban areas. Maori business enterprises were becoming more common as iwi and other groups and individuals recognised that Maori needed an economic base separate from the land-based activities of the past.

Latimer found, however, that with every new attempt by the Council to act as an advocate for Maori there was a social cost. Racial harmony was put at risk. Greater prominence produced what the news media called a white backlash, which they reported in full detail. Maori were criticised as a single homogenous group.

Winston Peters rose to national prominence when he revealed what he described as scandals in the Department of Maori Affairs. Attacks on Maori initiatives earned him headlines and instant popularity – deliberately appealing to latent prejudice in the community.

Latimer does not, however, believe that Peters, who is related to Emily, is personally anti-Maori. 'It's all a pose to win popularity and power. He would attend a hui and agree with the points being made and then at a National Party meeting would attack them. There's a word for that sort of thing. He actually wanted, as minister of Maori affairs [1990–1991] to do his best for Maori.'

While Peters was becoming one of the best-known Maori in the country for criticising Maori he was not making friends within his own party – because he was Maori. Muldoon believed that Peters could have been New Zealand's first Maori prime minister except for the jealousy of colleagues, the opposition of new right-wing groups and an element of racism in the National Party – a victim of the same anti-Maori feeling he was generating. Some MPs were happy with the attacks Peters made on Labour: Let the Maori boy do it.

Media interest in conflict and scandal had created a new theatre, a new arena in which personalities paraded their egos. When Wi Pere shouted out 'To hell with the damned Pakeha' in Parliament in the early 1900s nothing happened; no headlines, no interviews, no questions about why he was so upset, what land-grabs was he talking about? Today, there would be an uproar, the offending MP would be asked to apologise, would refuse, be suspended temporarily, appear on current affairs programmes, be the sensation-of-the-week, have his/her photograph on all the front pages, and finally disappear when a new sensation was fabricated.

The reporting of such non-events as earth-shattering dramas has widened gaps between Maori and non-Maori. The Maori warrior image has, also, been badly dented by reports of some Maori men beating and raping women and abusing children. While the great majority do not behave in this way, all are smeared.

At the end of the 1990s the Anglican bishop of Dunedin, the Right Reverend Penny Jamieson, expressed concern about attitudes within the church. She deplored the 'rash of political posturing' about child abuse that fed what she called a voracious news media and increased anxiety and division. 'The current situation is leading us towards a dysfunctional model that is giving many of us Pakeha excuses we too readily reach for, and which are quite frankly of terrible danger to the soul of this Church.'[25]

She noticed: 'among Pakeha, an increase in both overt and covert racism in the Church over the past 10 years.' She added: 'The partnership between the races was often being interpreted by Maori and Pakeha as "a-part-ness".'[26]

David Lange, former Labour prime minister, has linked low income with tensions and warned that Maori and Polynesians would not put up with being economic underdogs forever. He thinks the Maori reaction is likely to be radical, separatist and probably violent, and the pakeha response just as unpleasant.[27]

Similar warnings have been given for at least the last thirty years. Ranginui Walker said, as early as 1973, that race relations were explosive because of the 'warrior tradition of the Maori'. He said that when 'he is backed up against the urban wall, the Maori will fight – as he has already done in some of our major cities'.[28] Ken Mair has said he has no problem with the possibility of Parliament being blown up. Other leaders warn that they will not be able to hold their young people in check if they continue to be badly treated. Some Maori protestors placed their young people in the forefront of violence at Takahue in Northland in 1995.

John Clarke, race relations conciliator in 1995, said few people wanted a racially divided and acrimonious society. He condemned the willingness of those politicians, and others clamouring for public attention 'to exploit the prejudices of the few'. 'This,' he said, 'is a prospect I find deeply disturbing and potentially socially disruptive.'[29]

Dr Rajen Prasad, race relations conciliator in 1998, said in his annual report that some talkback radio hosts were encouraging callers to rebuke and ridicule other cultures under the guise of freedom of speech. 'Some individuals and groups have mounted a sustained attack on Treaty settlements and, by extension, on what some now see as Maori privilege. The cynicism displayed in the print media and talkback programmes is persistent.' Dr Prasad warned that collectively these signals, if not addressed positively, could expose the nation to race relations difficulties.[30]

The National government's attempt in the mid-1990s to pay off all Maori claims over ten years with a fiscal envelope of $1 billion entrenched a culture of anger, and inflamed Maori who would never have considered themselves radicals or extremists. National's leaders treated the Maori Council as an enemy. Latimer was not surprised in 1995 when two National MPs, one a cabinet minister and the other the chief whip, performed an anti-Maori double act on a Radio Pacific talkback show (*Banksy on Sunday*). Reviving the tradition of Pat Lawlor's *Maori Tales* and McCallum's *Half-Gallon Jar*, John Carter pretended to be a dole-bludging Maori who just loved loafing on the unemployment benefit while John Banks, the show's host, said really, and how interesting, Mr Hone.[31]

Carter's Hone said he didn't want Treaty claims settled 'otherwise what will I have to do? I won't get any more dole or anything like that if you settle that, Banksy'.[32] He went on to say he wouldn't have anything more to moan about. 'So don't you go and settle that thing too much.'[33] When Carter referred to the fiscal envelope 'Banksy' intervened, correcting him by saying 'fiscal grab', thus denigrating the policy that Banks supported as his own government's policy.[34]

The 'comic act' created an uproar, releasing pent-up anger against Maori demands. Frank Haden, a *Sunday Star-Times* columnist, said Carter was 'talking for the majority of New Zealanders' by putting the 'importunate Maoris in their place'.[35] Haden denied all feelings of guilt and blamed Maori for people being angry 'enough to make racist jokes we would never have dreamed of making until a couple of years ago'. He added: 'We used to make jokes about Maoris, but they were recounted with a fond smile. Now, when Maori jokes are told, they are told with a sneer. That's the difference.'[36]

The National Party's Maori immediate past vice-president, Jim Brown, demanded the resignation or sacking of both MPs. He said he suspected the talkback item was a 'set-up' (even though Banks denied that he knew Hone was Carter).[37] Carter lost his senior whip position for a time but retained the sympathy of most colleagues.

Doug Graham's reaction was noted by the *Evening Post* journalist, Brent Edwards: 'The image that sticks most in mind is Treaty Negotiations Minister Doug Graham and Maori Affairs Minister John Luxton – the two men charged with gaining Maoridom's trust and confidence – sitting in Parliament laughing at Labour's condemnation of Mr Carter's action. National will hope they have the last laugh.'[38]

Banks had a long history in Parliament and on radio of making anti-Maori jibes. He was still being censured by the Broadcasting Standards Authority in 2000 for saying that Maori had made New Zealand a third-world country and that tangata whenua were merely 'natives who have nothing better to do than wave spears on television'.[39]

Latimer says that both politicians had attacked Maori for years, openly appealing to the racist vote in Northland, an area of high unemployment and the venue each year for Waitangi Day protests. In 1987, Carter said in Parliament that he was worried about the increasing racial tension and that problems had to be faced 'head-on if we are going to avoid bloodshed'.[40] In 1992 both politicians accused church leaders of 'whingeing' about poverty, and they supported benefit cuts which hurt Maori proportionately more than others.[41]

Latimer believes that National, in spite of its members' mixed feelings about Maori, made real progress in the 1990s. He admires Jim Bolger for his personal support in remedying grievances. While Latimer considered the fiscal envelope policy was a disaster, he still respects the negotiated settlements reached with Tainui and Ngai Tahu, including the apologies from Bolger and his successor Jenny Shipley for past injustice. He also sympathised with Bolger when he was angrily abused in 1997 by a retired teacher for working with the New Zealand First Party and sucking up to Maori.

In a letter to Bolger, the Palmerston North man, who claimed he reflected the opinion of nearly everybody he came into contact with, said: 'Your continued attempts to appease this minority group at our expense has cost you your job. Your sell out to this group of mixed parentage, your slobbering, disgusting, nose-rubbing antics with the New Zealand Maori party [Winston Peters' New Zealand First] are the absolute pits. The facts are that the Maori population do not enhance our lives in any way.'[42]

Bolger observed that the letter 'tells us sadly, in the minds of maybe a few, we still as New Zealanders have some journey to go'.[43]

The writer may well have been right when he said that Bolger was seen as pro-Maori and that this contributed to his downfall, like McIntyre in 1972. A number of National MPs were unhappy with the government's Treaty policy. Bolger's support for Doug Graham, as Treaty negotiations minister, in working through the big iwi settlements at that time, lost him caucus votes when Jenny Shipley organised her coup and replaced him as prime minister.

Winston Peters was well aware of anti-Maori feeling within the National Party when he was still a member (he was expelled in 1993). Peters said in 1996 that National thought that Maori were only second-best: 'That's the kind of racism I rail against and despise.'

Michael Laws, a former National MP and an authority on Peters, said in 1998 that there was 'no shortage of National Party activists who dismissed the possibility of Peters ever leading their party precisely because of his part-Maori lineage'.[44] Laws said that a subterranean smear circulated that Peters would 'go native' if ever given a position of authority.

Some New Zealand First supporters had the same attitude according to Tuku Morgan, who left the party in 1998 with Tau Henare, MP for Northern Maori, to form their own shortlived political group. Morgan was told, he said, by the makers of a TV1 documentary that some Pakeha New Zealand First financial members had called its Maori MPs 'black monkeys'.[45]

Henare provoked anger within the party and the country when he flew to England with his wife and three officials to bring back eleven mokomokai. Cartoonists, letter-writers, editorials and commentators abused Maori generally, not just Henare, as hypocrites, racists, bullies and bludgers. While he did not create racial tension his actions hardened attitudes and provided ammunition for hard-core anti-Maori. As the journalist, Barry Soper, observed in 1996: 'Race relations is a sure winner – not for harmony but for headlines and popularity.'[46]

Rajen Prasad continued to issue regular warnings in the late 1990s about increasing tensions between the majority Pakeha population and Maori, linking them mostly to perceptions about Treaty claims and settlements. He repeated the calls from earlier years for more understanding of what was actually happening, and urged greater emphasis on education.

Speaking in 1998, Prasad said that current projections showed that within fifty years Pakeha would make up about 50 per cent of the population (dropping from 71 per cent), the number of Maori would double and the Asian–Pacific Islands population would treble.

Gregory Fortuin, another race relations conciliator, agreed in 2001 that education is important but said that race relations are fundamentally sound, that the great majority of New Zealanders from different ethnic backgrounds get along with each other very well. Like Latimer, he believes that exaggerated publicity given to racial incidents obscures the reality, that this is a country in which people co-exist remarkably well.

Forty years after the Maori Council was set up Latimer believes it is not possible to make any useful comparisons as to whether race relations are better or worse. 'It's a different country, and we're a different people.'

He points out that Maori and Pakeha have a much greater shared ancestry, and that New Zealand has a significantly different ethnic mix. More immigrants have arrived from Asia and the Pacific. The bigger cities are increasingly more cosmopolitan. New Zealanders travel widely and the country is less insular and narrow in outlook.

Latimer says that sport has changed racial attitudes. 'Maori and Pacific Islanders are admired as leading athletes, rugby players, netballers, golfers – many of them make successful careers from it. Parliament now [2000] has sixteen members who claim Maori ancestry, and some are gaining valuable experience and showing signs of independence of the party system.' Maori corporations and businesses are big contributors to the economy, with well over $10 billion in assets and capital.

He believes that the gaps identified in the Hunn Report still exist, and that some are wider than before. Health, education, housing and employment are still the big issues. Family violence and criminal offending (more than half all those in jail are Maori) are at crisis point. Some politicians are still appealing to race prejudice and Maori leaders have been singled out for attacks, for character assassination. The ACT Party continues to seek the anti-Maori vote by attacking the Treaty process and the National Party made the Treaty an election issue in 2002.[47]

Most people are still misinformed and confused about Treaty issues. Treaty negotiations minister, Margaret Wilson, is well aware of this and intends to give urgency to education programmes to improve understanding of the Treaty.[48]

Latimer supports this but believes it can be successful only with the full cooperation of the mass media. Until newspapers and television accept social responsibility for representing the community as it really is, instead of concentrating on the mad, bad and ugly – because of their entertainment value – sober educational efforts are not likely to be successful, he says.

He objects to the way in which the media focus on Maori enterprises which get into trouble, such as Tainui's financial problems with some of its investments from money received as part of its Treaty settlement. These are given as examples of bad business decisions made by Maori but the same approach is not adopted when other companies, like Air New Zealand, go bust. 'The huge losses of the late 1980s were not described,' he says, 'as Pakeha losses.'

The same point was made by a writer to the editor of the *Sunday Star-Times* (16 September 2001): the writer was waiting for the anti-Maori columnist, Frank Haden, to complain about the shocking standard of Pakeha mismanagement of Air New Zealand.

Latimer says that the Council has been doing its best to promote harmony since 1962. At a human level there is no obstacle to good race relations. 'We're getting close to the time when *all* of us will have some blood or marriage ties with each other.' He says that current estimates indicate that within the next fifty years about one-in-five New Zealanders will be Maori and more than about one-in-eight will be of Pacific Islands origin.

He does not believe that the main strands of Maori culture will disappear. 'Culture,' he says, 'is not a matter of blood, or colour, but of the way we identify with our tupuna, how we look at the past, and decide to live in the present.'

He says he sees himself first as a human being with a tremendous amount in common with all other human beings. He then feels like a member of a whanau, and, also a 'paid-up member of the New Zealand community as someone of both Maori and Pakeha ancestry'.

He has great respect for the courage of many of the early settlers from Europe. 'They took huge risks leaving their homes to come here to start a new life.' He does not believe they wanted to destroy Maori but nor did they make much effort to understand them. 'New Zealanders have no patience when it comes to understanding others, people of different cultures.'

Race relations in the future? He thinks it is a minor miracle that people actually get along as well as they do. 'We've gone a long way to resolving the injustices of the past. The Treaty process is working, slowly, and it can't be stopped. Race relations? They'll take care of themselves.'

Former prime minister Jim Bolger agrees with Latimer. Back in New Zealand in 2002, after finishing his term as ambassador to the United States, Bolger says this is the best period ever for New Zealand to resolve outstanding issues, for creating a better understanding between Maori and Pakeha. 'People *know* more.'

CHAPTER TEN

Reputations

1987–2001

> A man's reputation is not in his own keeping, but lies at the mercy of the profligacy of others. Calumny requires no proof. The throwing out of malicious imputations against any character leaves a stain, which no after refutation can wipe out. To create an unfavourable impression, it is not necessary that certain things should be *true* but that they *have been said*. The imagination is of so delicate a texture that even words wound it.
>
> William Hazlitt, 'Characteristics'[1]

> I've often felt like tossing it all in – who needs this sort of abuse, aggravation? But what was it all about? Where were all these attacks coming from? Mostly from people who knew nothing about what I was trying to do, who wanted the Treaty scrapped, wanted all the Maori nonsense about grievances to go away.
>
> Sir Graham Latimer, 1995,
> responding to calls for his dismissal as Maori Council president

FOR LATIMER, THE 1990S WERE TRAUMATIC. AS MAORI COUNCIL president, chairman and spokesman he was the first target for all those who resented the new directions forced by court decisions. Then, eight years after the Council's Court of Appeal triumph in 1987, he felt the full force of all the cumulative hostility.

In 1995, Latimer was fined $16,000 for negligently filing false tax returns and failing to register for Goods and Services Tax (GST). Opponents demanded that he be stripped of his knighthood. The *National Business Review* (NBR), a weekly magazine, launched a sustained campaign to have him forced out of public affairs. Three northern National MPs, all Pakeha, declared him unfit to be a Maori leader.

During the same year the National government's attempt to impose a financial cap on Treaty claims led to angry demonstrations, land occupations, arson and roadblocks. All the usual celebrities heightened the nation's blood pressure. News media coverage suggested civil war was just around the corner. The substantial Treaty gains made since 1987 were temporarily forgotten. To those who got most of their information from the six o'clock television news and newspaper headlines, Latimer's reputation and career appeared to be in shreds.

In the previous few years the political scene had changed dramatically and so had Latimer's life. After being treated with indifference by all governments since 1962 the Council had become a major force in national policy making and Latimer's position as president was transformed. His personal opinions, strategies, negotiating skills, business experience, attitudes toward the Treaty, knowledge of the ways of politicians and bureaucrats, suddenly had new significance.

Individuals and pressure groups courted him while others objected to his perceived role as a conduit for Maori opinion and as a negotiator for Maori – ministers wanted to deal, for convenience, with only one organisation, the Council. His critics, competitors and enemies multiplied rapidly as his position became pivotal.

Till 1987 Latimer had not been well-known to the general public. He was, however, extremely well-known within Maori communities. He had a presence on marae where, for thirty years, he had attended hui and tangi and was often called Te Rima Ratima rather than Graham Latimer. In the Tai Tokerau he was acknowledged to be a strong advocate for the north, with unequalled political connections in Wellington.

Within the higher ranks of the National Party he was a familiar figure, seen as an astute operator, not likely to rock the boat, and useful as a spokesperson in a party with a long record of distancing itself from Maori issues. To others, including National's northern MPs (John Banks, John Carter and Ross Meurant), he represented Maori interests they angrily opposed for political advantage.

Latimer's position as president of the country's only statutory pan-Maori body had been disputed for many years but this had never been an issue of public concern – the arguments took place within Maori communities, at marae level, district councils and trust boards and among some university academics. While he was respected for helping to keep the Council alive, opponents criticised him for failing to win greater self-determination for Maori.

He did not have a charismatic persona, instantly recognisable on television. He was not a celebrity. Few of the many organisations he worked with for Maori generated headlines. He did not demonstrate yearly at Waitangi, but sat with dignitaries while some of his friends, relatives and enemies angrily abused the establishment for oppressing Maori, and him, for sitting with them.

Many Maori, particularly those in urban areas, were not even aware of the Council's existence or its purposes. The best-known Maori were politicians and entertainers.

Winston Peters had achieved instant star status by attacking and diminishing the Department of Maori Affairs in the 1980s. Eva Rickard was up there for her vibrant personality, her occupation of the Raglan golf course, and her marches on Waitangi. Dame Whina Cooper had been dubbed Mother of the Nation by the Maori Women's Welfare League and made so by the news media, delighted to have finally found a friendly Maori face. Howard Morrison and Billy T James, highly successful entertainers, became household names, though both were under-rated for the contribution they made to Maori. Kiri Te Kanawa was everyone's favourite, representing New Zealand on the world stage.

Iwi leaders like Sir Robert Mahuta and Sir Tipene O'Regan spoke for Tainui and Ngai Tahu but did not have a national voice, or aspire to one. They were heavily involved in developing their own Treaty claims and building new iwi bodies to promote their people.

By 1995 Latimer had accumulated an imposing array of opponents. Politicians in both major parties were angry and frustrated because he successfully used courts to force them to do things they did not want to do: their resentment was palpable. Some claimants to the Waitangi Tribunal thought his position as chairman of the Crown Forest Rental Trust gave him too much power over the allocation of resources to research their claims, and accused him of favouritism.

His support for the Sealord fisheries deal was considered by many influential Maori to be an abuse of his authority as Council president, unsanctioned by Maori protocol or by legal precedent. Conflict within the Waitangi Fisheries Commission, set up to manage the new resources, pitted him directly against the chairman, Sir Tipene O'Regan. At stake was his pan-Maori vision as opposed to Sir Tipene's tribal weighting. He felt no great threat from the urban Maori groups. He always believed that a distribution system had to be fair to all Maori in order to be durable.

Banks, Carter and Meurant attacked Latimer continually, singly or collectively, for his leadership of the Tai Tokerau Maori Trust Board, his initiative in buying the Waitangi Hotel (Banks wanted to buy it personally), and his approach to a long-running controversy over a Maori claim to land owned by Alan Titford north of Dargaville. Carter asked the Serious Fraud Office to investigate Latimer and the Tai Tokerau Maori Trust Board. The fraud office cleared both.

He was strongly criticised for floating the idea of a Maori political party to take advantage of the new MMP electoral system. The charge was separatism, apartheid.

Jim Bolger tried to diminish the importance of the Maori Council, saying it was not representative and suggested that a new organisation was needed to reflect the views of all Maori.

The Department of Maori Affairs (later, Te Puni Kokiri), became increasingly hostile. Many senior staff wanted to represent Maori, as well as being the servants of their minister and the minister's party policies – a classic conflict of interest. Some had always resented the Council as a competitor, but, because the Department managed all the resources, the staff had not felt overly threatened till, after 1987, the Council became the prime adviser to government on what Maori wanted or would settle for.

Dr Ranginui Walker continued to be one of Latimer's most outspoken critics and condemned Latimer's involvement in the Sealord fisheries deal, arguing validly that nobody, traditionally, had the right to speak for Maori on such an issue.[2] Latimer agreed in theory, but with the other three negotiators felt that this was a once-only chance to give Maori a major stake, then about $200 million, in the fishing industry. He saw it as a practical compromise. (Walker has since modified his criticism, accepting that Latimer's negotiating skills gained a substantial economic resource for Maori.)[3]

In a *Metro* article in 1994 Walker called Latimer a political survivor, a man of 'humble' origins who learned how to use the system and became one of the first members of the 'brown table'. He said that Latimer had benefited personally when he persuaded the Muldoon government to give the Council sufficient funds to 'run a secretariat' and then paid 'himself an honorarium of $30,000'. Walker, who was a Council member at the time, says Latimer was criticised by district councils which 'thought the money should have been devolved to the grassroots'.[4] Dr Walker said that when he was a member he had tried to make the Maori Council more democratic but had been stopped by Latimer and the Council's conservative rural rump.[5]

He conceded that Latimer was 'often placed in the invidious position of having to guarantee overdrafts on the Maori Council's bank account for the payment of wages, travel and office overheads, pending the receipt of the government grant'.[6]

Shortly after Latimer's 1995 tax conviction, Dr Walker told Kim Hill on Radio New Zealand that Latimer was a 'false leader', unable and unwilling to fulfil the aspirations of Maori. When Kim Hill asked him whether Latimer treated the Council like a private club he said 'Oh, yes.' Walker has, however, also stated firmly and repeatedly that Latimer sincerely believes that he has acted in what he sees as the best interests of Maoridom. And: 'I like the man.'[7]

Latimer has rarely, if ever, responded to Walker's attacks, including the $30,000 honorarium charge. 'Rangi is family and I don't argue with family in public.'

Within the National Party, Winston Peters emerged as Latimer's main opponent. They held diametrically opposed views on the Waitangi Tribunal and the Treaty. Peters spoke against the Waitangi Tribunal's power being extended to cover claims from 1840, wanted it to be downgraded to little more than a research unit and said at the party's 1988 annual conference that the Treaty was long past its use-by date.[8]

Latimer saw the stand by Peters as a betrayal of legitimate Maori interests, and a move to gain personal popularity with the wider electorate. Latimer: 'Peters had stardust in his eyes and was all ego, in it for himself.' Though Bolger was unhappy about many of the implications of Treaty issues he supported Latimer and tried to appease conference delegates by passing a remit calling for all land and fisheries claims to be resolved within ten years. Peters resented Latimer's easy relationship with National's leaders, and his access to Labour cabinet ministers between 1984 and 1990. In political circles they were seen as enemies, though in the same party. When Peters, as minister of Maori affairs, said it was National's policy to abolish the mandatory powers of the Waitangi Tribunal with regard to claims over state-owned enterprises, Latimer threatened legal action against the Crown if it tried to do so.

Peters attacked Latimer's involvement in the Quality Inns deal (1991), which gave a number of Maori groups a big stake in the tourism industry. He raised legal issues and tried to present it as a scandal. (Peters is still angry about the deal today, 2002. He claims that if Latimer had only been willing to take advice Maori would now own the whole hotel chain – a view Latimer rejects.)[9]

When the personal and political relationship between Peters and Bolger broke down in 1991 Bolger sought and received Latimer's support in sacking Peters from his Cabinet. Peters believes that Latimer was directly responsible. Latimer had already publicly suggested that Bolger take over the portfolio of Maori Affairs because, he said, Maori were losing out as a result of the animosity between Bolger and Peters. Also, he said, the public thought Peters was belittling Bolger by his constant attacks on government policies – necessary for Peters if he was to maintain his personal popularity as spokesman for the people supporting his views.

Other voices offered contrasting perspectives on Latimer during the 1980s and 1990s. To those like Judge Durie and Justice Paul Temm, involved in Treaty claims, Latimer was respected for his efforts to set up the Waitangi Tribunal, to have its scope extended and its membership increased, and, as a founding member, to help develop Treaty principles.

Wira Gardiner said during the early 1990s that Latimer was one of the most important Maori leaders: 'He's taken advantage of opportunities and he's succeeded where others haven't acted.' Gardiner, former chief executive officer of Te Puni Kokiri and now Maori vice-president of the National Party, said Latimer was not afraid of failure, has the political experience to know when to try something, and has 'an impeccable capacity for opportunism, is a supreme optimist, and has been the driving force behind numerous developments'.[10]

Former race relations conciliator, Wally Hirsh, saw Latimer as a leader trying to bridge the gap between older leaders like Sir James Henare and younger, impatient radicals who provoked the non-Maori community with their angry rhetoric. He commented in 1992 that Latimer was more aggressive than earlier leaders, that he was a 'risk-taker' and that he wanted to see things happen in his own lifetime, but thought that was possible by working within the established system.[11]

Sir Henare Ngata, one of the Maori Council's leading members, praised Latimer's cumulative efforts, when interviewed in 1992 for this book. Ngata admired Latimer's ability to focus on essentials and not get tied up with details. He was impressed with his remarkable memory: 'Emily took prodigious notes but Graham just listened.'[12]

Ngata said Latimer 'always had an easy relationship with Pakeha and was able to get to know them far more quickly than I could'. Ngata was not aware that Latimer had been brought up more by his Pakeha mother and her family than by his Maori relatives.[13]

Dr Peter Tapsell, when MP for Eastern Maori, in 1993, said that Latimer had 'done as well as he could' considering the Council's weakness as an organisation. That, however, was not a great deal, he said, pointing to the huge gaps which still existed between Maori and the rest of the community in education, health, employment and housing.[14]

Tapsell agreed that Latimer's independent style as president had been a great strength. 'If he'd relied on consensus nothing would have been achieved. He had to do it on his own, even if it was not in line with traditional methods.' He had been able to maintain his position, however, because his competition on the Council was made up of so many 'lightweight' members.[15]

An argument developed when Dame Whina Cooper died in 1994, aged ninety-eight, after publicly telling Latimer to carry on her work for Maoridom, an action seen as passing on the 'mantle' of leadership that had been awarded to her by the news media. They were distantly related. Latimer was also aware of the help his own father had given her when she first arrived in Auckland in the late 1940s. When his father died in 1965 he passed on to her his 'mantle'.

Dame Whina's reputation was ambiguous. Particularly in her later years the news media presented her as a courageous fighter for unity between Maori and Pakeha, reprimanding noisy radicals, and loved by all. Not quite so. She was also viewed by some as arrogant, always interfering with the work of others and wanting to dominate everybody.

An *Evening Post* editorial writer, who may not have known Dame Whina personally, said Latimer was an 'odd choice' as her successor because he was 'seen not only as politically tainted' but had been at the 'centre of some of Maoridom's unspectacular financial investments'.[16] Dover Samuels, not then a Labour minister nor yet a figure with a public history, questioned Dame Whina's state of mind during her final illness, and said such a mantle had to be earned rather than accepted in 'some de facto way'. An angry Winston Peters called it a stunt.[17]

Some claimed there was no such mantle, that this was the last theatrical performance of a great actress. Latimer was, however, not willing to reject Dame Whina's symbolic gesture. She had made a career of being great during the last forty years of her long life and had tried to do her best for Maori. Defying the law, he killed a protected kereru and took it to her in hospital during her last illness, as a traditional gift to a dying leader. He said he would respect her call but did not think he could 'fill her boots'.

When Latimer's reputation became a public issue in 1995, Judge Lindsay Moore made it clear that the offences were not tax evasion but negligence, adding that the adverse publicity and 'loss of mana' was part of the real penalty.

Just how much mana was lost and in whose eyes are still open questions. David Baragwanath QC, representing Latimer in court, stressed that tax evasion was not involved and there had been no allegations of dishonesty. He said that the charges related to returns from 1988 to

1992, and had coincided with a period of intense involvement by Latimer in negotiations over state asset sales and fisheries negotiations.

Latimer believed he had been entitled to claim much of the money involved as reimbursement for the income he had lost, while being away from his farm, spending time on Maori issues. Judge Moore accepted that Latimer was under enormous pressure but said that he could not ignore the amount of money involved.

Most news reports of the case later referred to false returns, tax convictions and tax offences, without mentioning that no tax evasion was involved, that there had been no charges of dishonesty. Most of those who read about the case were left with the incorrect impression that Latimer was guilty of deliberate tax fraud.

Even before Judge Moore gave his decision, calls came for Latimer to resign from the Maori Council and other organisations.

Ross Meurant, then Hobson MP and leader of the recently formed Right of Centre Party, said the only honourable thing for him to do was resign. Meurant had been elected as a National MP, then resigned and set up his own party without going back to the electorate for a new mandate. (He has since lost both seat and party.)

John Carter, Bay of Islands MP, who was later forced to resign as National's senior whip in Parliament following his impersonation of a Maori on talkback radio, raised the question of Latimer's knighthood (awarded in 1980), and suggested that he take 'the appropriate action' because the 'offences are very serious'.

John Banks, MP for Whangarei, also demanded that the prime minister withdraw Latimer's knighthood. When Bolger did not do so, Banks said that he, personally, had stripped away the honour on his talkback show, which he named the 'People's Parliament'. Banks, then minister of tourism, no longer held any cabinet position by the end of the following year, described himself as an independent National MP, and left national politics at the end of 1999. He is now Mayor of Auckland City.

Peters, who had formed the New Zealand First Party, said Latimer should step down from all his positions. He said Latimer had been propped up by the National government for a number of years 'either out of naivety or a contempt for Maori'.

He said then and later that Latimer had come 'ill-equipped for the job [as president of the Maori Council] and had stayed far too long'. He claimed that Latimer had not encouraged young leaders to gain experience, to replace him in the future, particularly in Te Tai Tokerau (Northland) — that he did not want any challenges to his position or authority.[18] (Peters' political party fragmented after he went into coalition with National following the 1996 general election, but re-emerged strongly in 2002.)

Tau Henare, Northern Maori MP at the time, and a member of New Zealand First, joined the attack and agreed with Peters that Latimer should pull out of public life, and make more space for new, young leaders like himself. Henare later left New Zealand First, formed his own small Maori party with other dissident MPs, allied them with the National government of the late 1990s, and finally lost both his position and his party. In 1999, he said that older leaders were too concerned with Treaty settlements and grievances and should step aside for a 'new generation' of Maori. (He is now a member of the National Party, along with Latimer, and stood unsuccessfully for the Te Atatu seat in the 2002 elections.)

The most sustained news media attack on Latimer came in August 1995 from the NBR. Its billboard spelt out the message in large bold capital letters: 'Sir Graham Latimer: Public's Verdict Is In'. Inside, in smaller letters, the paper said that an NBR–Consultus survey revealed that '56 per cent of New Zealanders' polled wanted his knighthood stripped from him. Only 26 per cent opposed his losing his knighthood, while 18 per cent did not know. The paper interpreted this to mean that a majority of New Zealanders wanted the knighthood removed — on the basis of the opinion of 420 people, out of 750, questioned by its own polling organisation.[19]

In the accompanying stories the headlines said it all: 'The knight in tarnished armour'; 'Judge said Latimer at fault — not his accountants'; 'A matter of HONOUR'; 'dear Prime Minister, sack Sir Graham'; 'SAVED — by the old-boy network'; and 'Prime Minister alone decides whether to strip honours'. The editorial continued the theme: 'Why Honour is at Stake'.[20]

The paper's attack included criticisms, many anonymous, from his political enemies and rivals, accusations of mismanagement of trust board resources, and allegations of commercial incompetence, and unpredictability.

While Latimer was used to savage headlines he believed the NBR had planned a king-hit, a killer-blow that would shame and humiliate him so deeply that he would retreat back to his farm. He wondered why the magazine would go to the trouble. Who would benefit?

In a series of articles, journalist Fran O'Sullivan recalled the 'grim saga' she described as the 'Quality Inns Fiasco', which pitted Peters against Latimer 'in a vicious row', that led to the sacking of Peters from Cabinet. O'Sullivan admitted that the deal finally worked out successfully.[21]

Latimer, commenting today, says that the hotel chain now has more than $60 million in assets, about one-third owned by Maori investors. He considers it an extremely successful investment, his only reservation being about the way some of the profits are channelled through the office of the Maori Trustee. His answer to O'Sullivan's premature rush to judgment in 1995: 'A bad investment? The facts speak for themselves. She damned us too soon. I wonder why.'

O'Sullivan said that, in 1993, the Maori Council was 'technically insolvent' because it had gone into debt to fund early Waitangi fisheries law suits. This problem was resolved by a Crown payout but, she added, Ngai Tahu (Sir Tipene O'Regan) was unhappy about not being able to get a detailed breakdown of the way in which this money was used by the Maori Council, and Latimer.

Latimer says that the court action the Council had taken in 1987 had made possible further negotiations with the government, which led finally to the Sealord deal, and the creation of assets now valued at about $1 billion. The bulk of the money provided by the government paid the legal costs of all claimants. 'The Council had to go into debt, to become "technically insolvent", because that was the only way we could get the government to meet its Treaty obligations. Nobody is complaining now.'

O'Sullivan said that the Tai Tokerau Maori Trust Board was the subject of a special Audit Office review after a 'wrangle' over 'illegal' special payments made by the Board to Latimer and other members. The Board had paid more for travel and expenses, related to the purchase of the Waitangi Hotel, than it was authorised to make without special permission from the minister of Maori affairs. That permission was later given by the then minister, Doug Kidd, who said that payments would have been approved anyway, if the normal procedures had been followed.

Latimer responds today by saying that the regulations governing the Maori Trust Board expenditure are restrictive and cumbersome. 'Yes, we should have got permission first, but we were fully involved in negotiating for the Board, and we have a very small staff. The Board did nothing illegal and it was all approved. It wasn't a big deal, but some people wanted to make political capital out of it.'

O'Sullivan then criticised the Maori Trust Board's management of the Waitangi Hotel, which had many financial and organisational problems. The Board had bought it for just $600,000 in 1989–1990, knowing that a major capital input was needed. O'Sullivan quoted extensively from a 'secret' Ernst and Young report that raised questions about the Hotel's ability to survive, then added that 'after considerable doubts about the hotel's future, CDL [City Development Ltd] later bought in'.

Latimer agrees that the Board had great difficulty getting the hotel re-started after the Tourist Hotel Corporation sold it so cheaply, reflecting its condition. 'We believed it was a wonderful site at Waitangi, near the Treaty House and the marae. For the Board, for Tai Tokerau, it was more than a hotel. The site is part of our history. We were willing to go to a lot of trouble to hold on to it.'

And they did. In 2002 the hotel is valued at over $11 million and the Maori Trust Board still holds 51 per cent of the shares. 'Our biggest mistake,' says Latimer, 'was to try to actually run it ourselves. We didn't have the skills. Today it is our biggest single asset.'

He makes no apologies for their problems with the hotel, which had made a profit only once in the previous thirty-two years when it was run by a government corporation. 'We were under-funded, and the hotel industry is pretty fickle. Many companies with much more experience and money than we had have gone bust. Today it's part of the Copthorne Hotel chain [the former Quality Inns group] and is going extremely well.'

Latimer says that during much of the 1990s he and the Board were under continual attack by Carter, Banks and Meurant. 'You don't have to be guilty of anything to be defamed,' he says. 'You only have to be charged. And that's what happened with the enquiry. It was a typical smear campaign.' O'Sullivan also criticised Latimer's involvement with Maori International, a company set up to promote economic development, particularly in tourism, claiming it had made 'huge' losses in a fisheries deal. Latimer agrees that Maori International had a rocky start but says that it later played an important role in acquiring a stake for Maori in tourism through the Quality Inns deal. It has been making a modest profit for years and was still a useful instrument for Maori.

O'Sullivan repeated official and iwi-based criticism of the Crown Forest Rental Trust's performance in making money available for Waitangi Tribunal claimants to research their cases. She said some iwi doubted that money was being distributed fairly because there was no public breakdown of the amounts allocated. She also reported concerns by the Treasury and the National minister of finance, Bill Birch, that trustees' fees had the 'appearance of excess'. She said that some concern had been expressed at the slowness of the claims process, that only one had been made to the Waitangi Tribunal in the first four years of the Trust's existence.[22]

Latimer's answer to the unfairness claim is to point to the Trust's membership, which is determined by the government. Whenever decisions had to be made that could have involved a conflict of interest he absented himself. The slowness of the whole settlement process was, he says, the result of the government's own actions, and its demands for exhaustive detail supporting every aspect of every claim.

O'Sullivan's verdict on Latimer: 'The overall picture is of a dealmaker out of his depth in chairing important bodies.' She conceded that there were balancing factors in his business records. Some companies with which he was involved were doing very well, and he had played an 'adept hand, aided by Queen's Counsel David Baragwanath and Sian Elias, in successfully mounting legal challenges to the

Crown, preventing it from disposing of state assets until Treaty of Waitangi claims are heard'.

O'Sullivan said Latimer was protected by friends in high places, saved by the old-boy network, a 'political protection racket that goes all the way to the top of the Beehive'. She said that Bolger was responsible for not stripping Latimer of his knighthood, that he was ignoring serious allegations and that it was 'scandalous' he had survived with his title intact.

In an editorial in the same issue as O'Sullivan's articles, the NBR said that New Zealand's reputation as the 'least corrupt country in the world to do business in' was at risk unless Bolger took away Latimer's knighthood. 'Sir Graham's past reputation in Maoridom cannot be used as a shield to protect him from the consequences of his wrongdoing. The country's world standing should not be sacrificed on the PC [politically correct] altar of being victim to the double standards of ethnic patronage.'

O'Sullivan also mentioned that Latimer had a Totalisator Agency Board (TAB) account which amounted, over four years (1988 to 1992), to just under $80,000 – thus giving the impression that he was a big-time gambler with lots of money.[23] Latimer's response: 'Yes, I've been betting on horses for much of my life. That's not a secret, not a crime. But I've never spent a lot of money gambling. Emily and I used the TAB account like a bank. We could take cash out whenever we needed it. This was before it was possible to get money at any time through shops, using EFTPOS cards. After all the publicity given to our case the TAB stopped the use of accounts in that way.' And he still bets.

Latimer is angry that these articles presented him as a millionaire living a high life on the back of Maori claims. Today, he and Lady Emily own a farm of about 240 acres, land originally owned by his grandfather and father. This is their main asset, worth an estimated $750,000 at current market prices. It is also all that both of them own after working for sixty years. 'If we're millionaires,' he says, 'someone must be using a new definition.' They also have four race-horses, which they list as liabilities rather than assets.

Latimer says he has never been a 'real race-horse follower', and rarely went to race-courses. He is more interested in numbers, odds, probabilities. Former Archbishop Sir Paul Reeves comments: 'I've often seen Graham in church looking at the hymn numbers posted for the day and I've known he's almost certainly computing the odds for the next race meeting.'[24]

The *NBR*'s campaign of character assassination failed but articles attacking Latimer continued. In 1997 O'Sullivan predicted that Latimer's days as the most powerful kaumatua in the north were coming to an end. 'The government is preparing to bite the bullet on some of Sir Graham's high-profile appointments as they come up for renewal.' She said that the return of Winston Peters to power in the new coalition government 'has put the skids under the Maori leader'.[25] (Instead, Peters was sacked as National's coalition partner by Jenny Shipley after she replaced Jim Bolger as prime minister.)

The anonymous sources of information and opinion the *NBR* used have never been revealed but some were Latimer's opponents in the Waitangi Fisheries Commission and the Treaty Tribes Coalition. If the campaign had been successful then the main opponent of a coastline-based allocation would have been removed from the Commission, and Sir Tipene O'Regan's position would have been strengthened. An attempt was made within the Commission to have Latimer, then deputy-chairman, removed, according to one of O'Sullivan's sources, but was not supported.[26]

Latimer was not the *NBR*'s only target. The weekly has also published many articles on Donna Hall, a lawyer heavily involved in Treaty and fisheries issues, and her husband, Justice Durie. Libel suits have been filed and are still before the courts.

The Inland Revenue Department (IRD) had not finished with Latimer, charging him again, in 1997, over an issue that involved a technical question of whether some money from the Copthorne Hotel chain was loans or income. The case was finally dropped in 1999 but not before Latimer's reputation was again damaged, simply because his tax returns were being questioned for a second time.

Latimer told the *Sunday Star-Times* in 1999 that he felt the IRD 'really wanted to get me for some reason. They failed in the first place but they keep on coming back'. He said that every cheque he received was banked: 'Now if I was trying to hide anything I would try to move away from banks.'[27]

His legal costs for the two IRD cases were $145,000, and he still (in 2002) owes $30,000 to his lawyers.

He agrees with criticisms that the IRD, during the 1990s, developed a culture of vindictiveness, and believes that a number of Maori leaders have been 'picked on'. He has no proof of a conspiracy and wants to believe none was involved. However, he still has doubts about why the IRD pursued him and the way in which it pursued him over an extended period of five years. He compares this with the IRD's reluctance to investigate some of the country's biggest companies accused in the Wine Box inquiry of tax evasion during the mid-1990s (not just negligence in filing returns) involving many millions of dollars.

He believes that his public reputation has been damaged, solely because of the nature of the charges and the massive publicity they were given. He accepts Judge Moore's view that in 'his case, far more than most, the adverse publicity and loss of mana is both part of the real penalty and one of the prices to be paid for major involvement in public life'.

How much, if any, mana he has lost cannot be quantified or assessed with any certainty. He received continual expressions of public confidence in the months and years that followed the court case. He kept all his important elected positions. He is still president of the New Zealand Maori Council. He was again chosen (in 2000) for the eighth time in succession to be chairman of the Tai Tokerau District Maori Council.

He is still chairman of the Crown Forest Rental Trust and the Tai Tokerau Maori Trust Board, still a respected Anglican layman. Sir Paul Reeves holds him in high regard and considers he has made a substantial contribution to the wellbeing of Maori.

He is still a knight. Jim Bolger saw no reason to withdraw the honour. Bolger says today: 'I never gave it a moment's serious thought.' He did not feel under any pressure, in spite of the demands of a few of his party colleagues. 'Sir Graham had already earned his award for his great services to Maoridom and to the country.'[28]

Bolger had cooperated with Latimer on all issues involving Maori development, negotiations with the Crown and National Party matters. He was not surprised that Latimer continued to hold the respect of so many organisations and of the public. 'He brought a distinctive style to his role, and he was completely consistent in his desire to carry forward the hopes of Maoridom as he interpreted them.'[29]

Bolger also praises Latimer's skill as a negotiator, particularly during the Sealord fisheries deal in 1992, when totally conflicting principles and attitudes had to be reconciled in an agreement which, at first, seemed to please nobody. Bolger: 'He had endless discussions with his own people. The status quo was not acceptable. Change was inevitable. And so was the criticism he received.' Bolger says that during all that turbulence Latimer displayed great wisdom at crucial times. He was, he says, the only person with pan-Maori status, the only one seeking an agreement to benefit all Maori.[30]

Bolger also admires Latimer's flexibility: 'When he came to the negotiating table he wasn't confined to a particular grand strategy. He knew exactly where he was going but was prepared to consider each proposal or policy as it came. He was prepared to discuss them all.'[31]

Sir Henare Ngata, who worked closely with Latimer on the Maori Council for twenty years, still holds him in high regard and considers him one of Maoridom's outstanding leaders.

Sir Geoffrey Palmer, commenting on the constitutional consequences of Latimer's actions as head of the Maori Council, describes him as a 'very skilled negotiator' who has 'delivered a great deal for Maori'.[32]

Current leaders such as Prime Minister Helen Clark regularly discuss policy issues with Latimer, seeing him as one of the two or three most experienced Maori leaders in the country.

Shane Jones, a Waitangi Fisheries Commission member (and now chairman), said in 1995 that he could see no point in reviewing Latimer's knighthood. Jones cannot understand why Latimer was 'pursued', believing that any problems could easily have been settled by discussion with accountants. To him it is a 'lingering mystery'.[33]

Jones believes there was only a 'modest' impact on Latimer's reputation and never saw the whole episode as undermining his status as a Maori leader. Many Maori saw it as an example of 'dirty pool' and reinforced their belief that their leaders needed a hide as thick as a puriri tree.

Jones praised Latimer's efforts in securing the Sealord fisheries deal and says today that the economic base provided by fisheries is of immense importance to Maori.

Many senior kaumatua from leading iwi assured Latimer of their continuing support. Matiu Rata, a leading advocate of Muriwhenua claims in the 1990s, said that Latimer's tax offences were not wilful or deliberate but matters of a technical nature. Rata, who had also been fined on tax charges, said: 'He will survive this. Sir Graham is never one to run away from a battle. He is also not a person who would wilfully mislead the exchequer.'[34]

A few Maori leaders in Northland misread the mood among Maori and called for his resignation as chairman of the Tai Tokerau Maori Trust Board. One, Kevin Prime, of Ngati Hine, sympathised with Latimer and praised his past efforts but said that the Board's credibility would suffer if he remained.[35] Latimer refused to resign and retained the support of Board members and the great majority of Maori attending a hui which discussed his position. Latimer: 'If you're going to let that type of blip stifle you, then you should never have been there in the first place.'

Richard Prebble considers Latimer a tough and successful negotiator, taking full advantage of the leverage given by court decisions against his Labour government in the late 1980s. He sympathises with Latimer's problems in coping with the demands of Maori leadership and the demands made on him by his extended family responsibili-ties. Echoing other politicians, Prebble believes Latimer could have had a much happier life by giving up his Maori Council presidency many years ago.[36]

High Court judge Eddie Durie says Latimer is one of the last of an older group of leaders who put the interests of Maoridom first: 'He has always worked for Maori interests; not for his own, or for any district or group.' Durie admires his integrity, pragmatism, clarity of thought, and considers his commitment to principles is his major characteristic. Durie also acknowledges Latimer's willingness to compromise when he has to, to make progress: 'But everyone knew exactly what it was he stood for'. He never 'flinched from following his principles or beliefs'.[37]

Durie describes him as 'our most outstanding Maori leader' and says he has a 'deep understanding of traditional Maori thinking'. Commenting in 2001, he said that too much emphasis is placed by new younger leaders on commercialism, on the management of resources.[38]

Durie ranks Latimer, in terms of importance, with early leaders like Ngata. Each in his own time did what he considered necessary. Both took a full part in what many people see as the dirty business of politics, accepting what they believed was unavoidable, and biding their time till they could change policies. He sees the 1987 Court of Appeal case, so strongly advocated by Latimer, as the 'key decision in opening the way ahead'.

Dr Hohepa, chairman of the Maori Language Commission, has not changed his view of Latimer over recent years, though he believes that the IRD charges have damaged his reputation in some quarters. All Maori leaders need good accountants, he says. 'He's still Maoridom's most unusual leader,' he says, 'and I have great respect for him, and for what he's done.'[39]

Titewhai Harawira, one of the first women members of the Maori Council in the 1970s, says Latimer has 'done a good job' in spite of the 'pain and suffering' that came with his position. 'He had to take the blame for all sorts of things. He took a lot of criticism, particularly from Maori, and had to learn to roll with it.' Harawira believes he still has a lot to contribute and should continue as a leader, though she puts her energies into more direct, confrontational action.[40]

Latimer says he knows he is regarded with suspicion and doubt by some Maori just because he is president of a statutory body set up by a Pakeha Parliament. Maori hold a deepseated belief that governments, meaning the Crown, cannot be trusted because of their long record of broken promises. Therefore, anyone who cooperates with them is automatically suspect, a collaborator.

To these people Latimer is tainted by politics. To deal with politicians, to strike deals, to negotiate for Maori, he has to some extent become similar to them – has become a politician himself. Latimer: 'We all know the standing of politicians in the community, just a bit higher than used car salesmen, on about the same level as journalists.' (The October 2001 *Readers' Digest* poll of the trust accorded New Zealand's professions and occupations places politicians twenty-fifth out of twenty-five. Journalists ranked twenty-third.)

Hohepa, as the head of a state agency, is also familiar with this problem, but his elders tell him, when he goes home to the Hokianga, that he still 'doesn't have the stench of government on him'. So far, he says.

Sir Paul Reeves acknowledges the dilemma Latimer and other Maori leaders face in entering the snakepit of politics. 'Graham is not noble,' he says, comparing him with the late Sir James Henare, a scholar, a distinguished public servant, a man steeped in tradition and protocol – a very gentle person who stood, reluctantly, for Parliament as a National candidate and who was almost certainly relieved when he was not elected. 'But', says Sir Paul, 'Graham is a totally practical man. He is needed because he gets things done.'[41]

Shane Jones does not believe it is useful to make comparisons, to compare Latimer with Henare: 'Politics in New Zealand is a mad scramble for resources. It takes place in the trenches, not on mountains. Sir Graham is an independent thinker who saw his chance to help Maori and seized it ... . At the same time he's expected to play the statesman's role. Leadership isn't a question of nobility.'[42]

Winston Peters remains implacably opposed to Latimer. In an interview for this book he said Latimer had 'conspired' against him when, as minister of Maori affairs in 1991, Peters tried to introduce reforms in health, education and employment. Peters said he tried to change National Party policy on Maori issues but was forced out by Latimer. 'He has greatly disadvantaged the Maori people.'[43]

He argues that the Maori Council has not lived up to its potential under Latimer's leadership, that it has been a disaster. He did not know what its purpose was any more. He is angry that the Council had not supported his efforts to exercise greater control over immigration policy – 'to stop so many new people arriving when Maori are still faced with so many problems'.

He still criticises Latimer's advocacy of the Treaty, which he calls Maoridom's greatest handicap today: 'Treaty issues are forcing Maori to focus their energies back to 1840 instead of concentrating on the real things they need to deal with. All the emphasis on the Treaty is doing is to benefit the elite, not the people, Treaty policies are a rollercoaster to failure.'[44]

He says that Latimer 'hasn't been able to overcome feelings of jealousy and envy of other Maori who have been successful'.[45]

Asked whether he could say anything in Latimer's favour Peters said immediately: 'Yes. He's an excellent husband, a great father – and has few vices, except, perhaps, race-horses. Emily has been an absolute rock for him.'[46]

Latimer is very conscious of the perception that he has become a politician, that he lobbies ministers and pressure groups, that he sups at the same table as the devil, runs with wolves. Some politicians call him the 'fox'. He knows that every decision he makes, every opinion he expresses, is likely to be more criticised than praised: 'Being disliked or criticised is part of the price you pay if you want to change things.'

He deliberately maintained good working relationships with as many politicians as he could – Geoffrey Palmer, Mike Moore, Helen Clark, Jim Bolger, Jenny Shipley – because he saw no sense in alienating the powerful. He believes he has to work with everyone. Liking or disliking them has nothing to do with it.

During forty-six years as a representative of Maori groups, most of it at national level, he has worked with ten prime ministers, nine ministers of Maori affairs, six secretaries of Maori affairs, a few hundred cabinet ministers, even more members of Parliament, mayors and local body officers, heads of state departments and other officials.

He admired and respected many of them but realised early in his career that all were bound within their own organisations, their own parties and within their own views of what was possible. And, he reminds his critics and supporters, politics is the art of the possible. The alternative to being part of that political scene was to stand on the high ground and make grand pronouncements, and to do nothing about them – to remain clean, and noble, and a failure.

His reputation in business and as an administrator of companies and trust boards has survived the savage attacks of the 1990s. He admits he has taken on too many tasks and commitments and has not always given sufficient energy to each. He rationalises this by saying that at the time he felt he had to give the support of the Council presidency to some of them.

His reputation as a Maori and as an appropriate person to be a national spokesperson is still being debated, raising fundamental questions about what it means to be Maori at the beginning of the twenty-first century.

As a national Maori leader he is the first of his kind. Though he was the third person to be Maori Council president he was the only one with the time and experience to develop the skills needed to be a national leader. His significance comes from his revolutionary use of the courts from 1987 onward to force governments to recognise the legal and constitutional authority of the Treaty. He brought Treaty issues to the fore when he changed New Zealand's political equilibrium by focusing on *how* past injustices could be remedied and not on *whether* they should be remedied.

He is not particularly interested in how he will be judged in the future. Over the last forty years he has seen reputations flame and flicker, and then blaze again with the fashions of the day. He would rather be respected than not, but the person he has to live with is himself, not the public or his critics.

Interviewed in 1999 about his reaction to the abuse he had received over the years he said that he would have sunk from sight long ago if he had taken his critics to heart. His father had told him that so long as he could sleep contentedly at night he had nothing to worry about. He had been sleeping well, he said. Today, in 2002, he still sleeps well.

Epilogue
2002

SIR GRAHAM NOW LIVES WITH LADY EMILY ON FAMILY LAND NEAR KAITAIA.
The Latimers had sold their first farm at Tinopai after eighteen years and bought a bigger property at Taipuha, still in the Kaipara, in 1979. After the court judgment in 1995, they decided, possibly mistakenly, to sell the property to pay off the tax arrears immediately.

They also decided to settle at Pamapuria, where the Latimers had lived when they migrated from the gumfields in the 1930s. Latimer: 'We came back north because I need to be among my own whanau and hapu. They asked me to return. There's a lot going on with the Muriwhenua case before the Waitangi Tribunal, and arguments about who should negotiate settlements with the Crown. Anyway, this place is home and I can work from here just as well as from the Kaipara.'

They continue to support Ngati Whatua and Te Uri-o-Hau initiatives, including a successful claim to the Waitangi Tribunal for the return of land and resources.

Today the Latimers live in a small three-bedroomed house built in the 1950s. They bought it for about $15,000 when it was not considered good enough for a constable in Russell, in the Bay of Islands, and transported it to Pamapuria. Part of a new two-car aluminium garage serves as an office. One large built-in wardrobe in the main house holds Latimer's working clothes: formal suits, shirts, ties and shoes for his use as Maori Council president. Lady Emily still compulsively irons absolutely everything, a legacy from her laundress experience in the 1940s. Another old house on the property is used to store archives covering Latimer's more than thirty years of public service.

These records were the target of a police raid early in 1998 – the Waitangi Fisheries Commission believed Latimer had improperly leaked confidential files (he had resigned as a member a year earlier). Police also searched the home of Shane Jones, now, four years later, the Waitangi Commission's new chairman, and the office of lawyer Donna Hall.

Latimer says that at eight o'clock 'on the dot' five officers arrived. One stayed at the gate, one stood outside the garage-office, where working files are kept, one went to the second house where the archives are filed, and two came to the front door. None were locals; they came from Wellington and other centres. The senior officer told the Latimers that the search was at the request of the Waitangi Fisheries Commission. Sir Tipene O'Regan, no longer a member, was then chairman, and Robin Hapi was and still is the chief executive.

Latimer: 'Both Emily and I were ill at the time – it was during a long spell of illness for me. Quite distressing. No warning. I'd done nothing wrong. I'd just kept all my Fisheries Commission material in the same way I'd kept everything from all the other bodies I'd worked with – just a mass of stuff.'

A High Court review later decided that the search warrants were not justified, that the Latimer's privacy had been invaded, and that publicity about the search had damaged his reputation. Latimer: 'Not only was it found they [the police] had no business searching our place, but they had to pay the cost too.' Further legal action is pending. All files have been returned.

From his Pamapuria base Latimer travels every week all over New Zealand for the Maori Council and other groups he represents. The most important position he holds, apart from the Council's presidency, is chairman of the Crown Forest Rental Trust.

Latimer maintains that he is still carrying out the agenda laid down by elders in the nineteenth century – when in 1892 the four Maori MPs asked the government for a Maori forum, in despair of ever being heard in a Parliament dominated by a huge majority of British immigrants who knew nothing of the Treaty.

He says that this agenda was reconfirmed by the New Zealand Maori Council when it was set up in 1962, 102 years after the first national meeting of Maori leaders at Kohimarama in Auckland had asked for annual conferences. Good idea, said Governor Thomas Gore

Browne who returned to England the following year. Bad idea, said the new governor, Sir George Grey, who, soon after, illegally invaded the Waikato. Maori were semi-barbarian natives, he said, and it was unwise to call them together to frame a constitution for themselves.[1]

Latimer says that the Maori Council, in its current form, is not the best body to represent Maori interests nationally, but argues that it must remain in place as a statutory body to defend Maori against constantly changing governments. 'It must stay,' he says, 'until the Treaty is fully entrenched as part of New Zealand's constitutional framework and a new, more powerful, organisation is formed with the authority to form policies, with the resources to implement them.'

Because of Latimer's fears that future governments could reduce the Treaty's importance he favours a written constitution for the country under a republic. He believes this would allow for a full settlement of Treaty claims. He is afraid that if the existing system continues successive governments could 'go back' on Treaty settlements if it suited them. Consequently, he is in favour of dropping the Privy Council as New Zealand's final court of appeal, and believes the country is now mature enough to develop its own system.

He recognises the Maori Council's limitations but says they result from the conscious acts of politicians who still refuse to accept fully the court decisions of the last fifteen years.

He claims the work of the Maori Council is not finished and says that governments have consistently opted out of their responsibilities. Even when obliged to develop new policies after the court decisions of the 1980s they fought a tough rearguard action. Instead of collaborating with the Maori Council and other Maori organisations, the governments used their Crown powers to try to force Treaty claimants to accept their ultimatums.

The issues itemised in the Hunn Report forty years earlier still remain: housing, education, health and employment. He believes the Council has been stunningly successful in carrying out its statutory functions. Equally strongly he believes that most governments since 1962 have failed to fulfil their obligations to Maori and to the wider community. Latimer: 'Instead of forming the partnership laid down in the Maori Welfare Act 1962, governments have refused to fund the Council to do its job, and have only responded when forced to do so by the courts.¹ For the last ten years the annual budget of the Maori Council has been $220,000 and it uses rooms made available by Te Puni Kokiri. He senses great changes in the political and constitutional climate. Maori are still in a minority – about one in every six or seven New Zealanders are of Maori descent – but have much more influence on national policy than the Maori of 1926, when he was born (then about one in twenty-three, and almost all living in rural areas).

Maori are now an urban people: about nine out of ten live in cities or towns. Approximately one-third have not only lost their rural links – they no longer know their hapu or iwi affiliation. Their numbers, and the introduction of the MMP electoral system, have finally given Maori political clout. After the 1999 general election there were sixteen MPs claiming to be Maori or acknowledging Maori heritage in a House of Representatives of 120 members. Following the 2002 general election there are nineteen. They are still a minority but cannot be ignored.

Latimer's Far North today is dramatically different from that of his early world – then a much simpler place. Radio, in 1926, was an infant (four years old in New Zealand). The Ratana Church had been formally established in 1925. Massey Agricultural College was opened the following year and the Department of Scientific and Industrial Research was set up. The General Motors plant in Petone produced the first New Zealand-assembled car (a Chevrolet sedan). The government rejected a proposal to use planes for topdressing work (not practical).²

Low-income parents on four pounds a week were given two shillings a week for their third and subsequent children (nothing for the first two). Maori were officially second-class citizens. They received lower social benefits because they all lived in the country and could, it was argued, survive on fish and vegetables. They did not have the right to vote in secret (as did non-Maori) and they were not even obliged to register as voters, as everyone else was, until 1956.³

The status of all women was low, with Maori at the bottom of the scale. Women were also second-class. They were not eligible to be justices of the peace till 1926 and could not serve on juries till 1942, and then only if they were between the ages of twenty-five and sixty. Though they had the vote since 1893, not one woman was elected to Parliament till 1933. They had to wait till 1960 for equal pay to be introduced in the public service.

Bessie Te Wenerau Grace provided a different sort of model when she graduated Bachelor of Arts from Canterbury University in 1926, thought to be the first Maori woman to do so from a New Zealand university.

To protect itself, the country had an army of 493 (102 officers, 391 other ranks). Today the armed services number about 13,000. In 2000, about $800 million was budgeted for additional army equipment and services – almost as much as the $1 billion cap initially proposed by the National government in 1994 to settle all Maori Treaty claims over a ten year period.

In 1926 the New Zealand economy was solidly based on farming and, therefore, totally dependent on world market prices. When the New York Wall Street stock market collapsed in 1929, so did New Zealand.

Today, Latimer sits as often as he can in a small sunroom attached to the kitchen of his house, and looks over the paddocks and tree-covered hills lying to the north. Once hapu and whanau land, some was subsequently bought by his grandfather. In the 1960s, after his father's death, forty-five acres were sold by the Department of Maori Affairs, and the remaining 118 acres were leased for forty-two years for $50 annually, to recover $62 in unpaid rates. Latimer family members were not given the chance to buy. Now, acre by acre, the Latimers are buying it back, turning it into a dairy farm and restoring it as a place for their extended family, their turangawaewae.

Immediately opposite his home is an Anglican Church and cemetery, where many of his relatives are buried. He has thought of bringing his mother's body back from Auckland for re-burial but decided that 'no matter where she is she's still with me'. He often has, he says, silent conversations with her.

The Latimer's home is a centre of domestic and political activity. Latimer and Lady Emily have twenty-seven grandchildren and spend as much time with them as they can. Latimer's commitment to Maori issues came at a heavy cost in time to his own family and he still feels a sense of personal responsibility and guilt.

In spite of this, Latimer remains fully involved in national Maori issues and in Muriwhenua affairs as five Far North tribes try, with great difficulty, to settle their Treaty claims with the government and with each other. The Far North is still desperately poor, with one of the highest rates of unemployment in the country.

Political leaders visit regularly and sit with him in the sunroom or in his more formal lounge where the walls are covered with family photographs. His phone rings continually, often late at night and early in the morning. Friends and relatives try to avoid visiting at times when he is likely to be watching big rugby matches or horse races. Latimer admires Helen Clark as a person and as prime minister. 'She can really be the mother of the nation,' he says. 'She has the vision, intelligence and energy. And she understands the Treaty and the needs of Maori.' He believes Clark wants sincerely to reduce the gaps between Maori and the rest of the community, acknowledged by all political parties, and that her approach is positive and long term.

He maintains contact with his mother's Kenworthy relatives. One, in Perth, is buying and developing properties in Awanui, a small settlement just north of Kaitaia. This is injecting new life to the area, with the opening of craft shops and eating places for tourists going to Cape Reinga.

Latimer regularly drives over the ground on which he was born at Waiharara just north of Awanui. It is now covered by a tarsealed road. Friends suggest that if his name is ever commemorated a plaque could be inset in the middle of the road: Graham Stanley Latimer was born here.

He can also walk over the land on which he spent his first four years. All remains of the squatter shacks have long gone. The bush has been burned and much of the land has been planted in pine. The nearby cemetery in which family members are buried is well-kept.

Some descendants of the Dalmatian gumdiggers still live in the area or further south in or around Kaitaia. They are no longer ranked below Maori in the social and racial order. Now they own property, shops and tourist services. They are prominent in local politics and have produced notable mayors, such as Millie Srhoj in Kaitaia and James Belich in Wellington. Visitors to the Far North are greeted with Serbo-Croat road signs, Dobro Dosli, as well as Haere Mai and Welcome.

One relatively unimportant law passed in 1927 had a lasting impact fifty years later. Parliament made cannabis an illegal crop though little if any was cultivated then, or used, or sold. It was criminalised only to bring New Zealand into conformity with international law. Cocaine was made illegal at the same time. Opium was already banned.

Cannabis has in the last twenty years become a staple crop, probably bringing more cash into the region than any other single product – and, with it, crime, social dislocation and personal and family tragedy. The region has changed from a wasteland occupied by drifters and very poor Maori into an area with a thriving drug industry, complete with gangs, sophisticated systems of crop production, protection, distribution and money laundering.

Latimer wants the drug decriminalised and supports moves to have the law changed to stop the damage being done to Maori communities and the public. In the 1999 general election he and Lady Emily allowed a billboard to be placed on their land advocating cannabis decriminalisation. He is heartened by moves in some other countries, such as Britain, to make possession of cannabis no longer an arrestable offence, and allowing medicinal usage.

▲▼▲

How long does he expect to be actively involved in public affairs? There are still things he wants to do. He would like to see the funds held by the Crown Forest Rental Trust, a non-profit-making institution, used more for development purposes, and not so much for research into Waitangi Tribunal claims. He is also concerned about persistent attempts by successive governments to tax the Trust's income, and so reduce its ability to help Maori.

He feels that the Waitangi Tribunal has accepted far too many claims (more than 950) and will never be able to do justice to them because it does not have the necessary resources. New systems are needed, he believes, to cope with the claims, and he welcomed government moves in October 2001 to develop alternative methods.

Latimer also supports policies that will allow the Waitangi Fisheries Commission to use its massive accumulated resources as an economic and financial base for Maori, rather than dispersing all or most of it to competing interests.

He wants to follow up his request to government for more support for J Force veterans and their families where health problems can reasonably be linked with service in Japan between 1946 and 1948.

Latimer knows he can't go on forever. He dislikes the continual travel round the country and overseas. His health has been poor over the past few years and old rugby injuries are catching up with him. One journalist in 1999 commented that he was looking a bit dishevelled at Waitangi that year, noting that he was wearing white sneakers with a suit. 'No,' says Latimer, 'I'm not losing it. It was gout – not absentmindedness, not senility, not yet.'

He and Emily have thought of selling their property and moving into a small house in Kaitaia, which now has a population of about 5,000. 'I know we'll never do it,' he says. He wants to stay on family land.

Latimer responds to complaints that he should let younger people take over his leadership roles by saying that is precisely what is happening and mentions the large pool of younger people who have gained extensive experience over the last twenty years. He says they have a solid understanding of the political scene, know how to work with business and with civil servants, and are far more familiar than he was in the 1960s with the levers of power.

Shane Jones is one he considers has the experience and the judgment, at forty-one, to be a strong leader. 'He's intelligent, well-travelled outside New Zealand, and has a sound knowledge of the bureaucracy and of national politics. He will prove to be a very good chairman of the Waitangi Fisheries Commission.'

Jones believes that Latimer and other kaumatua and kuia have welcomed rather than opposed the involvement of young Maori in leadership roles: 'Most are delighted when the young show any interest or commitment.' Jones is aware of the sacrifices many of his elders have made in the past, knowing that they have experienced hardship and loneliness, years of impoverishment and frustration. And, he says, leadership positions do not lead to vast riches: 'Sir Graham and Lady Emily would have been far better off economically if they had not devoted their lives to public service, if they had just worked for themselves.'

Latimer believes that traditional leadership systems are still important but urbanisation and the experiences that most Maori today share with everybody else are creating a common cultural mix. People can still choose to hold on to as much as they want of their traditional cultural heritage, including language, but it comes at a cost in time, money and life options. In practical terms leaders have to develop new strategies to cope with an international environment. Nobody has a single inherited culture anymore: everybody shares parts of a mass world culture which changes daily.

Maori women will, he predicts, be much more prominent in future as leaders locally and nationally. 'That's where the strength lies. Many men have just opted out of family and community responsibilities and left the women to struggle on their own. There's a leadership vacuum and women are filling it.'

What does Lady Emily think about his future? 'He's still needed. Nobody has his experience. She remembers the instruction given by his early mentor, Kemp Nathan, in the Kaipara: 'You stay as long as your memory lasts.' Lady Emily says his memory is just fine.

She is also acutely conscious of the time they have left and the way they want to spend it. 'We need to be with our family and friends.'

Glossary of Maori Terms

aroha	love, compassion, affectionate regard
haka	dance
hapu	section of a large iwi, clan, secondary iwi
hui	assembly, meeting
iwi	nation, people, tribe
karanga	call, summon, welcome
kaumatua	elder (male)
kaupapa	rules, basic ideas, principles, plan
kawa	protocol
kereru	native wood-pigeon
Kingitanga	the Maori King Movement
kohanga reo	language nest
kuia	elder (female)
mana	power, influence, status
mana motuhake	autonomy
marae	meeting ground
moko	tattoo
mokomokai	preserved human head, collection of preserved human heads
pa	village
rangatira	chief
runanga	assembly, council, debate
tamahine	girl, daughter
tangata whenua	people of the land
tangi/tangihanga	funeral
taonga	treasure, property, artifact

tapu	sacred, forbidden
te reo	language (Maori)
toheroa	shellfish
tupuna	ancestor
turangawaewae	home-place
wahi tapu	cemetery, burial-ground, sacred place
wairua	spirit
whakapapa	genealogy, cultural identity

References

All quotations from the Latimer family come from interviews and discussions held between 1992 and 2002, and are not specifically dated. Statements made by Sir Graham in reports or articles are given specific references. Works frequently cited in the notes have been identified by the following abbreviations:

AJHR Appendices to the Journals of the House of Representatives

NZPD New Zealand Parliamentary Debates

INTRODUCTION
1 Interview with author, 27 February 2002.

CHAPTER 2 – TROOPER IN JAPAN: 1946–1947
1 Defence Department Poster, 22 February 1946.
2 Report to the Joint Chiefs of Staff in Australia, from Lieutenant-General John Northcott, late Commander-in-Chief, British Commonwealth Occupation Forces (Japan), 25 July 1946.
3 Personal Instruction from the Commander in Chief, BCOF: to all ranks of BCOF – Concerning Fraternising.
4 *American Caesar: Douglas MacArthur, 1880–1964*, William Manchester, Arrow Books Ltd, London, 1979, p 428.
5 *The Pacific, Official History of New Zealand in the Second World War 1939–45*, Oliver A Gillespie, War History Branch, Department of Internal Affairs, Wellington, 1952, p 314.
6 *Hone Tuwhare*, Janet Hunt, Godwit, Auckland, 1998, p 52.
7 Ibid.
8 *Children of the Ashes: The Story of a Rebirth*, Robert Jungk, Heinemann, London, 1961, p 141.
9 *Dominion*, 24 September 1993.
10 Report to the Joint Chiefs of Staff in Australia, from Lieutenant-General John Northcott.
11 *Jayforce: New Zealand and the Military Occupation of Japan 1945–48*, Laurie Brocklebank, Auckland University Press, Auckland, 1997, p 186.
12 'The Publication of "Hiroshima" in *The New Yorker*', Steve Rothman, http://www.geocities.com/Heartland/hills/6556/hiro.html.
13 *Hone Tuwhare*, Hunt, p 50.
14 *Regular Soldier: A Life in the New Zealand Army*, Frank Rennie, Endeavour Press, Auckland, 1986, pp 97–98.
15 *Jayforce*, Brocklebank, p 122.
16 *Hone Tuwhare*, Hunt, p 49.
17 Letter to author, 30 August 2001.
18 *Evening Post*, 2 December 1994.

19 *No Ordinary Sun*, Hone Tuwhare, Blackwood and Janet Paul Ltd, Auckland and Hamilton, 1964.
20 *Evening Post*, 2 December 1994.

CHAPTER 3 – MAORI IDENTITY: 1947–1956

1 *The Unauthorized Version: A Cartoon History of New Zealand*, Ian E Grant, Cassell New Zealand, 1980, pp 128–129.
2 *Maori Tales, A Collection of Over One Hundred Stories*, Pat Lawlor, New Century Press, Sydney, 1927, p 30–31.
3 Ibid.
4 Ibid, p 31.
5 Ibid, p 132.
6 Ibid.
7 Ibid, p 74.
8 *The Long White Cloud*, William Pember Reeves, first published 1898, this edition, Golden Press, Auckland, 1973, p 62.
9 *Appendices to the Journals of the House of Representatives*, 1879, Vol 1, D-3, p 1.
10 *Coates of Kaipara*, Michael Bassett, Auckland University Press, Auckland, 1995, p 133.
11 Letter to the author from the Hon George Gair.
12 Ibid.
13 *The New Zealand People at War: The Home Front*, Nancy Taylor, Official History of New Zealand in the Second World War 1939–45, Historical Publications Branch, Department of Internal Affairs, Government Printer, Wellington, 1986, p 1294.
14 *Letters From Private Henare Tikitanu*, Reverend JC Fussell, Worthington and Co, Printers, Auckland, 1917, p 1.
15 Personal communication, 21 February 1992.
16 *Grog's Own Country*, Conrad Bollinger, Minerva Ltd, Auckland, 1967, p 104.
17 Ibid, p 111.
18 *NZPD* 284, 1946, p 4225.
19 *Sir Apirana Ngata and Maori Culture*, Eric Ramsden, AH & AW Reed, Wellington, 1948, p 57.
20 *The New Zealand People at War*, Nancy Taylor, p 1244.
21 Ibid.
22 *More Minhinnick: Cartoons from the New Zealand Herald*, 1949, p 32.
23 *Jayforce Times*, 9 September 1946.
24 *The Billy T James Real Hard-Case Book*, Billy T James and Chris Slane, Beckett Publishing, Auckland, 1986.
25 Resource Planning Tribunal, hearing on Karikari Peninsula, mid-1980s.
26 Ibid.
27 *Te Iwi Maori: A New Zealand Population Past Present and Projected*, Ian Pool, Auckland University Press, Auckland, 1991.

CHAPTER 4 – BECOMING A NATIONAL LEADER: 1956–1987

1 *Maori Girl*, Noel Hilliard, William Heinemann Ltd, Auckland, 1960.
2 *Maori Youth*, David Ausubel, Victoria University of Wellington Publication in Psychology No. 14, Price Milburn, Wellington, 1961.
3 *The Fern and the Tiki*, David Ausubel, Holt, Rinehart and Winston, New York, 1965.
4 Interview with author, 6 November 1992.
5 *The First 50 Years: A History of the New Zealand National Party*, Barry Gustafson, Reed Methuen, Auckland, 1986, p 246.
6 Interview with author, 13 July 1993.
7 Interview with author, 23 June 1993.

8 *Report on the Department of Maori Affairs* JK Hunn, Acting Secretary for Maori Affairs, Government Printer, Wellington, 1961.
9 *NZPD* 139, 1907, p 520.
10 *NZPD* 148, 1909, p. 943.
11 *Te Iwi Maori*, Pool, p 123.
12 Ibid, p 186.
13 Interview with author, 7 November 1992.
14 *The First 50 Years*, Gustafson, p 246.
15 Interview with author, 7 November 1992.
16 Interview with author, March 1992.
17 Interview with author, 23 June, 1993.
18 Interview with author, 13 July 1993; reconfirmed in 2001.
19 Interview with author, 13 July 1993.
20 Interview with author, 13 July 1993.
21 Paper for Te Puni Kokiri, 1992.
22 Interview with author, 2001.

Chapter 5 – The Treaty Legacy: 1840–1987

1 *The Waitangi Tribunal: The Conscience of the Nation,* Paul Temm, Random Century New Zealand Ltd, 1990, p 3.
2 Ibid, p 113.
3 *New Zealand Herald*, 13 February 2001.
4 *Making New Zealand*, Vol 2, No 29, Department of Internal Affairs, 1939–1940, pp 30–31.
5 Ibid, p 31.
6 Ibid, p 31.
7 *New Zealand Official Yearbook*, 1946, p 252.
8 *New Zealand Official Yearbook*, 1970, p 30.
9 *New Zealand Community: An Integration of Geography, History, Civics, and Elementary Economics*, FG Spurdle, Whitcombe and Tombs, 1946.
10 *Diary of the Kirk Years,* Margaret Hayward, Cape-Catley Ltd and AH & AW Reed Ltd, 1981, p 30.
11 Interview with author, 10 October 2000.
12 *Aotearoa, A History of New Zealand,* Olive Baldwin, Heinemann Ltd, 1975.
13 Ibid.
14 Ibid.
15 *The Waitangi Tribunal,* Temm, p 3.
16 *The Rise and Fall of a Young Turk*, RD Muldoon, AH & AW Reed, Wellington, 1974, p 52.
17 Interview with author, 27 February 2002.
18 Interview with author, 9 October 2000.
19 Interview with author, 12 June 2000.
20 Interview with author, 27 February 2002.
21 Interview with author, 9 October 2000.
22 Letter from Chief Judge Durie to Sir Graham, 14 July 1986.

Chapter 6 – The Treaty Goes to Court: 1987

1 *New Zealand's Constitution in Crisis: Reforming our Political System*, Geoffrey Palmer, John McIndoe, Dunedin, 1992, p 78.
2 Interview with author, 26 March 2002.
3 *New Zealand's Constitution in Crisis*, Palmer, p 88.
4 *New Zealand Maori Council and Sir Graham Latimer v Attorney-General* [1987] 1, NZLR 641.
5 Ibid.
6 Ibid.
7 Interview with author, 27 February 2002.
8 Ibid.
9 Ibid.

10 *Ratana: The Man, the Church, the Political Movement*, JM Henderson, AH & AW Reed in association with the Polynesian Society, 2nd edition, Wellington, 1972, p 88.
11 *New Zealand's Constitution in Crisis*, Palmer, p 88.
12 Ibid.
13 *I've Been Writing*, Richard Prebble, 1999, quoted in the *Dominion* 1 June 1999.
14 Ibid.
15 Interview with author, 12 June 2000.
16 Speech notes, Jim Bolger, 14 May 1988, pp 20–21.
17 *Nga Tau Tohetohe: Years of Anger*, Ranginui Walker, Penguin Books, Auckland, 1987, p 264.
18 Interview with author, 26 March 2002.
19 Ibid.

Chapter 7 – Tupuna Maori: 1988

1 Statement made to Sir Graham, 13 July 1988.
2 Submission by Dr Joan Metge to High Court (Wellington) 19 May 1988.
3 Survival International letter to Bonhams Auctioneers, 12 May 1988.
4 Press release from Bonhams Auctioneers, 18 May 1988.
5 From request to High Court (Wellington) 19 May 1988, for Letters of Administration for Tupuna Maori.
6 Decision of Justice Greig, 19 May 1988.
7 Ibid.
8 *Observer*, June 1988, Bernard Levin.
9 *Overseas: The Magazine of New Zealand News UK*, 24 July 1988.

Chapter 8 – First Fruits and Backlash: 1987–2001

1 Annual Report, Sealord, 2002.
2 *Winston First: The Unauthorised Account of Winston Peters' Career*, Martin Hames, Random House New Zealand, Auckland, p 81.
3 Ibid.
4 Ibid, p 90.
5 *Rights of Passage*, Chris Laidlaw, Hodder Moa Beckett, Auckland, 1999, p 144.
6 Ibid.
7 *New Zealand Herald*, 9 February 1993.
8 *New Zealand Herald*, 10 February 1993.
9 *New Zealand Herald*, 19 March 1992.
10 *Trick or Treaty*, Doug Graham, Institute of Policy Studies, Victoria University of Wellington, Wellington, 1997, p 41.
11 Ibid.
12 *Listener and TV Times*, 31 October 1992.
13 *Trick or Treaty*, Graham, p 72.
14 Ibid, p 60.
15 *Rights of Passage*, Laidlaw, p 145.
16 Ibid.
17 *Trick or Treaty*, Graham, p 45.
18 Ibid.
19 Ibid, p vii.
20 *Sunday Star-Times*, 28 June 1998.
21 *Evening Post*, 19 March 1999.
22 *Evening Post*, 20 December 1999.
23 *Dominion*, 11 November 1999.
24 *Evening Post*, 19 March 1999.
25 *Dominion*, 20 April 2001.
26 *Dominion*, 6 July, 2000.
27 *Evening Post*, 11 February 1995.
28 *Bridled Power, New Zealand Government under MMP*, Geoffrey Palmer and Matthew Palmer, Oxford University Press, 1997, p 287.
29 Ibid, p 319.

CHAPTER 9 – RACE RELATIONS: A MINOR MIRACLE: 1926–2001

1. *Dominion*, 17 February 1995.
2. *A Labour of Love*, Mike Moore, MMMC, Wellington, 1993, p 130.
3. Ibid.
4. Ibid.
5. *New Zealand Values Today, the Popular Report of the November 1989 New Zealand Study of Values*, Hyam Gold, Monash University, and Alan ebster, Massey University, Palmerston North, Alpha Publications, Palmerston North, 1990, p 30.
6. *Northern Advocate*, 22 October 1992.
7. *Dominion*, 8 February 1995.
8. *Evening Post*, 7 July 1998.
9. *New Zealand Official Yearbook*, 1970, p 76.
10. 'The Maori Health Nursing Scheme', article in *The New Zealand Journal of History*, 1992, Alexandra McKegg, p 159.
11. 1956 Census.
12. *Poverty and Progress in New Zealand*, WB Sutch, AH & AW Reed, Wellington, 1969, p 226.
13. *Man of Two Worlds: Sir Maui Pomare*, JF Cody, AH & AW Reed, Wellington, 1953, p 144.
14. *The Half-Gallon Jar,* Hori (author W Norman McCallum), AD Organ, Auckland, n d, (probably early 1960s), p 1.
15. Annual Report, Department of Maori Affairs, 1960.
16. *The Fern and the Tiki*, Ausubel, pp 149–215.
17. Speech on New Zealand and its Race Relations, at Victoria University of Wellington, 15 September 1971 by Duncan McIntyre, minister of Maori affairs.
18. *Report on the Department of Maori Affairs*, Hunn, pp 32–33.
19. Speech on New Zealand and its Race Relations, McIntyre.
20. *The First 50 Years: A History of the New Zealand National Party*, Gustafson, p 248.
21. *John Marshall: Memoirs, Volume One: 1912 to 1960*, Collins, Auckland, 1983, p 164.
22. *Memories of Muldoon,* Bob Jones, Canterbury University Press, Christchurch, 1997, p 104.
23. Ibid, p 51.
24. *The Rise and Fall of a Young Turk*, Muldoon, p 52.
25. *Evening Post*, 6 September 2000.
26. Ibid.
27. *Evening Post*, 18 March 1998.
28. *Nga Tau Tohetohe: Years of Anger*, Walker, p 98.
29. *Evening Post*, 8 December 1995.
30. *Dominion*, 20 March 1998.
31. *Banksy on Sunday*, Radio Pacific, 26 March 1995.
32. *New Zealand Herald*, 30 March 1995.
33. Ibid.
34. Ibid.
35. *Sunday Star-Times*, 9 April 1995.
36. Ibid.
37. *Evening Post*, 30 March 1995.
38. *Evening Post*, 1 April 1995.
39. *New Zealand Herald*, 7 July 2000.
40. *NZPD*, Vol 483, 1987, p 176.
41. *Northern Advocate*, 11 January 1992.
42. Letter to prime minister, Jim Bolger, the *Dominion*, 1 April 1998.
43. Ibid.
44. *The Demon Profession,* Michael Laws, HarperCollins, Auckland, 1998, p 106.
45. *Dominion*, 24 August 1998.
46. *Sunday News*, 25 February 1996.
47. *National Times*, Mainfesto 2002, election leaflet, 21 July 2002.
48. *Evening Post*, 20 July 2002.

CHAPTER 10 – REPUTATIONS:
1987–2001
1 *William Hazlitt, Selected Writings*, J Cook ed, Oxford University Press, London, 1991.
2 *Metro*, February 1993, pp 124–127.
3 Conversation with author, 2001.
4 *Metro*, May 1994.
5 Interview with author, 13 July 1993.
6 Ibid.
7 Radio New Zealand, 15 March 1995.
8 *Winston First*, Hames, p 103.
9 Interview with author, 20 March 2002.
10 *Evening Post*, 24 March 1994.
11 Interview with author, 25 August 1992.
12 Interview with author, 6 November 1992.
13 Ibid.
14 Interview with author, 23 June 1993.
15 Ibid.
16 *Evening Post*, 5 April 1994.
17 Ibid.
18 Interview with author, 20 March 2002.
19 *National Business Review*, 4 August 1985.
20 Ibid.
21 Ibid.
22 Ibid.
23 Ibid.
24 Interview with author, 16 August 2001.
25 *National Business Review*, 28 February 1997.
26 Ibid, 4 August 1995.
27 *Sunday Star-Times*, 1999.
28 Interview with author, 26 March 2002.
29 Ibid.
30 Ibid.
31 Ibid.
32 Interview with author, 27 February 2002.
33 Interview with author, 1 May 2002.
34 *Evening Post*, 11 February 1995.
35 *Northern Advocate*, 28 March 1995.
36 Interview with author, 12 June 2000.
37 Interview with author, 14 March 2001.
38 Ibid.
39 Interview with author, 2001.
40 Interviews with author, various, from 1993.
41 Interview with author, 2001.
42 Interview with author, 1 May 2002.
43 Interview with author, 20 March 2002.
44 Ibid.
45 Ibid.
46 Ibid.

EPILOGUE: 2002
1 *AJHR* 1862, section 11, No 14, cited by Claudia Orange, *Treaty of Waitangi*, p 158.
2 *The New Zealand Book of Events*, Gordan McLauchlan, Michael King, Hamish Keith, Ranginui Walker and Laurie Barber eds, Reed Methuen, Auckland, 1986.
3 The Electoral Act 1956

Bibliography

Appendices to the Journals of the House of Representatives, 1879, vol 1, D-3.

Baldwin, Olive *Aotearoa, A History of New Zealand*, Heinemann Ltd, Auckland, 1975.

Bassett, Michael *Coates of Kaipara*, Auckland University Press, Auckland, 1995.

Bollinger, Conrad *Grog's Own Country*, 2nd edition, Minerva Ltd, Auckland, 1967.

Brocklebank, Laurie *Jayforce: New Zealand and the Military Occupation of Japan 1945–48*, Auckland University Press, Auckland, 1997.

Cody, JF *Man of Two Worlds: Sir Maui Pomare*, AH & AW Reed, Wellington, 1953.

Department of Internal Affairs *Making New Zealand*, Vol 2, No 29, 1939–1940.

Fussell, Reverend JC *Letters From Private Henare Tikitanu*, Worthington and Co, Printers, Auckland, 1917.

Gillespie, Oliver A *The Pacific, Official History of New Zealand in the Second World War 1939–45*, War History Branch, Department of Internal Affairs, Wellington, New Zealand, 1952.

Gold, Hyam and Webster, Alan *New Zealand Values Today, the Popular Report of the November 1989 New Zealand Study of Values*, Alpha Publications, Palmerston North, 1990.

Graham, Doug *Trick or Treaty*, Institute of Policy Studies, Victoria University of Wellington, Wellington, 1997.

Grant, Ian E *The Unauthorized Version: A Cartoon History of New Zealand*, Cassell, Auckland, 1980.

Gustafson, Barry *The First 50 Years: A History of the New Zealand National Party*, Reed Methuen, Auckland, 1986.

Hames, Martin *Winston First: The Unauthorised Account of Winston Peters' Career*, Random House, Auckland, 1995.

Hayward, Margaret *Diary of the Kirk Years*, Cape-Catley Ltd and AH & AW Reed Ltd, Wellington, 1981.

Hazlitt, William *William Hazlitt, Selected Writings*, Jon Cook (ed), Oxford University Press, London, 1991.

Hunt, Janet *Hone Tuwhare*, Godwit, Auckland, 1998.

James, Billy T and Slane, Chris *The Billy T James Real Hard-Case Book*, Beckett Publishing, Auckland, 1986.

Jones, Bob *Memories of Muldoon*, Canterbury University Press, Christchurch, 1997.

Jungk, Robert *Children of the Ashes: The Story of a Rebirth*, Heinemann, London, 1961.

Laidlaw, Chris *Rights of Passage*, Hodder Moa Beckett, Auckland, 1999.

Lawlor, Pat *Maori Tales, A Collection of Over One Hundred Stories*, New Century Press, Sydney, 1927.

Laws, Michael *The Demon Profession*, HarperCollins, Auckland, 1998.

Manchester, William *American Caesar: Douglas MacArthur, 1880–1964*, Arrow Books Ltd, London, 1979.

Marshall, John *John Marshall: Memoirs, Volume One: 1912 to 1960*, Collins, Auckland, 1983.

McCallum, W Norman *Hori, Fill it up Again!*, Sporting Life Publications, Auckland, no date, circa 1960s.

McCallum, W Norman *Hori, The Half-Gallon Jar*, AD Organ, Auckland, no date, circa 1960s.

McIntyre, Duncan 'New Zealand and its Race Relations', speech at Victoria University, 15 September 1971.

McKegg, Alexandra 'The Maori Health Nursing Scheme', *The New Zealand Journal of History*, 1992.

Moore, Mike *A Labour of Love*, MMMC Ltd, Wellington, 1993.

More Minhinnick: Cartoons from the New Zealand Herald, Auckland, 1949.

New Zealand Maori Council and Sir Graham Latimer v Attorney-General [1987] 1, NZLR 641.

Palmer, Geoffrey *New Zealand's Constitution in Crisis: Reforming our Political System*, John McIndoe, Dunedin, 1992.

Palmer, Geoffrey and Palmer, Matthew *Bridled Power, New Zealand Government under MMP*, Oxford University Press, Auckland, 1997.

Prebble, Richard *I've Been Writing*, Fraser Holland Publishers, Wellington, 1999.

Ramsden, Eric *Sir Apirana Ngata and Maori Culture*, AH & AW Reed, Wellington, 1948.

Reeves, William Pember *The Long White Cloud*, Golden Press, Auckland, 1973 (1898).

Rennie, Frank *Regular Soldier: A Life in the New Zealand Army*, Endeavour Press, Auckland, 1986.

Report to the Joint Chiefs of Staff in Australia, from Lieutenant-General John Northcott, late Commander-in-Chief, British Commonwealth Occupation Forces (Japan), 25 July 1946.

Sutch, William B *Poverty and Progress in New Zealand*, AH & AW Reed, Wellington, 1969.

Taylor, Nancy *The New Zealand People at War: The Home Front*, Official History of New Zealand in the Second World War 1939–45, 2 Vols, Historical Publications Branch, Department of Internal Affairs, Government Printer, Wellington, 1986.

Temm, Paul *The Waitangi Tribunal: The Conscience of the Nation*, Random Century New Zealand Ltd, Auckland, 1990.

Walker, Ranginui *Nga Tau Tohetohe: Years of Anger*, Penguin Books, Auckland, 1987.

NEWSPAPERS

Dominion, 8 February 1995.
Dominion, 17 February 1995.
Dominion, 20 March 1998.
Dominion, 24 August 1998.
Dominion, 11 November 1999.
Evening Post, 24 March 1994.
Evening Post, 5 April 1994.
Evening Post, 11 February 1995.
Evening Post, 8 December 1995.
Evening Post, 7 July 1998.
Evening Post, 20 December 1999.
Evening Post, 6 September 2000.
National Business Review, 4 August 1985.
National Business Review, 28 February 1997.
New Zealand Herald, 19 March 1992.
New Zealand Herald, 9 February 1993.
New Zealand Herald, 10 February 1993.
New Zealand Herald, 30 March 1995.
New Zealand Herald, 13 February 2001.
Northern Advocate, 22 October 1992.
Observer, June 1988.
Sunday News, 25 February 1996.
Sunday Star-Times, 9 April 1995.

Sunday Star-Times, 28 June 1998.
Sunday Star-Times, 7 August 1994.
Sunday Star-Times, 1999.

MAGAZINES

Listener and TV Times, 31 October 1992.
Metro, May 1994.

PERIODICALS

Jayforce Times, 9 September 1946.

RADIO

Radio New Zealand, 15 March 1995.
Banksy on Sunday, Radio Pacific, 26 March 1995.

Chronology

7 February 1926	Graham Stanley Latimer, born Waiharara, son of Lillian Edith (née Kenworthy) and Graham Latimer
February 1940	Attended Kaitaia College for two weeks in the third form
1943	Joined the New Zealand Army
1946–1947	Served with J Force in Japan
1948	Married Emily Moore Joined New Zealand Railways (resigned in 1961)
1952	Moved to Kaiwaka, Kaipara Harbour, as stationmaster Met the Nathan family (Kemp and Jessie)
1956	Elected as a spokesman for Ngati Whatua Became a Maori warden
1961–1979	Became a farmer (Tinopai, Kaipara Harbour)
1963	Elected to the Tai Tokerau District Maori Council
1964	Elected to the New Zealand Maori Council as one of three members representing te Tai Tokerau
1966–1975	Elected secretary, Tai Tokerau District Maori Council
1969	Elected vice-president, New Zealand Maori Council
1969–1972	Stood unsuccessfully as the National Party candidate for the Northern Maori electorate
1973–	Elected president of the New Zealand Maori Council
1977	Appointed as one of the first three members of the Waitangi Tribunal
1979–	Chairman of the Tai Tokerau Maori Trust Board
1979–1995	Farmed at Taipuha, Kaipara Harbour
1980	Knighted (investiture at Waitangi in 1981)
1981–1992	Maori vice-president of the National Party
1986	Passage of the State-Owned Enterprises Act
1987	Initiated a successful appeal against the State-Owned Enterprises Act, leading to a series of actions against the Crown, relating to land, forests, fisheries and te reo Maori

1988	Retrieved tupuna Maori from England, and stopped the public sale of human remains (artifacts) by auction houses
1990–	Became chairman of the Crown Forest Rental Trust
1993–1998	Member of the Treaty of Waitangi Fisheries Commission
1995–	Returned to Pamapuria (near Kaitaia)

Other positions and offices:

> member of the General Synod of the Anglican Church;
>
> member of the board of the National Museum;
>
> member of the Alcoholic Liquor Advisory Council, and director of various commercial enterprises.